UNSUSTAINABLE

How Big Government, Taxes and Debt are Wrecking America

James E. MacDougald

Marsden House
PUBLISHERS

UNSUSTAINABLE
How Big Government, Taxes and Debt are Wrecking America

James E. MacDougald

Marsden House
PUBLISHERS

First Edition, 2010

Although the author and publisher have made every effort to ensure that the information in this book was correct at press time, the author and publisher do not assume and hereby disclaim any liability to any party for any loss, damage, or disruption caused by errors or omissions, whether such errors or omissions result from negligence, accident, or any other cause.

Published in the United States of America

10 9 8 7 6 5 4 3 2 1

ISBN: 978-0-615-37368-3

Library of Congress Control Number: 2010907944

Cover design by Bryson Hale

Acknowledgements

The press is often pilloried for being biased or unfair, and there are those who believe the day of print media has passed. Most Americans seem to rely on quick sound bites on television or on talk radio for their "news." But where would we be without the intrepid reporters who go behind the scenes to tell us what lies hidden in the background and without the newspapers and magazines that bring those stories to light?

There would be no "UNSUSTAINABLE" book and no Free Enterprise Nation were it not for the story first told by Lucy Morgan and the *St. Petersburg Times*, or without the articles in *Forbes* magazine, or for the continuing reportage by the *Wall Street Journal*. We take these things for granted, and we shouldn't. We read a story and move on, enlightened by the discovery and reporting, and sometimes even infuriated by the point of view. But we learn things that we must learn, and we are richer because of it. So…here's to you, Lucy Morgan, and to the *St. Petersburg Times*! And to *Forbes*, and to the *Wall Street Journal*. And to Chris Edwards at the Cato Institute and Andrew Biggs at the American Enterprise Institute, and to the entire team of scholars at the Tax Foundation.

The book-writing experience tested my fortitude and that of my beloved wife, Suzanne. She allowed me to "head to the office" seven days a week for 8 months and supported me, without complaint, all the while. And it tested the fortitude of all those who supported the creation of this book, including Paul Watson, Bryson Hale, George Panagopoulos, Kathleen Mott, Debbi Gilmer, Jacky Tymon, Chris Erickson, Jo-Lynn Brown, Rebecca Stiteler, Jeri Risin, Noah van den Berg, Noelle Detko, Michael Symon, Gavin Scott, Bridget Smeltzer and Linda Brackett, each of whom had a role to play in the production of UNSUS-TAINABLE. Thank you!

Most of all, I want to acknowledge the efforts of my editor, research manager and critic, Donna Parrey. Her unbelievable ability to deal with my occasional frustrated rantings while working under tight deadlines that she never failed to meet was a wonder to observe. Thank you, Donna!

Jim MacDougald
St. Petersburg, Florida
June, 2010

Contents

Preface

Our nation is on an unsustainable financial path…and America is rising in protest. Millions of citizens are questioning and challenging the right of the federal government to interfere more and more with the rights of states and individual citizens. America is rising against the unsustainable levels of spending, deficits and debt at every level of our public sector: from school districts to cities, counties to states, and to the federal government itself. America is rising to assert that its Constitution means what it says. And America is rising to reassert itself as the world's most prominent bastion of absolute individual liberty and personal freedom, and as a land of unfettered free enterprise where the people control their own government.

It will take the bravery of many to preserve and protect what our Forefathers fought and died to leave us—a permanent legacy of enduring personal freedom. We are facing a transformative time in our history. A citizenry motivated to protect its own birthright is facing the forces that wish to change and employ strained interpretations of our Constitution, allowing government to assume unprecedented power over us all. It is a contest that will be fought at the polls and in the courts, not in the streets, because our democracy still allows each of us to be heard, and still peacefully responds to the will of the people. The battle will nonetheless be a fierce one because so much is at stake.

Like the Minutemen of 1775, citizens across the nation are rising to say that there's a limit to the authority that we will allow our elected governments to assert over us, and I'm proud to be one of them. How and why did a retired entrepreneur and business executive step forward to lead a fight to preserve free enterprise in America? It certainly wasn't planned to work out that way. It all began in early 2009. In the closing days of 2008, an article by Lucy Morgan appeared in my hometown paper, the *St. Petersburg Times*. The article disclosed that huge pensions were being provided to public sector employees in Florida and double dipping was permitted. In other words, retirees were taking pensions and lump sum payments, but then they were immediately returning to work in a salaried job, collecting money that taxpayers never agreed to provide.

I previously had no idea that public servants could collect lump sums as large as $800,000, and monthly pensions of $12,000 or more, and that they didn't even have to reach age 65 to collect them. Shortly thereafter, an article appeared in *Forbes* magazine, citing more examples of public sector pensions, including a police officer retiring at $65,000 a year, guaranteed for life, at the age of 42. I began to notice shocking revelations in other publications, too, such as the story of the New York city workers earning $100,000 in overtime in their final year of employment, triggering pensions greater than their salaries. Having spent my working career in the employee benefits area of the private sector, I knew that these practices did not exist for nongovernment workers. I also knew that such huge and early retirement benefits were so costly that they had rarely, if ever, been implemented in the private sector. Could this be why the federal and local public sector bureaucracies were all going broke and seeking more and more taxes for support? Just how widespread, nationally, were these practices, and what do they cost the taxpayers?

As a retired businessman, I was spending my time serving on numerous non-profit boards, working out of a small office with an assistant. Time was a commodity I had plenty of, and I was fortunate to have become financially independent as the result of starting a company, taking it public and then retiring soon after it was acquired by a larger public company. It seemed worthwhile to find out what was going on nationally with public sector pay and pensions. Were the stories I had read aberrations? Or was there a systemic problem? Was anyone even looking?

Within a few weeks I found and hired two recently-minted recipients of Master's degrees to do some research on a part-time basis. One was given "federal" and the other was given "state and local" categories to research. They were to develop information on the size and scope of public sector pay and pensions, including how they are reported to taxpayers and how they were funded.

> Each week, I would meet with my researchers as they brought in stacks of printed research documents. Usually they would begin with, "You're not going to believe this, but…" And they were always right–I couldn't believe what they were showing me. In case after case, they identified public sector pay and benefits practices that defied the imagination. There were massive liabilities to the taxpayer that had been created by promising health care and pension benefits to retirees without adequately funding for them. There were tricky and questionable accounting and reporting practices. There were benefits entitlements that went beyond any benefits I had ever seen before in the private sector. And I had been in the employee benefits business for 40 years!

It quickly became apparent that the information we were compiling had not been compiled before in any significant and meaningful way. We were learning that there is a systemic problem throughout the entire United States that has been generally unrecognized because no one had segmented the taxpaying population into "private sector" taxpayers and "public sector" taxpayers. What we had learned, and were constantly expanding our data to support, was that virtually no one had looked at the overall differences in compensation, benefits, reporting and disclosure by performing large scale studies of private sector versus public sector data. The problem was complicated by our discovery of the fact that many people in the private sector don't really know what the private sector is, and they don't even realize they are a part of it.

The online *Business Dictionary* defines private sector as:

> *"Part of a national economy made up of, and resources owned by, private enterprises. It includes the personal sector (households) and*

corporate sector (firms), and is responsible for allocating most of the resources within an economy."

The definition above sounds good at first blush, but America is now an economy where corporations and resources are increasingly controlled by the government, so we looked elsewhere for further definitions. Other definitions include:

"In economics, the private sector is that part of the economy which is both run for private profit and is not controlled by the state."

"All organizations in an economy or jurisdiction that are not controlled by government, including privately owned businesses and not-for-profit organizations."

None of the definitions we found fit the U.S. economy today. The government actually does control huge portions of what is usually called the private sector economy, and is actually preparing legislation to control it even more.

Perhaps if we looked for a definition of "public sector," we could define the private sector by process of elimination? We looked at public sector definitions and found several. These included:

"The public sector is that portion of society controlled by national, state or provincial, and local governments. In the United States, the public sector encompasses universal, critical services such as national defense, homeland security, police protection, fire fighting, urban planning, corrections, taxation, and various social programs."

A private sector organization, therefore, is one that belongs to the private sector, i.e. is not government owned.

The discovery that the U.S. free enterprise economy may no longer meet the actual definition of a private sector economy gave me a "WOW!" moment. Even standard definitions of the term private sector assume that government does not own or control it. What should we call it when government DOES control it, or major portions of it? We decided to pursue our efforts by using the definition that our government apparently employs in compiling statistical data: Institutions that are formed to serve the citizenry, at the expense of the citizenry, to serve the fundamental needs of the citizenry are the "public sector." That includes all governments at every level, and public education. Everything else, to our federal government, is considered the private sector.

> What we learned in our research is that the public sector is using the taxing authority that we gave it in ways that are extremely detrimental to those of us who formed the public sector entities in the first place. It became apparent that information this important needed to be shared with the generally uninformed businesses and taxpayers in the private sector. These private sector taxpayers are unknowingly providing huge disparate pay and benefits to public sector employees, and supporting programs initiated by the public sector to engender support for themselves–many of whom paid no taxes or were paid with tax dollars in the first place.

I knew it would be a difficult job to try to continue to amass and summarize the needed information and then to get it to the national media and directly to businesses and their employees in the private sector. It would take dedicated, full-time researchers to search for, evaluate and summarize examples and relevant data. It would take significant resources to get the message out. More importantly, it would take an organization that could unify businesses and individuals in the private sector to exercise their rights and effect changes necessary to level the playing field between private sector and public sector workers. Such an organization did not exist, so we started one. The Free Enterprise Nation (FEN) was established in April of 2009. Its mission would be to educate, unify and advocate on behalf of the broad economic interests of the private sector...the "free enterprise" portion of our economy.

While looking for more suitable offices for the new Free Enterprise Nation, I hired the first of 10 full-time researchers (growing to our present staff of 18) and information technology (IT) people to begin building our database of information. Gathered around a table in the small conference room adjoining my office were four researchers and our database developer, with computers and work papers all crammed at the same table. As our researchers began delving more deeply into pay and pension practices of public sector entities in various cities, states and school districts and those at the federal level, I would frequently hear the loud exclamation of "OH...MY...GOD!" or sometimes a softer "oh my God" as a researcher uncovered yet another piece of shocking information.

We were learning that pay and benefits disparity was not an occasional aberration, but that these disparities were virtually everywhere we looked. It might have been the drivers training teacher in Illinois earning a salary of $171,000 a year, eligible to retire at over $100,000 a year at age 59, with guaranteed 3% annual increases and free health insurance. Or it might have been the discovery that the largest public sector pensioner in California had a pension of $500,000 a year. It might have been the social workers in New York who were routinely earning overtime payments that tripled their total base pay, providing them with incomes of $200,000 a year and huge pensions. We began referring to these discoveries as "OH, MYs," labeling them as "OM" in our growing database. They went on...and on...and on.

The developing story was getting more and more complex. One discovery led to another and still another. As more and more pay and benefits disparity was uncovered, so were the accounting practices used to account for these benefits plans. And so were the misleading reporting practices occurring at every level of government including school districts, towns, cities, counties and states. Our discoveries included not only the pay and benefits entitlement provided to public sector workers, but also led to the discovery that the federal government misleads Americans about how they pay for and fund Social Security and Medicare. We saw the huge impact of public sector unions, and how they have created a "money pump" of taxpayer dollars paid to the public sector employee, then deducted as union dues and then provided by the unions as political contributions to those who support even more pay and benefits to public sector workers.

Constant references to the U.S. Constitution required us to reread the Declaration of Independence, the Constitution and the Bill of Rights, and to seek out and read books and articles written by constitutional experts. We began finding numerous research reports that had been prepared by think tanks dealing with the rights of governments and with looming and unsustainable government deficits and debt. We found that the creators of these reports had serious concerns that they agreed needed to be immediately acted on by elected officials. However, most are not permitted to engage in advocacy since they are 501(c)3 organizations the IRS says may educate but not advocate—so these reports have not been widely disseminated. These think tank reports are occasionally referred to in the *Wall Street Journal* or other business and economic publications, but they seldom reach the typical man and woman in the street.

Numerous books have appeared on the subject of the American economy. The problem is most are not relevant to average Americans who don't often chat about GDP (gross domestic product) and the significance of unfunded liabilities over dinner. They must rely on quick "sound bites" in the electronic media, headline articles in local papers and on their elected officials to do the right thing for them. What they rarely hear about is the concept of government as a "redistributor," that is, a government that takes from them and gives to someone else.

> America currently has "redistributive" governments at federal, state and local levels that employ their taxing powers to benefit themselves and their own public sector employees. They have redistributed so much to themselves and their own employees that tax revenues can no longer support the pay and pensions that they've promised themselves.

Key elements of the current financial crisis encompass:

1. Redistributive public policies that violate the Constitution.

2. Unfunded federal entitlement programs like Social Security, Medicare and the recently—passed health care reform legislation.

3. Pay disparity and unfunded retirement plans for military and civilian employees.

4. Pay disparity and unfunded retirement and health care programs for nonfederal public sector employees.

5. Unrestrained and irresponsible spending and debt at every public sector level.

6. The reliance on unionization of the public sector and coerced unionization of the private sector providing financial support to elected officials who will advance the redistribution cause.

7. The relentless demonization of corporations and individuals in the private sector and of any person(s) who oppose redistributive or unconstitutional public policy.

The combination of these factors has built a huge dependency, funded by the unknowing private sector employers and employees. Combined, they represent a clear and present danger to the survival of free enterprise and the personal liberty that comes with it. One cannot have true individual freedom and self-determination in a redistributive state. If individual achievement and risk-taking cannot be rewarded, they will not be employed.

Our research has convinced us that there is an ongoing struggle for political and economic control of the nation. It is a "cold war," with the eventual outcome determining whether the United States remains a free enterprise economy or becomes a social welfare state. The two are incompatible. On one side are the redistributors, consisting primarily of an increasingly unionized public sector and other beneficiaries of government support. On the other side are those who make up an "America Rising": those who insist on personal freedom, accept individual responsibility and demand the right of self-determination.

The Free Enterprise Nation launched its story in September 2009 with a full-page ad in the *Wall Street Journal* saying "We Are The Private Sector. And We Have Had Enough." We started sending tens of millions of emails, providing data to the print media and appearing on radio and television to tell the story about pay and benefits disparity, and of the huge liabilities that have been hidden from taxpayers. Stories began appearing almost everywhere. FEN's huge database, freely available to the press and public, was providing fodder and direction for the press, the media and for activist organizations.

Remarkably, and in spite of the dearth of information that is provided by governments to taxpayers, people across the nation have started to rise up in protest of uncontrollable government spending and debt at every level. From the Tea Party, to groups protesting at city halls and state capitols, to armies of talk show host followers, millions of Americans know that something has gone badly wrong. They don't have all the details, but they know that their future and the futures of their children and grandchildren are at stake. They are clearly motivated, but to be truly effective they need all the details to know exactly what it is they must seek to change. Most of all, they need to be unified.

We've seen an increase in activism by the Tea Party and other grass roots organizations. But what, exactly, do they stand for, and what are they trying to accomplish? They are obviously concerned about national deficits and debt, and fear the inevitable increases in taxes. But what, specifically, does that mean to each of them? It is heartening to see so many Americans expressing their rights of free speech, gathering to protest the dominance of big government. But where is the specific platform? What, specifically, do they all agree on? Is this "movement" a unified and coherent group, or is it a gathering of people who are embracing a generic message that is all-too-similar to the "Hope" and "Change" messages of 2008? Ambitious politicians naturally use the opportunity to speak before crowds of right-leaning activists in hopes of garnering their votes, but are their messages to these crowds so generic that no one REALLY knows what they stand for. Are public sector employees protesting side-by-side with private sector employees (or those who are unemployed) at Tea Party events, who are likely to part ways sharply when they read this book?

Many people will support a campaign or issue if it defines itself so broadly that everyone thinks that it embraces their own personal views. But when specific definitions on issues are presented, splintering inevitably follows. What, then, must be done to create a movement that consists of supporters who know EXACTLY what it stands for and wants to accomplish? Obviously issues need to be defined very clearly, and the campaign must have very specific goals and aspirations.

We discovered, in the months after launching FEN, that in spite of our efforts only small portions of the total story were being told. The press tends to focus on the "hot topic" of the day. They cover it for a few minutes then move on to what is happening with the latest Hollywood divorce scandal. It seemed that more coverage was given to the Tiger Woods apologies than to the fact that national debt and unemployment are at unprecedented levels, with no end in sight. Two or three minute interviews on the national media don't permit the disclosure of the varied and complex issues related to the problems that private sector taxpayers are facing. The impact of a myriad of public policies, at every level of government, was being overlooked. Pay and benefits disparity, and the unfunded and hidden liabilities associated with them, are only one part of a much larger national problem that is still generally unrecognized. As a result, attempts to define and "fix" the problem are not focused on the essential steps we need to rein in our out-of-control governments at every level.

UNSUSTAINABLE is intended for the average American. It is not written by or for economists. It is a ground-level overview of the many ways that employees in government and public education have been enriched at the expense of private sector business and individual

**taxpayers. Government and public education sectors
use their right to tax in order to feather their own nests.**

The result has been the creation of a growing privileged class with an insatiable appetite for more pay and more benefits that can only be satisfied by more taxes from the private sector. If left unchecked, like a parasite that devours its host, the public sector will destroy the private sector, resulting in government control and ownership of the entire economy. The United States of America will become a social welfare state, and the world's last bastion for free enterprise will fall.

The free enterprise nation needs information. They have to know why government spending and debt is out of control, and what they can do about it. The average person can easily understand, "If I'm paying taxes to give someone else more than I can ever have myself, something has to change, and it's in my best interest to make that change." They can also easily understand that if their own governments are hiding vital information from them, and that they are being impoverished because of it, they had best do something about it right now. WHY it is the way it is, and HOW voters can effect the right changes in public policy to fix it requires a deeper understanding of the complex series of issues.

The nation needs to know how we have allowed ourselves to be placed in a financial position that virtually every analyst and economist says is "unsustainable." Americans need to know how our government went wrong, and what to do to make it right. That is the purpose of this book.

*"Clearly, we are on an **unsustainable** path."*

—John C. Goodman, president and CEO of
the National Center for Policy Analysis,
Daily Policy Digest. May 21, 2009

_____ Chapter One _____

"Redistributive" Government vs. the U.S. Constitution

A "redistributive" government is one that extracts tax dollars from one citizen to give to another. We see it when tax refunds are given to taxpayers who paid no taxes, and when taxes are taken from some to provide rewards to others who support the government in power. We see it when the federal government determines that taxes should be taken from citizens in one state and given to the government of the citizens in another state, and we see it in national programs like Social Security and Medicare.

Once a redistributive government acquires power, it can maintain power by using its taxing authority to take from those who do not support it and give the money to those who do. A redistributive state is not necessarily a socialist state. Government does not need to own all property and business to be a redistributor. It can be a capitalist democracy, relying on the votes of the recipients of redistribution to retain control via officials elected by those receiving the benefits of redistribution. It can be a capitalist democracy with tax policies that allow it to extract money from opponents to provide to supporters.

The United States of America is becoming a redistributive nation. The only possible long-term result of a continuation of redistributive policies is a diminishing number of individuals and businesses from whom taxes can be taken, and an increase in those who depend on government for support. Ultimately, the entire nation will be forced to depend on government and a transition to a true socialist state will have occurred.

Most Americans are aware of the staggering deficits and debt faced by the federal government and by their own state. "Lost in translation" is recognition that these enormous deficits and debts have been caused largely by a relatively new phenomenon—the redistribution of tax dollars from taxpayers to those employed by government and public education.

There are 89,000 public sector entities employing 22 million Americans who are supported by taxes, fees and tolls. While issues related to federal spending and debt tend to get at least some national coverage, problems at the state and local level are treated as local news, and are rarely reported by the national press and news media. The result is that most Americans do not know there is a nationwide problem in almost every element of the public sector, brought about by providing unaffordable levels of pensions and benefits to government and public education employees. Most don't know that these problems directly affect them even if the financial crisis exists in another city, county or state. The reason is that the federal government and state governments tend to provide financial support to public sector entities with financial problems. This means that income taxes paid by Jeff in Alabama can end up supporting a ridiculously large pension for John in California. Or that property taxes paid by Amy in St. Petersburg can end up supporting a huge pension for Carol in Clearwater.

For the redistributors to win the war for control of the economy requires a degree of governmental control that is unprecedented in American history. Control can be taken by force as it was in Russia in 1917, or it can be elected into power as the savior of the economy, as was the case during the 1930s depression in the United States and in Germany.

History shows that voters often will enable a one-party strong central government and a significant abridgment of individual rights when an economy is under severe economic duress. Such an enabled government can choose to move quickly to alter the laws, the economy and even the society in a permanent way. For government to achieve such control without significant opposition, several conditions must first be met.

Conditions That Set the Stage for Absolute Government Control

- First, a serious and seemingly hopeless economic crisis must exist or be created. This is the key requirement. Happy people in a democracy with a thriving economy don't voluntarily allow government to interfere with their individual rights. When the economic conditions are the bleakest, the opportunity for convincing citizens to support unusually strong and active government intervention is at its greatest. Government as a "solution" facilitates the voluntary transfer of individual rights to the central government in hopes the government will improve the economic circumstances of its citizens.

- Second, for a strong single party central government to gain power, a large portion of the population needs to be either employed by government, dependent on government or in need of government support. These dependents will willingly grant more power to the government because it is likely to improve their personal circumstances. The larger this group can be made, the easier it is for government to use the "democratic process" to increase its own power.

- Third, to gain popular support for the government to engage in unprecedented interference with individual rights, "demons" must be identified as the cause of the problem, creating a basis for unification of a majority of voters. The premise is simple: *If something is badly wrong, someone is to blame for it, and government will find them and deal with them.* In the Russian revolution the demons were the bourgeoisie and the aristocracy. During the U.S. depression it was Wall Street, wealthy industrialists and big business. In Germany of the 1930s, it was the allies of World War I who imposed huge war reparations charges on Germany, and it was the Jews.

- Fourth, government must move quickly to change existing laws that could impair its strength or its growth. It must use the "crisis" and a unified opposition to the defined demons in order to gain popular support for abridging individual rights in favor of "the good of the people." Once total power has been achieved by the central government, the democratic process is no longer required.

In the United States, the preconditions for the potential establishment of absolute control by the central government over its citizens have been met:

1. **The first precondition is met. An economic crisis exists, and is expected to continue.** The U.S. has dealt with crisis upon crisis for the past decade. In 2001, it was the September 11th attacks and it was the "tech bubble" burst, followed by a decade of a generally flat stock market and an enduring fight against global terrorism. In 2008, it was the collapse of the financial and real estate markets. In 2010, it's hopeless government debt at virtually every level and continuing high levels of unemployment. One-fourth of American homeowners have mortgages greater than the value of their home. Social Security and Medicare are broke. The U.S. Postal Service is failing financially. Fannie Mae and Freddie Mac have trillions in unsecured risks the government has created and must support. If additional justification is needed by the federal government to capitalize on a continued "crisis," additional problems include the "need" for the federal

government to help the states with their unsustainable debt, the need to control the "demons" in the private sector, the need to deal with uncontrolled borders and the illegal immigration crisis, the need for domestic security and overseas military operations and the need for government to intervene strongly to prevent global warming (or climate change).

2. **The second precondition has been met because government is enlarging the "dependency" population.** More than 22 million Americans work for government or public education in the public sector. Approximately 47% of working American tax-filers pay no income taxes. Millions more exist on government-provided welfare. Millions are receiving government-provided unemployment benefits. Millions of individuals and companies rely on contracts with the government for their living. Millions of government and private sector workers are paying dues to unions, who provide 95% of their financial support to the political party that favors redistribution. And every political candidate and elected official is dependent on raising funds for political campaigns, money that unions provide to pro-redistribution candidates by the bucket-load.

3. **The third precondition has also been met. "Demons" have been identified and are routinely attacked by federal government officials and the president of the United States himself.** The demons are "profits," capitalists, Wall Street, insurance companies, investment banks, greedy doctors, "fat cats" and "the rich." The demonization message has broad appeal to union members and union organizers, to those who don't pay taxes (most students, welfare recipients, low-income earners), to most public sector employees and to everyone who feels that they should get their "fair share" via a government reallocation from others to themselves.

4. **The fourth condition has also been met. Government has moved quickly to strengthen its power by capitalizing on current economic difficulties.** The political advisor to President

Obama, Rahm Emanuel, has been quoted as publicly stating, "You never want a serious crisis to go to waste." Economic turmoil and the accompanying social unrest have justified the central government in taking over the automobile industry and much of the financial sector. Through government-sponsored enterprises (GSE's) Fannie Mae and Freddie Mac, it has taken control of the mortgage financing market, gaining support from more and more voters as it guarantees unsustainable low down payment, low-interest loans provided by the central government. It has enabled the president to appoint 26 "czars", unelected officials not confirmed by Congress and reporting directly to the president, to oversee almost every aspect of American life. It has allowed the president to sign Executive Orders requiring unionization of the private sector with no opposition from his majority Congress.

The citizens who formed our country never ceded power to the government, allowing it to control our entire economy. The government's power to levy taxes is based on the limited authority given to it by the people. The government was never given the authority to regulate personal behavior, other than to create and enforce laws designed to uniformly protect all citizens. The federal government has used its taxing authority to regulate personal behavior, and to force compliance by citizens in ways that were never intended when the Constitution and Bill of Rights were ratified.

We cannot address the issues that affect the survival and prosperity of the American free enterprise economy, and the preservation of "the American dream," without first looking at the authority that was given to our federal government by the people in our Constitution, Bill of Rights and amendments. (The text of these important documents—the Declaration of Independence, The Constitution of the United States and the Bill of Rights/Amendments—are included as Appendices.) We hear little about the private sector vs. the public sector because they are not terms commonly employed by elected officials or the press.

We do hear about big government vs. small government, and we do hear about federal and state deficits and debt. The nation is currently engaged in a fight between those who want big government and those who want small government.

The debate evolves around a central question:

What power did "*We The People*..." grant to government when we formed it in the first place?

The role of central government, or any government, has been debated throughout history. In the U.S. the debate ended in a crescendo when the 13 original colonies decided to declare themselves one nation and independent of British rule. The result was the formation of a republic unique in world history. It was a new nation, so it could start from scratch. It was based on a government that would be in place, and remain in place, only if the citizenry willed it to be so. The government itself was specifically limited in its powers by the states and the people who formed it. It was to be a "government of laws, not of men." Every aspect of federal government power was clearly enumerated and clearly limited, and the separation of powers between legislative, executive and judicial branches of government were intended as a series of checks and balances that could prevent a recurrence of the oppressive conditions the colonies had experienced under British rule.

It's impossible to address the debate concerning big vs. small government without taking a brief look at the Declaration of Independence and the U.S. Constitution. The Declaration of Independence was an angry document, signed by very brave people. The original signers were fully expecting that they might hang for having signed it. How many elected officials have such courage today?

The Declaration presented a justification for the overthrow of British rule centering on individual rights, on oppressive taxes and on the rights of the citizens to choose their government. A few excerpts from the document, explaining why the colonies decided to go to war, set the stage for the explicit language used in our Constitution, signed 11 years later.

Contained in the Declaration of Independence are the reasons for the action:

> "...All men are created equal, that they are endowed by their creator with certain inalienable rights, that among those are life, liberty, and the pursuit of happiness. That to secure these rights, Governments are instituted among men, deriving their just powers from the consent of the governed...Governments long established should not be changed for light and transient causes...But when a long train of abuses and usurpations...evinces a design to reduce them under absolute despotism, it is their right, it is their duty, to throw off such government, and to provide new guards for their future security."

The Declaration of Independence continues:

> "The history of the current King of Great Britain is a history of repeated injuries and usurpations, all having in direct object the establishment of an absolute tyranny over these states."

The writers gave numerous examples of the "repeated injuries and usurpations." Here are a few:

> "He has erected a multitude of new offices, and sent hither swarms of officers to harass our people and to eat out their substance."

> "He has combined with others to subject us to a jurisdiction foreign to our constitution, and unacknowledged by our laws, giving assent to their acts of pretended legislation."

> "For cutting off our trade with all parts of the world."

> "For taking away our charters, abolishing our most valuable laws, and altering fundamentally the forms of our government."

> "For suspending our own legislature, and declaring themselves invested with power to legislate for us in all cases whatsoever."

It is crucial to recognize that the 13 colonies each had their own governments. They were attempting to establish a central government that would only be permitted to do those things the newly-formed states could not do for themselves. There was great fear that a newly-formed central government would take power away from the states and their citizens, and establish a ruling government similar to that they were escaping from.

When the Constitution was approved by Congress in 1787, it subsequently had to be ratified by each state. There were many who still feared the new central government would be a replay of royal rule, allowing a diminution of individual and states rights. James Madison, with the strong support of Thomas Jefferson, introduced 10 amendments that were designed to explicitly limit the role of the federal government, and explicitly protect the rights of the individual and of the states. These amendments were essential to obtaining ratification of the Constitution by three quarters of the states. Known as the Bill of Rights, they became effective in 1791.

The "Welfare Clause"

The Constitution, in Section 8, gave Congress the right to "lay and collect taxes, duties, imposts, and excises, to pay the debts and provide for the common defense and general welfare of the United States."

The sentence above has become known as the "welfare clause." It has been interpreted by some (including Supreme Court Justices!) to imply that it gives Congress virtually unlimited power. Its entire meaning can be changed by selectively choosing certain words and rearranging the sentence to say: "provide for the...general welfare," rather than reading it strictly as it was written. This was about STATES as well as citizens having rights, and the sentence deals with common defense and general welfare of the United STATES.

> You don't have to be a Constitutional scholar to know that **"provide for the common defense and general welfare of the United States"** does NOT mean that Congress can do anything it wants to, to individual citizens, thus taking away all the individual rights that are clearly spelled-out throughout the Constitution and Bill of Rights. It certainly

does NOT give Congress the right to take from certain citizens and give to others.

The "Commerce Clause"

Section 8 also gave Congress the power to "regulate commerce with foreign nations, and among the several states, and with the Indian tribes."

Remember this phrase, too. It is known as the "commerce clause" and is used by many to justify Congressional authority to do absolutely anything it wants to. It was originally intended to prevent states from establishing trade barriers to protect their own in-state interests. It says Congress has the authority to "regulate commerce...among the several states." But Congress has often used that clause to assume power to regulate PEOPLE. The Congress can and often does claim that virtually everything we as INDIVIDU- ALS see or touch or use is somehow connected with something in another state. That means, to some, the things we see or touch or use are "interstate commerce" and that gives them the right to regulate any individual who sees, touches or uses them. Many in Congress think that this empowers them to tax, require or mandate ANYTHING they want to in order to "regulate commerce among the several states."

The welfare clause and the commerce clause have been used by various presidents and Congresses to take the power to legislate anything they want. When one party is in power, it has the capability to pass any law it wishes, regardless of what the Constitution says. Everything in the Constitution and Bill of Rights is specifically intended to limit the power of our central government to those specific things that we gave them the right to do. When government overreaches by imposing taxes and regulations that affect our individual rights, we can only rely on the Supreme Court to save us. And, as we shall see, that is a scary thought!

If one reads the Constitution without its amendments, it can appear to grant authority to Congress that can abridge individual and states rights. To make it absolutely certain that Congress's authority was **limited** to the things the Constitution specifically authorizes, the Bill of Rights added strong statements as to what Congress could NOT do:

- **Amendment V.** "…nor shall private property be taken for public use, without just compensation."

This amendment was later impacted significantly by Amendment XVI in 1913, which gave Congress "the power to lay and collect taxes on incomes, from whatever source derived…" Unfortunately, the amendment doesn't state a limit on the amount of taxes they can impose, but it didn't repeal or replace the amendment that says that private property cannot be taken for public use "without just compensation." Presumably that would mean that the income taxes imposed by Congress would provide "just compensation" for all citizens because it provides services equally to all of us. But when they take income taxes from one citizen expressly for the purposes of giving to another, what is the "just compensation" to the person whose personal property (their income) is taken?

It is certainly arguable that when the federal government takes income taxes from a citizen, it is still obligated to provide "just compensation" to the person from whom it was taken. And redistribution to others doesn't comply with the 5th Amendment. The Constitution and Bill of Rights strictly delineate what Congress can and cannot do. When the 16th Amendment was ratified, it didn't mean that when we gave Congress the right to collect income taxes, we simultaneously gave Congress the power to take from some and give to others. Neither did it mean that Congress could use their taxing authority as a "penalty" to be applied selectively against those individuals and businesses that they wish to control.

- **Amendment IX.** "The enumeration in the Constitution, of certain rights, shall not be construed to deny or disparage others retained by the people."

- **Amendment X.** "The powers not delegated to the United States by the Constitution, nor prohibited by it to the states, are reserved for the states, or to the people."

The last two amendments say essentially the same thing. They were obviously trying to make that point well understood and clear. The point was to restrain Congress from engaging in tyrannical and despotic practices like those that were enumerated in the Declaration of Independence. This presumably includes preventing Congress from erecting a "multitude of new offices", or sending "swarms of officers to harass our people and eat out their substance," or to "cut off our trade with all parts of the world," or "abolishing our most valuable laws and altering fundamentally the forms of our government" or investing itself "with power to legislate for us in all cases whatsoever."

> The key here is to recognize that each state also has laws, taxing authority and its own constitution. The framers of the Constitution and the Bill of Rights wanted a central government that could do only those things that were specifically enumerated, leaving all else to the states and to the people.

Nowhere in the Constitution or Bill of Rights does it say a person has a "right" to food, clothing or shelter, although those are basic human needs. These documents do NOT say that it is the obligation of government to provide any individual with their basic human needs. Rather, our Constitution says that individuals have a "right" to "life, liberty, and the pursuit of happiness."

In the big vs. small government debate, it is important to distinguish wants and needs from rights. If Congress has the right to tax virtually without limitation, and if it determines that all citizens have the right to food, clothing and shelter (and even the right of getting someone else to pay their doctor's bills), the natural consequence is a redistributive state ... one in which Congress takes from one citizen and gives to another to "regulate commerce" or to "provide for the general welfare."

The question concerning the right of a government to determine that its citizens, or its own government employees, have rights that require a redistribution from one citizen in favor of another, is not restricted to a question of Congressional authority. Each city, school district, county and state has chosen to distribute services by taxing all citizens to provide a benefit to all citizens. The person who pays $20,000 in income taxes gets the same services as one paying none. The person paying $20,000 in property taxes gets the same

> In the big vs. small government debate, it is important to distinguish "wants" and "needs" from "rights."

services as one paying far less. The key, though, is the basic premise that the services are provided equally to all citizens and are paid for by all citizens. A major step in the redistributive process is made when government takes from only certain citizens and gives to only certain others. In this case, government decides that "for the public good" I will take money from Mary and give it to Ralph. Or even worse, "I will take money from the taxpayer and give it to myself."

There have been many circumstances when Congress has determined that to provide for the general welfare or to regulate interstate commerce, it can pass laws and/or impose taxes that are essentially redistributions from one citizen to another. And they have used their right to levy income taxes to accumulate huge amounts of money that they can offer to individual states on the condition that the states adhere to federal direction. That is, in essence, bribing a state to behave a certain way, using money taken from citizens in another state. We saw this method employed in Congress when key votes were needed from senators in Louisiana and Arkansas, among others. It was done under the guise of providing "for the general welfare."

Despite thousands of words intended to protect the rights of individual citizens and individual states, the welfare and commerce clauses have been treated as loopholes that can allow the party in power in Congress, and the president, to interpret what they mean and enact laws accordingly. In the event of a challenge, the Supreme

Court (five of nine judges) can decide whether the Congress and the president had the Constitutional authority to do so. Does that mean the federal government can redistribute wealth? The answer, so far, is YES.

Tax rebates to people who paid no taxes, and Social Security and Medicare programs are just a few examples of legislation that does just that. Can Congress and the president create a socialist state if they choose to? The answer, so far, is YES. They have taken over direct control of numerous companies in the past two years. Can they go farther? Of course they can if they can establish one party rule to pass laws and get them signed by the president, and get people appointed to the Supreme Court who support their objectives. It all depends on what the Supreme Court determines the Constitution means when it says, "provide for the common defense and general welfare of the United States" or to "regulate commerce among the several states."

Thomas Jefferson commented on the general welfare clause in 1791. Here's what he said:

> *"They are not to do anything they please to provide for the general welfare, but only to lay taxes for that purpose. To consider the latter phrase not as describing the purpose of the first, but as giving a distinct and independent power to do any act they please which might be for the good of the Union, would render all the preceding and subsequent enumerations of power completely useless. It would reduce the whole instrument to a single phrase, that of instituting a Congress with power to do whatever would be for the good of the United States; and, as they would be the sole judges of the good or evil, it would be also a power to do whatever evil they please... Certainly no such universal power was meant to be given them. It was intended to lace them up straitly within the enumerated powers and those without which, as means, these powers could not be carried into effect."*
>
> —Thomas Jefferson: Opinion on National Bank, 1791. ME 3:148

And James Madison commented on the commerce clause:

"Do not separate text from historical background. If you do, you will have perverted and subverted the Constitution, which can only end in a distorted, bastardized form of illegitimate government."

—James Madison

In the case of the recently passed health care reform legislation, the commerce clause is being used to justify the right of the government to require individuals to purchase individual health insurance. How does the government get interstate commerce into this picture? It says it has the right to regulate anything that crosses state lines. That means the government can claim that all hospitals and doctors use things that cross state lines, and we individual citizens use things that cross state lines (medical equipment, prescription drugs), they can now regulate anything that these things touch, including you. Sound far-fetched? It is, as is the fact that the federal government is also claiming it can tell states what to do.

Currently, 20 State Attorneys General are challenging this claim. Think about that. State Attorneys General suing the federal government for violating the Constitution. That is not an every day event! But it didn't stop Congress from passing the legislation or the president from signing it into law. Time will tell if the Supreme Court upholds the constitutionality of the new legislation. If they do, it will mean the Supreme Court actually supports the president and Congress in abrogating free choice, self-determination and individual responsibility, and there is no limit to where government can go from there.

Lest you think these are scare tactics, recognize that many of these constitutional questions were raised during the "New Deal" of Roosevelt when he led the enactment of Social Security and other government programs. Social Security was a redistribution of income from those who worked to those who no longer did. Under the "Great Society" of President Lyndon Johnson, Congress enacted Medicare, a redistribution from workers to those who no longer worked. What was clearly unconstitutional was enacted "for the public good," even though it became immediately clear that those businesses and workers who would have to pay taxes during the ensuing decades were unlikely to get a direct benefit from their contributions. The same questions have been raised again in connection with health care reform, and could lead to the ultimate abridgment of individual rights if the Supreme Court does not rule the legislation unconstitutional.

Roosevelt "ruled" for 13 years, dying in the first year of his fourth elected term as president. In his second term, during the Great Depression, he had overwhelming majorities in the House and Senate. But the pesky Supreme Court sometimes ruled against some of his new programs, one of which included allowing select industries to agree to establish uniform and higher prices, eliminating competition. His solution was to attempt to add five additional Supreme Court justices hand-picked by him and approved by his Congress, so that the Supreme Court would allow ever-increasing federal government authority. In the "Constitutional Crisis of 1937," he eventually lost because even his political majorities could see their voters getting terribly concerned. He did succeed in getting Congress to agree to provide lifetime salaries to Supreme Court justices even if they resigned, encouraging older justices to leave. By 1941, eight of the nine Supreme Court Justices had been appointed by Roosevelt, giving him four more years of power with a friendly Supreme Court standing by. He succeeded in enacting the national minimum wage law, Social Security and the establishment of numerous new government agencies and programs that exist to this day.

In Lyndon Johnson's one and only term in elected office as president, with the support of overwhelming majorities in Congress, he enacted Medicare and Medicaid as part of his "Great Society" programs, in spite of constitutionality questions that were raised at the time. And during Kennedy's "New Frontier" in 1962, he signed Executive Order 10988, giving federal employees the right to unionize. Executive Orders, as we shall see in later chapters of this book, have the force of law yet are never brought before or approved by Congress. It is one-person law-making power, exercised by the president of the United States that most Americans don't even know exists. By using large majorities in Congress and a sympathetic Supreme Court, a president from the same party can use (misuse?) his assumed right to enact laws with an Executive Order, achieving PERMANENT change. Once established, these programs are almost impossible to undo.

Government's Multitude and Swarms

Can the government go even farther, abridging more and more individual rights in favor of the general welfare or to regulate interstate commerce? The answer is found by asking another question: what could happen if one party had majorities in both houses of Congress and the presidency, as well as five or six on the Supreme Court who believe the Constitution should be interpreted to mean that all income should be redistributed, or that the central government should control all education and all business enterprises? Is that happening now? And even if that should happen, couldn't the voters elect a different president and a different Congress to change things? Well, yes, if the voters could gain a majority in Congress and the Presidency, AND if the Supreme Court concurred with their actions. If a different president isn't elected, they'd have to get votes from two-thirds of Congress in order to override his veto and repeal laws and programs that they want to reject. I repeat…that means gaining two-thirds of both the House and Senate to act in unity. Can that happen? And what about dealing with the Supreme Court ruling? How many have been overturned by a subsequent Supreme Court?

Remember the quote from the Declaration of Independence, where our Founding Fathers said that they had to declare their independence from Great Britain because the King "…has erected a multitude of new offices and has sent hither swarms of officers to harass our people and eat out their substance?" Doesn't the Internal Revenue Service (IRS) immediately spring to mind? Especially the part about sending "swarms of officers to harass our people and eat out our substance."

But our federal government has one-upped nutso King George. Our central government not only has the IRS (who at least collects some taxes), but they also have set up a multitude of new offices that either don't do anything of value, or do something that the constitution expressly forbids them to do. Even King George wouldn't agree to pay for that! Congress has created so many government agencies that "eat out our substance" or that have declared themselves as invested "with power to legislate for us in all cases whatsoever"—we can't analyze them all in this book. Let's look at just two examples of government "erecting a multitude of new offices."

The U.S. Department of Energy— What Does It Do?

Here's a federal bureaucracy that has accomplished virtually nothing that it was established to do, yet has continued to grow and prosper and has "eaten out our substance" for 33 years. The Department of Energy (DOE) today has 16,000 employees earning average compensation and benefits of $120,000 each, and a $27 billion overall annual budget. PLUS, they recently were given $37 billion in "stimulus money" to spend! What fun! That is, indeed, "swarms" and they do a lot of "eating out our substance."

What is its purpose, you ask? It was formed in 1977 to make us "independent of foreign oil." You'll enjoy this story if you can overlook the fact that you have been paying for this idiocy for more than 30 years.

By 1977, we had undergone several energy crises. In 1973, the Yom Kippur War had led to OPEC (Organization of Petroleum Exporting Countries) creating an oil embargo with resultant high gasoline prices and lines at the gas pumps. In 1973, President Nixon launched "Project Independence" aimed at making the U.S. energy-independent by 1980. I repeat: **1980.** Congress also approved the Trans-Alaska pipeline amid tremendous opposition over the havoc it would supposedly wreak on wildlife.

By late 1974, Nixon was gone and Ford was in. We were suffering nearly unprecedented inflation. Our government was doing the usual things that they do when in crisis mode: passing new laws, making up new taxes, providing new subsidies and hiring more government workers. And it was also establishing price controls. Price controls work great. They tell people to sell things at a loss. Of course people stop selling those things. A severe shortage–a crisis– results. As usual in difficult economic circumstances, government always decides that it must do even more.

Among the many goofy things President Ford did was to give a speech to the nation wearing a huge "WIN" button on his lapel, urging us all to "Whip Inflation Now," as if by wearing buttons and thinking positively, inflation would go away. President Ford also signed the Energy Reorganization Act of 1974. (When in doubt, reorganize!) He also continued energy price controls that Nixon had begun. Neither the "WIN" buttons (I never saw anyone but President Ford wear one) nor the price controls worked. It was time for a regime change and we found ourselves with President Jimmy Carter to lead the way in 1977. It took him only 6 months to "reorganize!" and create the Department of Energy, which opened for business on October 1, 1977. This new bureaucracy was a monster, and it had a monstrous job description: To make us INDEPENDENT of foreign oil. You've got to read at least some of his speech to the nation to appreciate how extraordinarily nonsensical it all looks today with the benefit of 20/20 hindsight. Here are some choice excerpts:

> *"Tonight I want to talk to you about a problem unprecedented in our history...this is the greatest challenge our country will face during our lifetimes...I will present my proposals to Congress...the most important thing about these proposals is that the alternative may be a national catastrophe...This difficult effort will be the moral equivalent of war...The oil and natural gas are running out...we now believe that early in the 1980's the world will be demanding more oil than it can produce...Because we are now running out of gas and oil, we must prepare for a third change...and to the use of*

coal and permanent renewable energy sources, like solar... World consumption of oil is going up. If it were possible to keep it rising during the 1970's and 1980's by 5% a year as it has in the past, we could use up all the oil in the world by the end of the next decade (1989)... We must reduce our vulnerability to potentially devastating embargoes... making the most of our abundant resources, such as coal... Government policies must be predictable and certain... We need to shift to plentiful coal while taking care to protect the environment... Goals for 1985: Increase our coal production about two-thirds to more than 1 billion tons a year."

—President Jimmy Carter, televised speech, April 18, 1977

So, what happened next? In January 1979 the Shah was forced from Iran, and another oil crisis ensued. We had huge shortages again. Then, in March 1979, the Three Mile Island accident occurred. The anti-nuclear crowd got, and stayed, very active. Price controls, started by President Nixon, were still in effect. By July, 1979 President Carter had proclaimed a shortage in our energy supplies and established temperature restrictions in office buildings, and announced plans for government to spend $88 billion to produce synthetic fuels from coal and shale oil reserves. Back in 1979, $88 billion was really serious money.

Meanwhile, the governments' efforts to force a transition to coal were working, because thankfully they had left that up to the private sector to accomplish. By 1976, coal production increased to 860 million tons a year, closing in on Carter's original target of 1 billion. The government implemented a mandate that required power plants to convert to coal or natural gas. Once again, the private sector did as they were asked. By 2009, 90% of all electric power plants had converted to coal. We had reached a billion tons a year of coal production by 1994, later than Carter's goals, but we got there. From Carter's "We are all doomed" speech in 1977, the price of coal had DECREASED 15% by 2003 and 23 states are today involved in coal mining.

Our imports plus production of oil went from 15.4 million barrels a day in 1981 to 17.8 million barrels a day in 2008, an increase of only 14% in 27 years. But did we achieve independence? During this period the U.S. **imports** of oil grew from 6.9 million barrels a day in 1981 to 12.9 million barrels a day by 2008, while U.S. **production** decreased from 8.5 million barrels a day to 4.9 million during the same period. Let's see…oil imports UP 6 million barrels a day, U.S. production DOWN 3.6 million barrels. Today we have a heavy reliance on coal, which is now a VERY BAD THING, and our government is going to fix it by punishing those who use coal and will undoubtedly create a NEW bureaucracy to deal with the windfall from enormous new "Cap and Trade" taxes.

But, never fear, the government and Department of Energy are loaning money to private companies to develop new cars. The Secretary of Energy is a lucky man…he gets to loan out $25 billion. Now that is real power! Our government has committed $25 billion in loans (borrowed from you and me, because they actually don't HAVE any money) to help auto manufacturers build more efficient cars. One of them, TESLA, got a loan of $465 million. Ford got $5.9 billion and there is always more where that came from. When was the last time the government gave YOU a $450 million loan to start a new for-profit business? **The government created the Department of Energy to make us independent of foreign oil and we didn't take even a tiny step in that direction.**

What have we accomplished? The bottom line for our current energy policy is:

1. We won't drill in the Alaska National Wildlife Refuge (ANWR) or anywhere else that there's oil. Of the 19 million acres in ANWR, about 1.5 million acres (8% of ANWR) would be an oil bonanza. It is estimated to contain 25 billion barrels of oil. We import 6 million barrels of oil a day from overseas, or about 2 billion barrels a year. 25 billion barrels of domestic production would be a huge difference. We also have reserves of about 200 billion barrels of oil offshore and in Wyoming and Colorado. But environmentalists have stopped the drilling in most places, and prevented any chance of drilling in ANWR, even though

Alaska WANTS to drill there. Environmentalists argue that it would harm wildlife, as they did in 1977 when the Alaska pipeline was approved. Wildlife has flourished since then, but that doesn't matter. No drilling in ANWR!

2. We won't drill offshore. Even though Mexico and China and Japan and virtually every other nation will, and they will do so in the same places that we could. They will drill and sell it to us. We hate offshore drilling, but don't consider that we do need oil, and we do buy oil, and that oil comes to us on SHIPS that enter our waters and our ports and represent the same threat to the environment that offshore drilling does. Environmentalists have taken over our national energy policy. There's nothing wrong with environmentalists. Norway, for example, is quite "environmentalist." They get 90% of their energy needs from hydroelectric power. They don't need much oil. But they drill for it off their own coast in the most inhospitable environment you can imagine and sell it to everyone else. They don't need oil, and do drill offshore. We do need oil, and don't drill offshore. Huh?

3. We won't build any new refineries, so even if we do stumble across some oil, we can't refine it. (The last U.S. refinery built was in 1976.) We know we need gasoline for many, many years to come, but we won't refine it.

4. We will use windmills! No matter that it takes TEN THOUSAND of these enormous wind turbines to (at their peak, meaning it is windy) produce what ONE standard power plant produces today. We've got 626 power plants. Let's see, if it takes 10,000 windmills to replace one power plant, we would need 6,260,000 windmills to replace them, IF it were windy 24/7. These wind turbines can't store power to use when we need it, and they can't produce more power when we need it for peak usage, and they can't produce less power when we don't want it. It is based on: "Hope it's there when we need it," and "Use it or lose it when they are generating, because we can't store it"

(Can you imagine how many batteries that would take?). And 6½ million windmills! Wow, that will be a pretty sight!

5. We will NOT use nuclear energy. In the United States, only 19% of our energy needs comes from nuclear energy. In France it is 80%. The EU averages 30%.

6. We WILL use solar energy. Except at night.

7. We will PUNISH utilities that use coal with new Cap and Trade taxes, even though we FORCED utilities to switch to coal, and spent more than $100 billion of taxpayer money to make it happen. That's not a real problem for public utility monopolies, because they can raise their rates to charge us whatever it takes.

8. Government will promote the use of electric cars, even though we know that some means of energy must be used to produce the electricity needed when everyone plugs their cars in over-night. The electricity can't come from coal. It can't come from oil. It can't come from solar (because the sun isn't out at night, silly.) Sure hope it's windy!

And there you have it: The U.S. energy policy and no national energy plan. A government bureaucracy of 16,000 people and an annual cost of $25 billion spending 33 YEARS to make us "independent of foreign oil."

The U.S. Department of Education— Unconstitutional

There is not one word in the Constitution that gives the U.S. Congress any authority, whatsoever, to involve themselves with, interfere with or influence the education of our children. There's a good reason for that. If a central government takes over what our children are taught, it can teach our children its own "preferred" version of history, freedom, responsibility and "rights." And it can teach our children to fear and to depend on it. It's a very dangerous thing to allow government to control what and how our children are taught.

Lenin once said, "Give me four years to teach the children and the seed I have sown will never be uprooted." I don't know about the "four years" idea, but I know that TWELVE years means that the ENTIRE education is influenced by the central government, and that is enough time to create a whole new world of people who believe what their government has said they should believe.

The Constitution says that unless we (the people and the states) specifically give the federal government the right to do a thing, it MAY NOT do it! To quote the 10th Amendment: "The powers not delegated to the United States by the Constitution, nor prohibited by it to the states, are reserved for the states, or to the people." How, then do we have a Department of Education, run by our central government, supported by income taxes that they take from us by force? And what is their mission?

> There is something that the federal government does do effectively with our tax dollars. It builds a larger and larger dependency.

The Department of Education states its purpose this way: "While most of the responsibility for education is vested with state and local school districts, the U.S. Department of Education establishes the policies for federal funding assistance programs and enforces education-related civil rights and privacy laws." Its mission is to "promote student achievement and preparation for global competitiveness by fostering educational excellence and ensuring equal access." They reach 56 million elementary and secondary students at 99,000 public schools and 34,000 private schools in about 14,000 school districts.

Although the Department of Education only employs 4,000, they have a $63 billion budget in discretionary appropriations, and $97 BILLION in "stimulus" funds to give away (also borrowed. Remember, they have no money.) More than 10% of all "stimulus" funds were given to the Department of Education by Congress to give to states. How does the federal government get the right to take our income tax dollars and give them to the Department of Education? And how does handing out our federal income tax money to states "stimulate" the economy? Well, it does provide money to "save" the jobs of teachers and other public sector workers who belong to the largest unions in America.

> If the federal government does not have the authority to engage in the education of our children, where do they get the authority to charge federal individual and corporate income taxes that it then gives to the states? It is obviously and intentionally coercive for the government to offer taxpayer dollars to states that "volunteer" to comply with federal government imposed conditions related to education. How can it charge us taxes to do something it is constitutionally forbidden to do? Isn't that exactly what the Constitution was written to prevent? I'll answer that for you. "Yes, it was."

Government Is Out of Control

As demonstrated by a quick look at the Department of Energy and the Department of Education, the federal government does do things that it shouldn't be trying to do at all. And with most of the things it should be doing, it doesn't do very well. (Don't get me started on the Securities & Exchange Commission (SEC) and Bernie Madoff!) The fact that they do not do many things well does not prevent them from continuing to take more tax dollars and attempt to do even more. **Cost is never an object...they can always take more from us when they want to. And effectiveness is not an object...there is no requirement that they actually deliver what they promise.** There is something that the federal government does do effectively with our tax dollars. It builds a larger and larger dependency.

The current economic crisis, fueled by the need to destroy or control demons (in this case, "profits," insurance companies and greedy doctors), has enabled Congress to pass health care reform legislation that establishes central government control over 100% of its citizens, the insurance industry and 17% of the economy. It enables the central government to put an estimated 16,000 new Internal Revenue Service employees on an already-bloated government payroll, giving them extraordinary rights to examine personal finances and interfere with individual rights. It gives them the right to tell doctors how to practice medicine.

It has also enabled them to justify taking control (thus eliminating more private sector "demons") of all student loans, making a huge and voting segment of our population directly dependent on government, while enlarging the government bureaucracy itself. In previous years, the federal government had gained control of much of public K–12 and higher education via strings attached to funding and grant-giving. They had coerced states into accepting federal mandates that are generally prohibited by the Constitution by telling the states that they could voluntarily comply to receive federal funds. Where did the federal government get the authority to use its taxing powers to take money from citizens and businesses in order to bribe states to do what it wants them to do? Where is the "just compensation" to taxpayers?

In the following chapters, we'll show how multiple factors impact the private sector corporate and individual taxpayer and why they must act as a unified force to defend themselves and free enterprise in America. We'll address:

- Government abridgment of Constitutional rights
- How tax policy is killing the private sector and jobs
- The huge pay and benefits disparity that exists between public and private sectors
- How governments hide costs from taxpayers
- How government creates dependencies to get more votes
- Why the Social Security crisis will create havoc for decades
- How health care "reform" became a debacle, and how it can be fixed

- How unions and government work together to milk the taxpayer
- The need to restrain insane government spending, debt and taxation
- How government demonizes capitalists and profits to create voting allies
- Why we must fix America, and how we can do it

We can all work together to prevent one-party rule, the inevitable dominance of a redistributive government and the death of free enterprise as we have known it. Informed and motivated voters can effect change, and they can do so rapidly. But the voter must know exactly what to demand from elected officials, and must make these demands known to those running for office.

This book contains a series of recommendations for demands that every voter should require from every elected official, at every level, in the nation. We are still a democracy, and we elect our school boards, Mayors, Council members, Governors and legislators. The entire House of Representatives and one-third of the Senate must stand for reelection every two years. We can truly change anything we want to. We can be a nation that, once again, is rising. Our destiny lies in our own hands.

*"We're still on a long-run trajectory that's **not sustainable**."*

—Rudolph Penner, former director of the Congressional Budget Office. 1983–1987

Chapter Two

Private Sector Dying + Government Thriving = the "Jobs Squeeze"

The private sector in America is dying. It has been dying for about 25 years, and no one seems to have noticed. Ten years ago, 1.5 million more workers were employed in the private sector than were employed there in 2009, while the public sector grew by 2 million during the same time period. As the private sector shrank between 2000 and 2009, government continued to grow. The private sector lost 2.4% of its workforce during that time span, while the government grew by 8.5%.

While the private sector has seen bankruptcies, huge business losses, lower pay, a decrease in benefits and huge unemployment, the public sector employees have enjoyed job security, high pay, unbelievably generous health insurance plans and pensions that are payable as early as age 40, and routinely payable at age 50 or 55.

> The taxes charged to those in the private sector to support public sector pay and benefits represent the largest claim on all taxpayer dollars, and also one of the largest claims on public sector debt and unfunded liabilities.

The continuous expansion of the public sector, including the pay and benefits to its leadership and its own employees, and the expansion of government entitlement programs, have led to the ruinous taxation of the businesses and workers in the private sector. It is literally destroying our free enterprise economy and replacing it with a redistributive state…and, if the path continues, ultimately a socialist state.

Labels: Private Sector / Public Sector

A fundamental problem in dealing with the issues presented in this book is that we are forced to use terminology that is used by government in providing statistics to us. The terms private sector and public sector gives legitimacy to the idea that there are sectors to our economy.

> The private sector is not a "sector" of the economy.
> It IS the economy!

We should never have allowed the term private sector to become part of the national vernacular, and especially not to be used by our own government. It creates the illusion that the private sector is a part of our economy, and the public sector is another part. It puts the public sector on equal footing as a component of our economy.

There is ONE economy in the United States and it is made up of free citizens, engaged in free enterprise, who HIRE people to serve us in government and public education. We are a free enterprise economy, and what is called the public sector should be identified as what it is, a COST to the free enterprise economy. It is an "expense item" that must be borne by those in the private sector, and it must be carefully managed. When Hillary Clinton said, "It's the economy, stupid," she really should have said, "It's the PRIVATE SECTOR economy, stupid!"

We elect people at every level whose primary job is to represent us in managing and controlling the costs of our governments and public school districts. From school boards, to cities and towns, to state governments and to federal offices, we elect people to see to it that we are taxed fairly and appropriately to provide the services that we require, and that those services are well provided. They

have failed us terribly, allowing costs, deficits and debt to get completely out of control. They appear to have thought that we elected them to go make new rules and pass new laws. We didn't. We elected them to represent us, to see to it that there was full transparency so that we would know exactly what was happening with our tax dollars. We elected them to see to it that our public servants were providing us with what we hired them to do.

Elected officials have allowed compensation and benefits programs to be implemented for our public servants that are unconscionable in their largesse and in their disparity to what the vast majority of private citizens can ever have. They have permitted bogus bookkeeping and Ponzi scheme entitlement programs, hidden from taxpayers and saddling the country with debt for generations to come. They have permitted public education unions to determine virtually every aspect of our children's education, from textbook choices to classroom hours. They have allowed government pay and pensions to be hidden, and their expenses and unfunded liabilities to become a financial anchor that will endure for a hundred years. They have allowed taxes to increase even at times that it is absolutely clear that private sector employers and workers can bear no more. If and when we say "no" to more taxes, they threaten to decrease the services we hired them to deliver in the first place.

> We elect people to see to it that we are taxed fairly and appropriately to provide the services that we require, and that those services are well provided. **They have failed us terribly.**

We must not allow these extortionate tactics to be used. That is why we must be very specific in our requirements of those who seek our votes. We must tell them specifically what we want them to accomplish (the last chapter of this book contains a list). We must then elect officials who "know what their job is" and agree to be held accountable for doing it well. This book is a primer for all of them.

I will sometimes be required to use the term private sector in this book because that is how almost all statistical analysis has been done, and I must use the terminology employed by the statisticians. I grit my teeth when I use the words, and wherever possible I will use the term free enterprise to define the people or businesses who do not work for government or public education.

Each elected official and government agency deals with its own issues, and reports to the taxpayer or the voter. But there are two kinds of taxpayers and two kinds of voters, and we're not talking about Republicans and Democrats. We're talking about private sector voters and public sector voters. It is because the private sector is not a unified force that it is being taxed and legislated out of business by those who want more and bigger government—a bigger government paid for by a smaller and smaller private sector. Increase taxes from decreasing sources. We hear it almost every day. "We have to get more from the greedy corporations and the rich," they say. "Don't worry, we're not going to tax you. We are going to do MORE for you. And THEY will pay for it."

In the traditional definition, the people who are employed by the citizens to provide governance and public education are "public servants" and work in the public sector. They are supported by taxes willingly paid by taxpayers to provide essential services. They are fully supported by taxes, fees and tolls. Although public servants themselves pay income, property and sales taxes, they are doing so with dollars provided to them via taxes in the first place. In that sense, public servants are "recyclers" of tax dollars.

In the traditional sense, everyone who is not a public servant makes up the private sector, and the government uses this approach in categorizing those elements of our economy. It sounds quite simple: If you work for a government or in public education, you are in the public sector, and if you don't, you are in the private sector. The concept is that businesses and individuals who work in the private sector hire, pay and manage their public servants. It is all about taxes. Taxes from the private sector pay the people who work for them in the public sector.

What really confuses the definition of private sector is the stunning growth of "Government Sponsored Enterprises" (GSE) and "non-profits." The federal government uses GSE's to create quasi-government agencies, but forms them as independent corporations, thus moving them out of the public sector category and into the private sector. The United States Postal Service, Fannie Mae, Freddie Mac and a host of other GSE's have been moved into the private sector category, although controlled by Congress and supported by the taxpayer.

Then there is the Federal Reserve Bank (the Fed). Unknown to most Americans, it is a private company not a government agency–and not a GSE–that virtually controls U.S. monetary policy. It has cushy relationships with the government that actually has it buying U.S. debt when (as is true now) Congress has major money problems. Astonishingly, even though our currency is issued at the instruction of the Federal Reserve Bank, and all of our currency says "Federal Reserve Note" on it, Congress does not have the right to audit the Fed! This private Federal Reserve Bank earned a profit of $53 billion in 2009, on top of their $37 billion profit in 2008. That's BILLION! Why isn't Congress complaining about "excessive profits" and "greed" at the Fed? Don't you wonder how much they pay their top officials? We'll never know.

Then there's the non-profit corporation that files for exemption from income taxes on the basis that it is providing a public service. In most cases, these exempt organizations are defined as a public charity and pay no income, sales or property taxes, and can receive additional tax benefits because corporations and individuals can give them money and take a tax deduction for it. Many receive a significant amount of their revenue in the form of government contracts or grants. Some of these public charities are among the largest and (dare I say it?) most profitable institutions in the nation. Like governments, these non-profits tend to provide their employees with benefits well beyond those provided in the real private sector. They can afford to . . . they don't have to pay any taxes. We'll provide some examples of enormous non-profits later in this book.

In higher education, public colleges and universities are added into government tallies of the private sector because they earn income from tuition, even though they pay no taxes and receive enormous financial assistance from tax dollars. They are "quasi-government" institutions that are identified as being in the private sector. The key is that they get tax dollars, but they don't pay tax dollars. They are partially "recyclers," too, as they were paid, in large part, by tax dollars or with Pell Grants and government-issued student loans in the first place.

> So, who actually creates the incremental "new" tax dollars to support the public sector? The answer is that they are all supported, in whole or in part, by the REAL private sector businesses, consisting of all the businesses that are not GSE's, not government agencies, not public education and not "non-profits." And it consists of all of the individual taxpayers who do not work for government or public education. This is the "free enterprise" nation. This is the private sector that is being literally destroyed by the public sector and taxpayer-supported non-profit sector which is out of control.

Our public servants have higher pay, better benefits, earlier retirement and larger pensions than most people in the private sector (who pay the taxes to support them) can imagine. It is a colossal transfer of income and power from the private sector to the public sector that has resulted in the creation of an "aristocracy" that has taken control of the citizens who hired them. Public servants are enriching themselves and using their legislative power to control and burden those who employed them in the first place.

This aristocracy likes their power and benefits, but they need votes to stay in control. To maintain control, they have become redistributors, taking from some and creating dependents of others. They need allies who support redistribution. As we will see later in this book, there are many such allies, not the least are the public sector employees who are organized by well-financed national unions. These organizations receive revenues from dues paid by other employees at other public sector entities elsewhere in the

United States. They use these financial resources to add more public sector entities to their dues-paying stream. The dues are used to promote even more unionism, and to support political candidates. The result is huge voting blocs who make huge political contributions to advance their own interests.

Fewer Jobs in the Private Sector

According to the U.S. Bureau of Labor Statistics, there were 1.5 million fewer employed in the private sector in 2009 than in 1999. About 10 million jobs had been created and then lost during that decade. During that 10 year period, the economy needed to create approximately 2 million new jobs every year to keep up with population growth.

> The really frightening statistic is that while 20 million NEW jobs needed to be created in the private sector in the last decade, we lost 1.5 million jobs. The difference is 21.5 MILLION jobs that should exist today but don't.

Had the needed jobs been created, we'd have 21.5 million more people paying income and payroll taxes and buying goods and services. Our country would be a very different place than it is today. "Help wanted" ads would reappear everywhere. Jobs would be plentiful, because more jobs would be created than people available to fill them. Workers would be in a sellers market, able to command higher wages, and employers would be able to pay them, because 21 million workers become 21 million consumers. Government would breathe a sigh of relief because tax revenues would POUR in. But that didn't happen, and isn't going to happen if we continue on the path we are on.

Government grew by 2 million jobs during the last decade. Those 2 million public sector jobs had to be supported by taxes paid by a much smaller number of companies and workers in the private sector. With every year that passes, a smaller number of private sector workers and companies must support a larger number of the unemployed and public sector workers. The strain on them results in fewer companies and fewer jobs.

The cause of the loss of 1.5 million jobs in the private sector? Obviously, when the housing bubble burst, the real estate and construction industries virtually shut down. And the financial services and stock market meltdown cost Americans trillions. They stopped buying, and the economy stopped growing. Certainly added to the difficulty was the impact of 40% corporate taxes (the second highest in the industrialized world), together with government interference in virtually every aspect of their operations, causing these large employers to fail, shrink or take their operations offshore. That meant fewer jobs, and big trouble for private sector workers and for all public sector entities that are faced with an ever-shrinking tax base.

> With every year that passes, a smaller number of private sector workers and companies must support a larger number of the unemployed and public sector workers.

Less Pay Earned by Private Sector Workers

The Bureau of Economic Analysis reported that in the first quarter of 2010, the pay earned by private sector workers provided the smallest share of personal income (42%) in U.S. history. In the first quarter of 2010 private sector workers earned $300 BILLION less than private sector workers in the last quarter of 2007! Imagine that. A "free enterprise" economy that earns only 42% of national income yet provides all of the **production** for the ENTIRE economy.

What does that all mean? It means that companies are not growing as they once did. The large corporation with its security, perks and benefits has been replaced by much smaller enterprises, including millions of people who started their own business because jobs have not become available as population growth requires. Many millions of these small businesses are LLPs, LLCs, and S corporations. All of these entities must show their profits on personal income tax returns. This means that their business results, appearing on personal returns, have created an illusion that the most successful of these firms should be defined as "the rich," and taxed to redistribute more to those who need it. When smaller employers cannot invest their profits back into their own growth (because it was taken away in taxes), they will not grow and they will not create new jobs.

The Jobs Squeeze

We all know that we have a jobs problem, but we haven't really dealt with the jobs squeeze that lies ahead in the next decade. **Three monstrous forces are at work:**

1. The currently unemployed, desperately seeking a job;
2. The older workers, especially "baby boomers" who will not leave the workforce as expected because they can't afford to; and
3. The young people attempting to enter the workforce.

In Chapter Six we'll show you how three legs of the baby boomers retirement stool have been cut off, and that many won't be able to retire at age 65. Some large portion of the 5 million people reaching age 65 every year for the next 15 years will either postpone retirement, or literally work until they die.

We know there are 10–15 million unemployed persons looking for jobs today. And we know that older workers can't afford to leave the workforce by retiring. That creates a "squeeze" in itself. But when you add the 2 million younger workers graduating from high school and college every year, where will their jobs come from? In an article in the *Wall Street Journal* titled "The Kids Are Not Alright," Daniel Henninger reported that the current unemployment rate for workers under 25 is 20%. Although he agrees that a new "green" economy will create some jobs, he reminded us that, "Since 1990, roughly 80 million Americans have been born. They can't all be organic farmers or write scripts for *30 Rock*." Well said, Mr. Henninger.

Robert Reich, the former Secretary of Labor agrees. He wrote in a *Wall Street Journal* op-ed piece that the jobs picture still looks bleak. He agrees that 150,000 jobs a month need to be created to keep up with population growth, and notes that since December 2007, we have lost 8.4 million jobs. According to Reich, "even if we create 300,000 new jobs a month, we could be looking at 5-8 years to catch up." By my math, he's overly optimistic. His assumptions undoubtedly are based on the premise that many people currently in the workforce will retire and that the economy will improve. I don't think they can or it will.

Right now, we need about 21 million more jobs than we have in America. And we need about 2 million more new ones to be created every year. Imagine what would happen if all those jobs were created? Everyone could get a job. Every employee would be a "hot commodity," getting paid more and with a wider choice of employment. The economy would soar. People would have money to spend. Governments would be flush with tax revenues. Businesses would prosper and grow. But that can't happen unless we make some very big changes.

The searing question for the next decade is: **How do we allow our free enterprise economy to grow and to create more jobs?**

Can government induce the private sector to create jobs? Can government hire 25 million more people? Unless you are absolutely and totally a socialist, and want yourself and everyone else to be employed by the government who will allocate resources as they see fit, you know that government cannot create enough jobs to solve our economy's problems. Government can't create jobs, but it can destroy them. Free enterprise creates jobs. If government interferes less, and taxes less, business will prosper and jobs will be created.

So how do we create jobs? Do we use government coercion and tax penalties to stop companies from sending jobs overseas? Virtually every economist agrees that won't work. Like it or not, we are in a global economy. You, and consumers everywhere, will buy the best product you can get for the dollar that you have available. We cannot force employers to stay in the U.S. and pay a higher wage base and expect to compete in the world marketplace. If we try to mandate that, the large U.S. companies doing business worldwide will simply "re-flag." They will become foreign companies, selling some of their products in the United States. That happened years ago with our shipping industry.

America used to have plenty of ships. But requirements that they hire only U.S. unionized crews resulted in the end of an entire industry. American companies couldn't compete with the fleets of other countries because our costs were so much higher. Other than the U.S. Navy, most American-owned ships are today "flagged" in another country, and those ships can hire anyone as crew that they feel are qualified for the job. In attempting to mandate hiring practices we lost ships, ship-repair businesses, all the jobs associated with them, and we lost a national maritime heritage. That can easily happen again, but this time, it won't be just ships. It will be entire corporations. There's an old Mississippi saying, "Business goes where it is invited, and stays where it is welcome." They know a few things down in Mississippi, and they need to share their wisdom with the folks in Washington, D.C.

> Free enterprise creates jobs. If government interferes less, and taxes less, business will prosper and jobs will be created.

Jobs: Here and Abroad

We read about the evils of American companies sending jobs offshore quite often. But companies don't send jobs offshore–you do. The consumers of the world do. And governments do so by creating tax policy that attracts or repels business investment and growth. Back in 1987, I moved our very small company of 12 people from New Jersey to Florida. We were a "back office" operation and it didn't matter where we were, but our charges to our customers DID matter to them. By moving to Florida, we cut our occupancy costs in half, and our personnel costs in half. It was the 1987 equivalent of "going offshore." We went where our costs were lower so that we could survive and ultimately prosper. We did survive and we did prosper, creating more than 1,000 jobs that are still there today. If we had stayed in New Jersey, we would have failed. You can't have DOUBLE the overhead and charge higher prices and survive. Competition would have killed us, because the buyer wants the best price he can get, and if we had stayed in New Jersey someone else (probably in Florida!) would have been the success story, not us.

The automobile industry is a good example of how costs and tax policies can kill a business. It's been well known since the 1980s that the "Big Three"—Ford, GM and Chrysler—had huge labor costs. They had agreed to some very quirky and expensive work-place rules and high rates of compensation. They were also faced with legacy costs of paying for health insurance and pensions for retirees that effectively doubled their total labor costs. They had a hard time competing with cars shipped here from countries whose labor costs were far lower. But using good old American ingenuity they survived by selling cars that Americans wanted. For the most part, they were uniquely American cars...big, comfortable, long-range cruisers; fast, sporty convertibles; and practical "soccer mom" multi-purpose minivans.

The American driving market is vastly different than European and Asian markets. In the U.S., we are generally not constricted by narrow roads through our cities and towns, so we can build our cars larger. We have a massive interstate highway system, so we can build cars designed for long range driving comfort. Our nation is 3,000 miles long and borderless. We can drive from Maine to California on wide and fast-moving highways. Texas is as big as France, one of the largest countries in Europe. It is quite easy to drive 600–700 miles in a day in the U.S., but in Europe, with few exceptions, you'd be traveling through small towns and villages and could never achieve those long-range results. America is 2 ½ times the size of all of Europe. We have a lot of land, and because of that we have a huge suburban lifestyle. We drive to get almost every-thing we need. Many of us don't live in cities where you can walk to the local supermarket or the corner butcher shop. We depend on our cars. We depend on getting to work in our cars in any weather conditions. And we depend on them for everyday living. And, maybe most important of all, we love our cars. They are not just basic transportation to most of us. To many Americans, cars represent freedom. We can go where we want to, when we want to and how we want to. Cars for many of us represent absolute freedom of self-expression and self-determination.

Because of our nation's massive size and the widespread nature of our population around cities, public transportation in many places is impractical. The result of all this is that we developed uniquely American vehicles including the station wagon, the minivan and the SUV, and we created the light truck as a vehicle capable of meeting all the same needs as our other vehicles plus serving as a "truck." For those who didn't need large vehicles, we developed cars like the Mustang, the Camaro and the Barracuda. For others, we created the Jeep. We made cars fun, or luxurious, or tough, or fast. If you wanted it, we made it. In spite of the fact that U.S. automakers had HUGE labor costs, they survived by creating American cars for the American market. And people bought them.

As foreign automakers eyed the U.S. market, they said, "We can build minivans, too, and we can build light trucks, jeeps and comfortable cruising cars. We can copy those ideas. But these will be built primarily for the American market. They won't work well in Asia or Europe. We need to build them in America."

So, "Coming to America" to open new plants were Mercedes and Toyota, Honda and Nissan, and so many more. Labor costs weren't a problem. Even if they had to unionize, they wouldn't have the legacy health care and pension costs for retirees that American automakers had. That meant total labor costs of less than one-half of the Big Three. And if they located plants in non-traditional places, like Tennessee or Alabama, they might not have unions at all. Since they'd be building new plants from scratch, they could eliminate much of the manual labor by building state-of-the art assembly lines and quality assurance techniques. And best of all, government would PAY them to come here to create jobs.

So, the state governments of Alabama and Tennessee and other states started bidding wars to get the new foreign-owned plants built in their states. They might give land, or provide tax incentives or tax breaks, or training subsidies to the foreign automaker. What an edge! Of course Nissan, Toyota and other foreign-owned companies could have an advantage in competition and they could make huge profits. You bought those cars. What happened is that the demanding consumer combined with the tax policies of some states (designed to "create jobs" in their own state) caused the automakers in other states to go out of business.

One key "takeaway" here is that tax policy in one state can wipe out jobs in another state. Since every state gets federal money, and money is "fungible" (i.e. money is money is money), are we, the national federal taxpayers, giving huge tax incentives to foreign-owned companies to create jobs in one state at the expense of wiping-out jobs in other states? If that is the right solution, South Dakota should raise a few billion dollars (borrowed from the federal government?) and give an incentive to every automaker in the world to come there, start a new company and build cars. They could give them free land, tax breaks and even train the entire workforce. They could create jobs and become a boom-state. What's wrong with this picture?

Another key "takeaway" is that consumers will buy the best product at the best price for them. They did not buy television sets built in America because they wanted to "support American workers." They did not, and do not, buy manufactured goods that are made in the U.S. if an equal product made elsewhere costs less. That's why we manufacture very little in the U.S. today. People work for less in other countries. Virtually every product made must be sold on the world market in competition with companies elsewhere in the world. Only those offering the best value will survive.

So, if preventing jobs from going offshore is not the answer, what is? Can government create jobs? Recently the federal government said they were going to help create jobs by providing tax credits. Duh! How does a tax credit benefit me if I'm already losing my shirt and don't pay taxes, anyway? What businesses are saying is, "I need customers to come through the door!" People that have jobs and money to spend, spend money. So, how do you create customers?

That brings us to "the chicken or the egg" dilemma. Which comes first, the jobs or the people spending money that create the jobs? Jobs create prosperity, and prosperous people spend money and create more jobs. People working and spending pay taxes, and government likes that.

No jobs mean no prosperity, no spending, no growth and fewer taxpayers. It's a "death spiral" and we're in it right now. How do you start a jobs creation cycle? Get government to hire everybody? That won't work unless you are willing to accept, fully and completely, the idea of becoming a socialist country. To avoid that result, free enterprise must prosper. That means government must get out of its way. But government is IN the way. Its spending, deficits and debt require taking more and more and more from the only productive element of our economy, the private sector.

In the chapters that follow, we'll show you some stunning revelations of how government is hiding the facts from taxpayers and killing our free enterprise economy.

*"… Congress has shown no sign it intends to meaningfully address the oncoming fiscal train wreck from the **unsustainable** growth in entitlements."*

—Jim Nussle, Director,
Office of Management and Budget
March 3, 2008

_____ Chapter Three _____

Disparity of Public Sector / Private Sector Pay and Benefits

There is a huge disparity between public sector and private sector pay and benefits caused mainly by overly generous and largely unfunded early retirement plans for government and public education workers, and by abuses routinely tolerated in these plans.

It is important to point out that those employed in government and public education did not create the problem. They accepted employment according to the terms provided by the public sector institution that they chose to join. While it is fair to attack the public policies and accounting and reporting practices that have led to massive taxpayer liabilities, it would be unfair to imply that such criticism is aimed at those who work in the public sector. They did not make the rules, and are not individually responsible for the determination of the pay and benefits they receive. What follows is aimed at bad policies, not bad people, and we have not used individual names in the examples we'll cite because we are not attempting to blame or criticize individuals who choose to work in the public sector.

> The myth of modest compensation in public sector jobs versus private sector riches is an absurdly inaccurate one. Study after study has shown that average public sector pay and benefits are significantly higher than can be provided in the private sector.

The federal government has become adept at deflecting attention away from its own excesses and in pointing a collective finger, instead, at corporations and executive pay. It's easy to stir community outrage when singling out a well-compensated CEO. Congress loves using its bully pulpit to denounce excesses in the private sector, especially when it can use (misuse) its authority to summon, and then browbeat, private industry executives in an environment that has Congressmen firmly in charge, seated at a higher level and with ownership of the microphone. It provides Congress with control of the conversation, the opportunity to be uncommonly rude to executives who may have done nothing wrong or illegal and to amass "sound bites" for play on network media. The added hysteria of complaining that executives of multi-billion dollar corporations have come to Washington in their company-owned and paid-for private jets, while the Speaker herself commands a 757 jet entirely at taxpayer expense, is mind-boggling in its hypocrisy.

While Congress can claim that these companies should be summoned to testify because these companies are "broke" and in need of help from the taxpayer, the corporate financial problems pale in comparison to those created by many of the same Congressmen and women who enjoy pillorying the private sector. All this congressional interest in private sector pay takes place while being remarkably silent on questioning the pay at companies controlled by Congress, such as Freddie Mac and Fannie Mae. In spite of their huge losses, insurmountable debt and business practices that virtually sank the entire U.S. economy, executives of these companies made, and continue to make, many millions of dollars a year. Since Fannie Mae and Freddie Mac are directly controlled by Congress, it would appear reasonable to assume that Congress might want to look into executive compensation practices in these companies because taxpayers are "on the hook" for hundreds of billions, probably trillions, of dollars of losses being incurred while these execs make millions.

Private companies either go out of business or their stock drops if and when payment to executives, or other employees, cannot be supported and justified by increasing profitability. Stockholders can and do fire CEOs who are at the helm when losses are sustained, and reward them when stock prices increase. Virtually all executive compensation in the publicly-traded private sector is tied to increases in stock prices, and that practice benefits the shareholders.

We often hear about the "outrageous" pay to corporate CEOs. Here's an example of how misleading those stories can be: Let's say that the board of directors of a company whose stock is trading at $10 a share gives one million stock options to its CEO. Typically, the options will say that if the CEO is still employed when choosing to exercise these options, he may exercise the right to buy the shares from the corporation, for the next 10 years, at $10 a share. The idea is that giving him or her the future right to buy stock at today's price is only of value if the stock goes UP. If the stock stays at $10 or decreases in value, the options are worth ZERO. The idea of the options is to motivate the CEO to do what it takes to make the stock go up, benefitting the shareholders. Now we get to year two: The stock has increased in value by $2 a share. Since the stock went up by $2 a share, the corporation must take an "expense" charge for compensation to the CEO of $2 a share, times one million shares, or $2 million dollars. The executive actually received nothing. He did not exercise his options. He did not sell any stock. The corporation gave him nothing. But the corporation must show, as an expense for compensation to the CEO, **two million dollars**. It's an accounting rule that tends to mislead, but it's the rule. That's how almost all of these stories about "excessive" executive compensation get started. The company actually did not give him/her that money. The shareholders gained $2 a share. That's what they hired the CEO to accomplish. So, when you hear of the OUTRAGEOUS compensation to CEOs, take it with a grain of salt.

No one is forced to buy stock in a private company. If they don't like the way the company is run (either in executive compensation or otherwise) they are free to sell their stock. The practices related to the compensation of executives in private sector companies are the right of the owners of the company, and not of the government. But government, by keeping the focus on the "excesses" of the private sector, can attempt to keep the taxpayer distracted from what it is doing with taxpayer dollars in the public sector. What government is often doing is giving the tax money to itself.

Public sector institutions employ approximately 22,000,000 people. About one-half are employed in public education and the other one-half by various local and state entities and by our federal government. An estimated 17 million of these public servants have guaranteed defined benefit pension plans and are allowed to retire before the age of 65. There are 2,543 nonfederal pension plans covering a variety of employee types, including teachers, police, firefighters and general government employees. Almost all the public sector early retirees also receive free or subsidized health insurance benefits.

> The true cost of maintaining the retirement pay and benefits of these public servants represents one of the largest claims on taxpayer dollars of all kinds in the United States.

The Public Sector Tends to be Unified While the Private Sector is Not

The public sector is generally unified. It consists of many large monolithic organizations that are connected to each other by common purpose, by dependence on federal and local taxes for funding and by unions that combine disparate elements, like teachers in Arizona with teachers in Maine, or police and firefighters in Utah with those in Florida. **They have a common purpose: to get more from taxpayers.**

Such unity of purpose does not yet exist in the private sector. Large corporations, smaller companies, entrepreneurs and workers in the free enterprise portion of the economy have never presented a united front in order to achieve public and tax policy changes that would benefit their own collective interests. Everyone in the private sector should be in favor of lower corporate taxes. They should all be in favor of smaller, less expensive government. They should all oppose pay and benefits disparity between public sector workers and themselves. But the private sector lacks unification, and instead has tended to concentrate on individual personal or corporate interests.

In doing our research concerning public and private sector pay disparity, the biggest problem was trying to find out what actually is provided to public sector workers as benefits, and what they cost. With 89,000 different public sector entities there is little hope than anyone could ever look at all them. Even restricting our research to pension plans wouldn't narrow the scope enough, as there are more than 2,500 different public sector pension plans.

Making the job even more difficult is the fact that this information is not publicly disclosed in any meaningful way. The information we have been able to find has come from many sources. Important ones have been the *St. Petersburg Times, Forbes* magazine and the *Wall Street Journal*. Other significant resources have been think tanks that delve deeply into public sector spending and debt, like The Cato Institute, The American Enterprise Institute and The Tax Foundation. Key additional information for this book has been obtained through individuals who found out that something "smelled bad" and decided to do their own research. People like Bill Zettler in Illinois made himself an expert on Illinois public education pay and benefits, and then started looking into the other areas of the public sector. And Jack Dean in California created an organization and a website to disclose the "pension tsunami" that is destroying California financially.

The essential problem is that there is no uniform disclosure requirement that forces public sector entities to tell us exactly what their pay and benefits practices are, and there is also no uniform requirement that makes them use acceptable accounting and reporting standards to tell us what the unfunded liabilities of these benefits programs are. Much of the information that has been gathered has been obtained under the "Freedom of Information Act." Think about that. In order to find out where our tax dollars are going, we have to use the Freedom of Information Act to find out.

As we have discovered, things are very good in the public sector! Employee satisfaction increased in 71% of federal organizations between 2007 and 2009, according to *The Best Places to Work in the Federal Government 2009*, a report produced by the Partnership for Public Service and American University's Institute for the Study of Public Policy Implementation. During that time period about 8 million private sector workers lost their jobs. I wonder who is asking how content they are?

> *"That's extraordinary...the American taxpayer is paying for exorbitant benefits, compensation and pay scale that are double their own average salaries. That is utterly mad. That's the stuff of revolutions, I believe."*
>
> —Lou Dobbs, CNN

Lou Dobbs was reacting to the report by the Cato Institute's Chris Edwards who had done a study of Bureau of Economic Analysis data. The study showed that **as of 2008, the average federal worker received $119,982 in compensation and benefits compared with the private sector average of $59,909.** Most striking was the "benefits" component of compensation. The federal worker won with $40,785 for benefits compared with the private sector worker at $9,881. This difference in the total annual compensation between federal and private sector workers was $60,073 in 2008. With a total of 1.9 million federal workers, the **difference** in annual compensation was $114 BILLION a year, taken from the private sector businesses and their employees to pay federal workers.

Is the difference due to excessive government generosity, or is it due to the private sector's unwillingness to pay its workers fairly? One way to answer that question is to assume that all private sector workers would receive pay and benefits to equal average federal worker levels. But that would not be possible to do. For private sector employers to match the pay and benefits of the federal government and pay their workers the same as federal workers, their payrolls would have to increase by an impossible $7 trillion a year, or about one-half the GDP (gross domestic product) of the United States. Clearly, that could not be done.

But what if pro-government pundits are right when they say that's an unfair comparison because federal workers do not mirror the private sector workforce? While they don't say this directly, they imply that federal workers are smarter and/or better educated, and that average compensation comparisons are unfair. Let's suppose we concede that federal workers are smarter and that average direct compensation to federal workers of $80,000 a year is appropriate, even though it is $30,000 a year more than the average private sector worker's $50,000 annual pay. How do we explain that the federal workers receive an additional average of $40,000 a year in employee benefits, while the private sector worker receives $10,000? Should federal workers receive benefits equaling 50% of their salaries that are 4 TIMES the level provided in the private sector? (Remember that public servants are paid from taxes of those in the private sector.)

Just the $30,000 per year difference in benefits costs between federal and private sector workers amounts to $60 billion a year. **That's $60 billion a year (and increasing every year) taxed to income tax payers, 85% of whom are in the private sector, to provide federal workers with benefits they don't have themselves.** It would cost private sector employers $3.5 trillion a year just to increase the benefits of private sector workers to federal employee benefits levels. That's clearly impossible.

No matter how the disparity is examined, private sector workers are charged taxes to provide federal workers with a disproportionately high level of benefits. Federal pay and benefits policies exist in a world of unending access to funds, and an unending requirement from federal employee unions to do "more."

> Despite the devastating impact of near-record unemployment levels in the private sector, the federal government actually grew in 2009, and significantly increased compensation and benefits to their own employees. Knowing the private sector was literally dying, unemployment was at near record levels, and the government was incurring absolutely impossible new debt loads, they gave themselves all raises, anyway.

To rub salt in the wound of the private sector, federal workers were rewarded on January 1, 2009, with a 3.9% cost of living raise (an average of $3,000 each); again in March with an increase in paid time off for child care; and again in October when they began being allowed to save unused sick and vacation days and be paid for them in their final year before retirement. This actually gave them a "twofer:" being paid for unused days at a much higher rate of pay than when they were earned, and increasing their final earnings and therefore their pension benefits.

During the year federal workers also qualified for "step grade" raises averaging another 3%, for a total average annual increase of 6.9%, plus their improvement in benefits! Late in 2009, government workers were told that their cost of living raise on January 1, 2010, would be "only 2%," providing them with another average increase of $1,600, in addition to their step-grade 3% raises that would be earned during the year as time-in-service raises would become payable. That is a payroll increase (not counting benefits) of 11.9% in 2009–2010 when federal worker benefits and compensation were ALREADY MORE THAN DOUBLE the average private sector benefits and compensation at the end of 2008.

2010 Base General Schedule Pay Scale (Incorporating a 1.50% pay increase)

Effective January 3, 2010

Note: The following is a BASE pay scale. All U.S. locations receive additional pay adjustments above the base pay ranging from 14% to 35.15%.

Grade	Step									
	1	2	3	4	5	6	7	8	9	10
1	17803	18398	18990	19579	20171	20519	21104	21694	21717	22269
2	20017	20493	21155	21717	21961	22607	23253	23899	24545	25191
3	21840	22568	23296	24024	24752	25480	26208	26936	27664	28392
4	24518	25335	26152	26969	27786	28603	29420	30237	31054	31871
5	27431	28345	29259	30173	31087	32001	32915	33829	34743	35657
6	30577	31596	32615	33534	34653	35672	36691	37710	38729	39748
7	33979	35112	36245	37378	38511	39644	40777	41910	43043	44176
8	37631	38885	40139	41393	42647	43901	45155	46409	47663	48917
9	41563	42948	44333	45718	47103	48488	49873	51258	52643	54028
10	45771	47297	48823	50349	51875	53401	54927	56453	57979	59505
11	50287	51963	53639	55315	56991	58667	60343	62019	63695	65371
12	60274	62283	64292	66301	68310	70319	72328	74337	76346	78355
13	71674	74063	76452	78841	81230	83619	86008	88397	90786	93175
14	84697	87520	90343	93166	95989	98812	101635	104458	107281	110104
15	99628	102949	106270	109591	112912	116233	119554	122875	126196	129517

Source: Federal Research Service, http://www.fedjobs.com/pay/pay.html

Pay rates for Senior Executive Service (SES), Senior Level (SL) and Scientific & Professional (ST) positions range from $119,554 to $179,700.

Note: SL & ST employees receive the appropriate percentage pay adjustment for their area.

Let's take a look at how federal step grades work and how "location pay" boosts these ranges even further, as described on the Federal Research Service Website. Even the LOWEST pay level shown here is boosted by an additional pay adjustment, typically ranging from 14% to 35%. For example, if you work in Chicago, you'll get 25.10% tacked on to your base pay. Houston? It's 28.71% higher than what's noted below. San Francisco? Tack on a whopping 35.15%. And if you're not in one of the 33 locations with specific location adjustments provided, well, heck, you'll get 14.16% added to the base pay rates noted below anyway!

Pay rates for Senior Executive Service (SES), Senior Level (SL) and Scientific & Professional (ST) positions range from $119,554 to $179,700, with SL & ST employees also receiving location pay adjustments.

So, if you are a GS-10, Step 1 in Atlanta, your base pay is $45,771 and the location adjustment for Atlanta is 19.29%, so you'll multiply:

$$\$45,771 \times 0.1929 = \$8,829.22$$

You'll add the result back to the base pay:
$$\$45,771 + \$8,829 = \$54,600$$

Therefore, the starting salary for a GS-10, Step 1 in Atlanta is $54,600

The Recession and Economic Downturn Did Not Affect Pay of Federal Workers

The economic impact of the current record-setting recession and accompanying high-unemployment rates has not adversely affected federal workers.

> Nearly 20% of federal workers now have salaries of $100,000 or more. According to Dennis Cauchon in a USA Today article on December 11, 2009, "Defense Department civilian employees earning $150,000 or more increased from 1,868 in December 2007 to 10,100 in June, 2009."

That is a 500% increase in the number of Defense Department employees earning more than $150,000, occurring in an 18 month period. And that's just the Defense Department!

In 2000, the average federal employee earned compensation and benefits that were 60% higher than the average in the private sector. Eight years later, by 2008, the difference had grown to 100%. The disparity continued to broaden in 2009 as government increased direct payroll and benefits costs by more than 6.9%, far greater than the 1.5% average of the private sector.

Health care benefits and other perks provided to public sector workers (at taxpayer expense) are far superior to those that private sector companies can afford to provide their employees. The federal government offers most employees the choice of a 4 day work week; generous holiday and vacation benefits including 10 holidays, 13-26 vacation days, and 13 sick days; flexible work schedules; and tax-free "forgiveness" of up to $100,000 in student loans for employees who stay 10 years. In addition, more than 200 federal agencies offer on-site childcare centers.

What's more, federal workers have a three-tiered pension program—a defined benefit plan, a Thrift Savings Plan and Social Security. In addition to a generous defined benefit pension plan, retirement at 55 and subsidized health insurance after retirement, their "Thrift Plan"—a government version of a 401(k)—allows for a 5% pre-tax contribution, matched by the government. Even if an employee chooses not to participate, the government will contribute 1% of pay to the account.

A Closer Look at Government Generosity Towards Its Own

To appreciate the subtle ways that government can provide benefits to their own employees that taxpayers don't see, you sometimes have to "peel back the onion" and look at the details of some of these benefits. Let's look at just one of them–the "Thrift Plan" provided to federal employees. It is **in addition** to the pension plan that is provided, and by itself is far superior to the typical 401(k) plan that is generally provided for retirement in the private sector.

The government Thrift Plan matches up to 5% of the employee's pre-tax contribution. The employee has several investment choices, one of which is the "G Plan." The G Plan consists of federal securities that are not available to anyone but government employees, and pays interest 2%–3% higher than the returns that nongovernment investors receive when they buy a Treasury. They are fully guaranteed government securities that have no risk of loss. The benefits of this program are significant. If you invested an average of $4,000 a year, matched with a $4,000 government contribution, and earned 4.5% a year (easy to accomplish with the G Plan), you'd have $517,000 at retirement at age 55. That's age 55. You would have contributed $120,000. Most of the remaining $397,000 **comes from the taxpayer** through matching contributions and interest rate payments that exceed the rates you would receive if you were a private sector employee and bought the Treasuries available to the public. Remember, this is a "supplemental" plan, in addition to the pension plan that pays about 50% of pay beginning at age 55 with cost of living increases. The federal government is very generous to their employees with taxpayer money.

State and Local Government Pay/Benefits Disparity

State and local governments and public education can be even more generous with our tax dollars. They can and do provide pre-age 65 retirement pension for public servants of $100,000, $200,000, $300,000 and even $500,000 a year. They can provide public school teachers with the benefit of working 9 months a year while also getting spring and winter breaks and umpteen holidays as well as with retirement at age 58 with a pension of $100,000 or more a year, free health insurance and a guaranteed 3% pension raise every year. They can provide police and firefighters in many cities with retirement in their 40s or early 50s with pensions of $100,000+, and guaranteed increases every year. And we have seen that federal workers can work a four-day workweek with fabulous vacation, sick-pay and health insurance benefits, and then retire 10 years earlier than private sector workers at monthly pensions four to six times higher than private sector workers get under Social Security and with heavily subsidized health insurance.

It is impossible to overstate the significance of the cost of pre-age 65 retirement for public sector workers. Almost every one of the 89,000 public sector establishments allows their employees to retire well before the age at which Social Security benefits become payable for private sector workers. This practice results in the need for these entities to accumulate, during the abbreviated working years, enough money to pay the retiree for an extended period.

> It is impossible to overstate the significance of the cost of pre-age 65 retirement for public sector workers.

Average U.S. mortality is 80 years of age. Retirement at age 65 (moving to age 67, depending on the year of birth of the individual) in the private sector results with Social Security benefits payable for an average of 15 years, and entitlement to Medicare simultaneous with the retirement date. In the public sector, retirement begins earlier and thus is paid longer.

In the public sector, pre 65 retirement, (during which time Medicare is not available), necessitates that health insurance be made available, at least until age 65. That places an added burden on public sector entities providing BOTH pension payments and free or heavily-subsidized health insurance to their pre-age 65 retirees. The combination of earlier retirement at amounts well in excess of what Social Security provides, with continued health insurance, is a staggering cost to taxpayers, as will be illustrated later in this chapter.

Why does the public sector allow retirement before age 65 in the first place? The reason is there are sound public policy reasons for doing so in certain limited situations, such as "high-risk" occupations. Let's examine some of them.

The obvious justification for early retirement is the military. The military, of necessity, must be composed of those who are physically able to endure the rigors of combat and combat training. It must be kept young. As a result, the military must create an environment where they routinely "kick out" heroic people who have risked their lives in service to us to continuously make room for young additions to the forces. It makes absolute sense to provide retirement pre-age 65. It serves three purposes: It is a "risk premium" paid for gallant services; it makes it possible to recruit people into the military in the first place (who would take a job if they knew they would be "fired" at age 45–55?); and it creates room for the upward mobility of younger servicemen, servicewomen and officers.

It can be convincingly argued that we do not do nearly enough for our military and their families. I am particularly sympathetic to that cause, as I grew up as an "Army Brat" and know firsthand of the enormous hardships endured by our military and their families. Suffice it to say that early retirement for the military makes great sense, and we as taxpayers should be absolutely in favor of this practice, and we should recognize that double dipping (i.e. retiring and then taking a full-time job with the government or elsewhere), makes absolute sense in this case. Military retirement benefits are inadequate to provide full and absolute retirement income for life, and those who are too old to remain at combat-ready status can continue to serve us in the civilian world as they use their training and experience to continue to contribute to our nation's best interests.

A second category is "high-risk" public sector jobs, including police and firefighters. They, too, should be eligible for pre-age 65 retirement for many of the same reasons that they are provided to the military, but there are some important differences. Most police and firefighters are unionized, and have a broad array of benefits and work rules that do not apply in the military. They also generally receive higher pay and overtime pay, during their working careers.

The military does NOT pay overtime. In addition, pensions are significantly higher for most police and firefighters than are provided to our military. And although their personal risk can be high, they are not sent to distant assignments in the U.S. or on overseas tours-of-duty that require an abandonment of their families for months, or even a year, at a time. And they are never involved in daily combat situations for weeks and months at a time. While we certainly want to reward those who risk life and limb in service to us, we also want to be treated fairly by those who receive the benefits that are willingly and generously bestowed by grateful taxpayers.

The problem is that many police and firefighter pension plans also tend to allow widespread abuse, from "spiking" final pay with overtime to earn larger pensions, to trumped-up "disability" retirement. Our police and firefighter pension plans are enormously expensive, in part because of the gamesmanship that is permitted in order to obtain pensions that are far higher than the taxpayer ever intended. Our police and firefighters definitely should be entitled to pre-age 65 retirement, and pay commensurate with the skill and high-risk requirements of their jobs. They should not be allowed to abuse or "game" pension plans that have been provided to them.

> With the exception of the military, firefighters and police, what is the justification for providing EVERY public sector worker and EVERY schoolteacher with retirement before age 65? There is none. Private sector taxpayers have never been asked if they wanted to provide these benefits to 20 million public sector workers who are NOT in high-risk occupations, and many taxpayers do not know that they pay taxes to provide early retirement pensions and benefits to their public servants that they cannot afford for themselves.

An editorial in the March 26, 2010 *Wall Street Journal* reported, "In 2008, almost half of all state and local government expenditures, or an estimated $1.1 trillion, went toward the pay and benefits of public workers" and that according to the Bureau of Labor Statistics "the average state or local public employee received $39.66 in total compensation per hour versus $27.42 for private workers." That's an average of $82,492 per year for state or local public sector employees versus $57,033 for the private sector, for a difference of $25,489 per year. **With 19 million workers in the nonfederal public sector, that means that the excess in pay and benefits totals about $484 BILLION a year.**

Since the total of all nonfederal public sector pay and benefits costs in 2008 was an estimated $1.1 trillion, that means approximately 42% of all state/local expenditures went to provide pay and benefits to public sector workers at levels in **excess** of the pay and benefits received by the private sector. **That is worth contemplation: More than $484 billion a year is taken in taxes to provide public sector workers with MORE than they would have if they were in the private sector.** Add that to the $114 billion resulting from the $60,000 a year pay and benefits differential that exists between federal and private sector workers, and we end up with a transfer of a nice, neat $600 billion from taxpayers to public employees, just to pay for the difference between their pay and benefits and those in the private sector!

Those figures assume that government representations to us as to their payroll and benefits costs are accurate. They are not, because government greatly understates the unfunded liability of its retirement plans. We will see later that these liabilities are often understated by as much as 600%-800%. Thus, it appears that the pay and benefits differential is an average of $28,000, when it is actually far greater than that. What is the REAL cost difference? No one knows for sure, but we can make an estimate, based on other studies that have been done.

Let's start with the total taxes paid by all taxpayers to nonfederal public sector entities. In 2008, that was about $2.2 trillion. About half, or $1.1 trillion was for pay and benefits. According to their own misleading accounting practices, these entities had an additional $400 billion in unfunded liabilities, which we assume (but can't guarantee) were included in the benefits portion of their calculations. Unfunded liabilities are promises that have been made for which no money has been set aside. The need to pay these benefits from current revenues (because money to pay them has never been set aside) will show up each year as a "new" increase in the cost of government. **Independent studies show the true unfunded liabilities is closer to $3.5 trillion, than $400 billion…a $3.1 TRILLION difference.** What does that mean? It means that when we see the cost of benefits for public sector workers, we are seeing a grossly understated number. So, the person who looks as if they "only" cost $28,000 more in pay/benefits than a private sector worker, could be multiples of that number.

> If unfunded pension plan liability calculations prepared by outside experts are correct (we'll see these numbers in the next chapter), it means that **more than 100%** of all taxes received by governments could be going to provide for their own pay and benefits. How could it be MORE than 100%? It's actually quite easy. They just borrow the rest. They can hide the truth from us, borrow what it takes to "run the government" and continue to raise taxes when they need even more. It is called "deficit spending" and every government is doing it.

And it requires more and more debt and more and more taxes. If we complain about tax increases, they'll say, "OK, we'll just cut back on employees and cut services." But they won't cut back on their own pay and benefits. They are virtually all unionized, they work on seniority and the senior people make the rules. They will cut services to us, and they will fire those with the least seniority if they have to, but the top folks (can we call them fat cats?) will keep what they've got.

According to 4th quarter 2009 data from the U.S. Bureau of Labor Statistics, many states have average total compensation per job figures that are higher for government jobs than for private sector jobs. In most states, it is the value of the rich state benefits programs that leads to this disparity. These total compensation figures include wage/salary disbursements and supplements such as employer contributions for employee pensions and various insurances. When looking at wages/salaries only, annualized from hourly rates, private sector jobs averaged $40,373, and the value of employer-provided benefits averaged $16,640. For state/local government jobs, wages/salaries averaged $54,309, with benefits averaging $28,059, or 69% higher than that of the average private sector job.

In Rhode Island, the total compensation per job averaged $73,540 for government jobs in 2008 but only $50,814 for private sector jobs, according to calculations using data from the U.S. Bureau of Economic Analysis. The value of government-provided benefits averages 146% higher than that of average private sector jobs. In West Virginia, the value of benefits is a whopping 212% higher for government jobs. Similar compensation disparities were noted in many other states, including Montana ($53,568 for government jobs versus $39,363 for private sector) and Florida ($63,960 versus $48,696). In Hawaii, the value of government-provided **benefits** averaged $24,991 in 2008, **or 231%** higher than that of the average private sector job.

Even when benefits are excluded from comparisons between public and private sector employees, compensation levels to public servants can be jaw dropping. A *San Francisco Chronicle* article by Rachel Gordon (April 26, 2010) cited some examples of high pay and resulting budget woes. She reported "more than 1 in 3 of San Francisco's nearly 27,000 city workers earned $100,000 or more last year," up 800% over the last decade. "And that doesn't include the cost of...benefits such as health care and pensions." According to Gordon, a police chief retired in 2009 with a $516,000 payout for unused vacation, sick days and comp time. The average city worker salary was reported to be $93,000 a year, before benefits costs are added. The head of the Municipal Transport Agency is the highest-paid at $322,000 last year. The current mayor, while running for reelection in 2007, negotiated a 23% pay increase for police and firefighters over the next four years, in spite of the fact that he knew that San Francisco would be dealing with a $483 million deficit looming ahead in its upcoming fiscal year.

> Examples of pay and benefits that have gone totally out of control are everywhere, and the tax burden to pay for all of this is literally killing the private sector and our country. How did this happen? In a nutshell, because we let it happen and because our elected officials of both parties, for decades, have allowed it to happen.

Unsustainable—and Immoral

The fact is that we have created an almost insurmountable financial problem for our nation's taxpayers. It has been called **unsustainable** by virtually everyone that looks at it. Our debt and unfunded liability load is truly **unsustainable** even if we accept the lower estimates arrived at by financial experts and think tanks. If the real liabilities were exposed and identified as the debt that they truly represent, the federal government and virtually every city, state and school board in America would be technically bankrupt.

We know that it is not right, morally, for our public officials to take advantage of the privilege we gave them to tax us and then to use our money to provide themselves with levels of compensation and benefits far greater than we have for ourselves. We also know that it is **morally wrong to hide these benefits from the taxpayer** or to mislead the taxpayer into thinking that the costs are much lower than they really are. But the public sector IS hiding the facts concerning the pay and benefits that are provided to public sector employees, and is also misrepresenting the costs and liabilities to taxpayers for the unfunded liabilities for the continued health insurance and pensions that they have promised to themselves and their co-workers.

> The public sector has adopted and defended accounting and disclosure practices that prevent the taxpayer from seeing the true costs and enormous unfunded liabilities

> of these plans. To make matters worse, abuse of public
> sector pension plans is rampant.

Public sector pension plans have many loopholes that can allow abuse of already overly-generous plans. Many of these loopholes result in creating inflated earnings in the last years of employment, triggering an even higher pension than the plan intended. Some permit retirement followed by a return to work, thereby double dipping. Many plans permit spiking, allowing the accumulation of untaken sick pay or vacation pay, or enormous amounts of over-time paid in the final year before retirement, thus increasing the final year's pay on which the pension will be based. Many (particularly police and firefighter plans) allow disability designation to the majority of retirees. A disability designation can provide earlier and/or larger benefits, and often allow proceeds to be received free of state income taxes. Some even allow grandchildren (grand-children!) to be named as beneficiaries (lifetime recipients) of the deceased public employee's pension. The public sector entity that allows this could pay a pension for 100 years!

What struck us most forcefully when we looked into double dipping was WHO was doing the double dipping and the AMOUNTS of the windfalls given to these people. The first program we found was the Florida program called DROP (Deferred Retirement Option Program). Similar programs exist in at least 19 other states. As reported by Lucy Morgan, the Florida DROP program…"was created in 1998 to encourage retirement of highly paid, senior employees to make room for advances among younger, lower paid employees. To enter, employees who reach retirement age or 30 years of employment agree to retire within five years. When they leave the program, they usually collect hundreds of thousands of dollars in deferred compensation."

Let's parse this deal. Let's say you are covered under the state retirement program. You are age 50 or have accumulated 30 years of service. You're told, "If you will agree to retire in five years, we'll keep you on the payroll and you keep doing your job. We will take the retirement amount you would have received if you retired today and put it in an account with guaranteed interest compounded monthly and give it to you in a lump sum when you really do retire in five years." Come again? Did I read that right? Do you mean that the state worker will continue to receive their pay and to stay at work, but ALSO receive retirement pay (put in a guaranteed savings account) at the same time? Do you mean to tell me that I'm paying for a Florida teacher or government employee to retire 15 YEARS before I can, and to give them a pension that is much larger than my own, and I'm paying it TWICE?!!

Well, no. "Thrice" might be a better word to choose. It gets better than just the DROP deal. There's also the, "Y'all come back!" deal. About 9,000 Florida public sector employees have improved upon the DROP deal: (1) Signed up for DROP, thus getting a huge check in 5 years; (2) Started receiving their monthly pensions when they "retired" after 5 years; and (3) come right back to salaried work! It is a "threefer", compliments of the unwitting taxpayer! And this doesn't even count the lump sum check for unused sick and vacation pay, or the lifetime free or heavily subsidized health insurance. (I had a former public official tell me he has seen "cash out" deals for unused vacation and sick pay in amounts approaching a million dollars.)

Let's look at a couple of specific DROP examples, and remember that these people hadn't reached age 65, because public sector workers can "retire" at age 55 or earlier:

- A Florida Supreme Court Justice collected $426,852 as a DROP payment, commenced receiving a retirement pension of $7,596 a month, and returned to work, collecting his salary of $161,000 a year.

- Twenty-two other sitting judges joined in receiving a similar windfall from the taxpayer.

- The Sheriff of the county in which I live collected $382,256 in DROP payment, a pension of $8,958 a month in retirement pay and a salary of $158,000 a year.

- A community college president collected $893,000 (!) in DROP, a monthly pension of $14,600 and a salary of $328,000 a year.

These are "public servants?" The **private sector worker, who pays for all this,** gets Social Security after 44-48 years of work, at an average of $1,200 a month. Did we ever VOTE to spend our tax dollars this way?

To get some context as to how much money that all adds up to, let's consider the cost of just one successful triple dipper to the average homeowner in Florida. In 2008, the average Florida homeowner paid $1,400 in property taxes. The community college president "triple-dipper" collected $893,000 in a DROP lump sum. That took **all** of the property taxes paid by 637 homeowners. He also gets a pension of $175,000 a year. That takes **all** of the property taxes for 125 more homeowners every year. Then, there's his $328,000 salary. It takes **all** of the property taxes paid by 234 more homeowners to pay his annual salary. So, **it took all of the property taxes paid by about a THOUSAND homeowners** to pay the DROP payment, plus the first year's pension and salary, for ONE person! Keep in mind that the average homeowner is a typical American who will retire at age 65 with a Social Security check of about $1,200 a month.

We've mentioned DROP plans in Florida, but 18 other states have them, too (Alabama, Arizona, Arkansas, California, Colorado, Connecticut, Indiana, Iowa, Louisiana, Maryland, Michigan, Missouri, Montana, Ohio, Oklahoma, Pennsylvania, South Carolina and Texas). Here are a few more examples:

- **ALABAMA:** Two Alabama Education Association administrators are slated to receive DROP payments of $1.2 million and $1.3 million when they retire.

- **ARIZONA:** A Phoenix police chief retired in January in 2007. He cashed out of the DROP program, began collecting his pension check and quickly took a job as a public-safety manager. According to the Associated Press, his expected pension was $90,000 a year, in addition to the $165,000 salary he earns.

- **ARKANSAS:** A budget director who retired in 2006 with a pension of $2,000 a month and a DROP payment of $160,000, still works for the same agency with an annual salary of over $96,000. New pension laws will merge the police pension plan into the Arkansas Public Employees Retirement System. This merger will greatly increase the number of police employees who are eligible to participate in the generous DROP program, thereby increasing costs to taxpayers exponentially.

- **CALIFORNIA:** Two sheriff officials in San Luis Obispo County collect a combined nearly $1 million in pension payments every year. On top of that, they get a salary. One earns over $70 an hour. They are participants in the county's DROP program. The county has $299 million in unfunded pension liabilities. San Diego may go bankrupt if unions and the city can't negotiate lower costs, says Councilwoman Donna Frye, according to the *Union-Tribune*. In the next fiscal year the city will need to contribute $231.7 million into the public retirement fund; $19 million more than projected. The increase was a result of a rush of employees entering the DROP program.

- **FLORIDA:** 5,000 double dippers also participated in DROP. The 5,000 double dippers who participated in DROP received about $585 million in one-time payments. They began collecting their pensions. And then they went back to government jobs. At the start of 2009, according to the state data, 920 government employees who had been retired were working again after each collected DROP payouts of at least $200,000, including 107 who did so before returning to work in government jobs in Orange, Osceola, Lake, Seminole, Volusia or Brevard counties. Charlotte County's tax collector, (Get it? A tax collector) received a lump-sum DROP check of $306,908 last year. Re-elected without opposition in 2008, she sent a letter of resignation to Gov. Charlie Crist, took a month off and started a new term with a $119,706 salary and a $5,740 monthly pension.

- **MARYLAND:** The DROP program, open to police and firefighters only, costs the city of Baltimore approximately $10 million every year. In March 2009, there were 980 participants. A police officer with a $61,000 per year salary is eligible for a DROP payment of $215,000.

- **OHIO:** The DROP payment alone could cost the city of Columbus, Ohio $8 million in 2011. This figure is just an estimate, since data on the exact numbers are available to police and fire agencies only. A retiring police chief and a retiring fire chief, both of Columbus, Ohio, are eligible for DROP payments estimated at $900,000 and $1.1 million, respectively. A retiring police chief in Cincinnati will be eligible for a pension estimated at $92,000 annually, $235,000 from unused holiday, vacation and sick time, and a DROP payment of $929,261. Another retiring police chief in Cincinnati will be eligible for a pension estimate at $89,000 annually, $106,000 from unused holiday, vacation and sick time, and a DROP payment of $905,760.

- **PENNSYLVANIA:** Philadelphia Board of Ethics (Board of ETHICS?) decided to rehire its general counsel after he took a DROP payment estimated at $200,000 and "retired"—for one day. The deputy executive director of the Philadelphia Parking Authority received a DROP payment of $250,768.45, and then returned to work the next day at her $147,934 salary. There are currently 6 council members in Philadelphia enrolled in DROP, expecting to receive a combined total of $2.2 million in benefits. One council woman already collected her DROP payment in 2008 in the amount $274,587 when she retired for one day and was then reelected to work.

We've talked about DROP, but there are plenty of other examples of such "pension inflators" used routinely by public sector pension plans. Spiking is the practice of applying unused sick days, vacation days, overtime or "graveyard promotions" to arbitrarily increase the final year's pay. Many public sector plans provide pensions based on the final year (or 2–3 years) pay. By working the system and increasing the last year's paycheck through overtime, or cashing in unused vacation and/or sick days, the final pay can be so high that the pension is actually larger that the final year salary or base pay was!

Over-the-top salaries, particularly in the education sector, also contribute to the problem of outrageous pension obligations. CalSTRS, the largest pension system for teachers and administrators in the country, has nearly 3,100 members receiving more than $100,000 in pension benefits.

The entitlement to disability benefits is another case where the plan assumptions often don't meet any reasonable test. For example, nearly every employee that retires from the Long Island Rail Road (LIRR) collects disability payments and a pension. An estimated quarter of a billion dollars in federal disability money has been channeled to previous employees of LIRR since 2000. This includes people working at desk jobs, too. For example, a married couple collects $280,000 annually in combined disability and pension payments. One worked for management and one worked in labor. Many workers with long service records are eligible for retirement at age 50. Passengers could soon face another fare increase, and the transportation authority is seeking more taxpayer money, in addition to the half of a billion dollars a year they already collect. The disabled also get an Access Pass, allowing disabled workers free admission into sports facilities in state parks. The *New York Times* reported in 2008 that many of these "disabled" workers frequently take advantage of the golf greens.

Public sector pension practices that leave you shaking your head in disbelief are not isolated incidents. Such practices are widespread, as is the detrimental impact of what has been allowed to occur. The following pages depict examples from dozens of states, showing **how public sector pensions can end up providing benefits that were never intended:**

- **ALABAMA:** A former Washington County schoolteacher is currently serving a 10-year sentence in prison for enticing a 14 year old former student for sex. Because she is a tenured teacher, union rules require a hearing before an arbitrator before the state can stop paying her salary. This hearing cannot commence until after all of her legal appeals have been settled. In addition to receiving her salary, if she is able to drag out her appeals for another 2½ years, she can retire at half her current salary.

- **ARKANSAS:** As of June 30, 2008 the Arkansas Teacher Retirement System had unfunded liability of $2.015 billion and recently passed an increase in benefits for 28,000 members at a cost of $19.5M.
  - As of June 30, the Arkansas State Police Retirement System had an unfunded liability of $82 million and a planned merge into the Arkansas Public Employees Retirement System will increase the amount of police who are eligible for DROP, which will only add to the debt.

- **CALIFORNIA:** More than two-thirds of the 50 highest paid retirees in Stanislaus County are receiving pensions larger than their salaries were when they worked. According to records obtained by *The Modesto Bee*, retirees earning $100,000 or more in pensions often spiked their final year earnings (and therefore their pensions) by cashing in unused vacation, a practice that can add significantly to their lifetime earnings. *The Bee* says, "The average pension increase from spiking was 22.5%, driving up lifetime pension costs for the top 50 retirees by an estimated $20 million."
  - And the highest paid employee in San Francisco's public sector? The top earner in 2009 was a Police Department

deputy chief, who retired midyear. He earned $516,118. According to city records, he received most of that from unused sick days, vacation days and comp time.

- **CONNECTICUT:** The New Haven Board of Education spent approximately $70,000 within the last year for early retirement bonuses. After retiring, previous employees are able to keep this bonus, collect a state pension and then return to work collecting a new salary. Current district data shows about 25 retirees are back at work collecting a pension and salary.
  - Connecticut has approximate 1,000 double dippers collecting both a pension and a paycheck.
  - At UConn, there were 29 double dippers collecting 6-figure pensions in 2008. One of these, a professor, collected a $162,000 pension and a $138,000 salary for 120 days of work.
- **DELAWARE:** According to the Delaware state auditor, taxpayers spend $17 million to pay for over 1,000 state employees who are double dipping.
  - The highest paid retiree in state of Delaware, as of 2009, is a Court of Common Pleas Judge making a salary of $168,835 while also receiving a pension.
- **FLORIDA:** During an investigation by the *St. Petersburg Times* in 2008, it was discovered that a Miami-Dade community college president is also a retiree who has been double dipping. His annual salary of $441,538 is nicely supplemented by his $14,631 per month pension. He also had received a partial lump sum of $893,286 upon his initial retirement.
  - An Indian River State College president was also a retiree who has been double dipping. Upon his initial retirement, he received a partial lump sum payment of $585,000. Now that he is back at work, he not only continues to receive his monthly pension of $9,823, but he is also paid $286,470 annually.

- A north Florida State Attorney changed his mind about retirement after leaving, and has now returned as a double dipping retiree. Upon his initial retirement, he received a lump sum payment of $519,995. Now that he is back on the job, he also collects an annual salary of $153,139, and a monthly pension payment of $7,749.

- **GEORGIA:** In Gwinnett County, the Sheriff's office paid eight retired deputies and one retired IT associate a total of $557,000 in 2008. Of that amount, $44,000 was overtime pay. This year, the Sheriff's office has already paid more than $354,000 in salaries to retired workers.

  - In 2008, county employees of Gwinnett County in Atlanta earned $1.2 million in county pay as they drew pensions at the same time they were drawing their paychecks. This year, employees who are double dipping have already cost the county around $800,000.

  - Three university presidents ranked within the top 25 highest paid university executives in the country, with total compensation packages ranging from $604,864 to $634,138, according to the *Chronicle of Higher Education's* 2010 annual executive compensation survey. These compensation packages included base salaries as high as $515,000 as well as deferred compensation, retirement pay, relocation allowances and perks such as the use of a house and car as well as club dues.

- **ILLINOIS:** In Illinois, taxpayers support some hefty teacher salaries, according to the Illinois State Board of Education's Teacher Service Records for the year ending June 30, 2008, compiled by consultant Bill Zettler. Some examples are:
  - 420 physical education teachers in Illinois make over $100,000 per year, with the top one earning $163,000.
  - 332 English teachers earn more than $100,000 per year, with the highest paid at $164,000.

- 94 driver education teachers in Illinois make more than $100,000 a year. The highest paid is $170,000.
- What's more, a $100,000 salary averages a pension benefit contribution of $27,440, other post-employment benefits, such as retiree health care, of $11,250 and estimated life, health and disability insurance benefits of $6,500, producing a total compensation package of $145,190.
- Illinois State University Retirement System (SURS) pensioners pay nothing towards their pensions or for health benefits (including vision, life insurance and dental), and still have the top 10 pensions in Illinois ranging from $243,000 to $379,000 per year.
- In addition SURS pensioners hold 84 places out of the top 100. There are more than 5,200 public university and Chicago City Colleges employees who, in 2007-2008, earned more than $100,000, all the while contributing nothing to their pensions.

- INDIANA: Secrecy laws were passed in 2001 that block any public access (is this even legal?) to information regarding Indiana's state and local pension funds which are valued at $13 billion and cover about 220,000 current and former public workers. Although taxpayers fund these generous pensions, they cannot see any information about payments.

- KANSAS: The Kansas Public Employees Retirement System (KPERS) faces $10.25 billion in unfunded liabilities. The funding ratio is only 49%. The total unfunded actuarial liabilities more than doubled from $4.8 billion in 2008 to $10.25 billion in 2009.

- MARYLAND: The city of Baltimore's 2009 pension tab of $81.9 million for police and firefighters could more than double to $164.9 million in 2010. City officials predict an 11% increase in property taxes and other service cuts just to pay the pension bill. Baltimore is attempting to increase the retirement age for police officers, increase employee contributions to pensions and eliminate the DROP program. Unions are planning to sue. In particular, unions object to eliminating the DROP program and increasing the retirement age to 55 (police and firefighters currently can retire after 20 years, regardless of age.)

- **MASSACHUSETTS:** A police chief in Pelham, Massachusetts triple dips after retiring at 51. When he retired in April 2007 he became chief in Topsfield yet was still listed as a part-time officer in the Pelham Town Report. At retirement he started collecting a $90,000 pension and making about $100,000 as chief, while still filling in as an officer when needed in Pelham.
  - A former commissioner of the Department of Corrections, took advantage of a retirement loophole that allowed her to spike her pension by $25,000 and collect payments of $106,202. She left her job one year and seven months before her official retirement, and took a job at an administrative opening for the Bristol County Sheriff's Office.
- **MISSOURI:** Missouri taxpayers spend $375 million annually on pension payments and are expected to contribute $460 million in 2010.
  - St. Louis alone spends 14% of its budget on its three pension funds.
  - Missouri's state pension plans are facing $200 million in unfunded liabilities and as of January were only 33% funded.
  - Despite the retirement system losing $1.8 billion last year, the Missouri State Employees' Retirement System handed out $160,000 in staff incentives, in addition to the $460,000 already paid in staff bonuses in 2008.
- **NEBRASKA:** The new police chief of the Bryan Police Department will be making $122,000 annually, in addition to his $104,000 yearly pension from his 25 years spent

working as an Omaha police officer, a position he retired from in August 2009. His pension was initially $98,000 per year, but due to his bankable hours and overtime it will actually be $104,000.

- A very generous contract in 2004 allowed Omaha police and firefighters to spike their pensions with overtime. A police sergeant in Omaha retired in 2008 at age 45 with a final base pay of $66,815. His annual pension was approved at $84,405. If he lives to the age of 85, that makes his pension (without considering cost of living increases) $3.4 million for 22 years of work.

- **NEVADA:** A handful of retired firefighters in Nevada are suing due to changes in their pensions. The Public Employees Retirement System changed the criteria regarding retirement contributions and adjusted the retired workers' pensions to make up for overpaid funds. Two of the firefighters saw their pensions go from about $11,000 a month to about $9,500 a month and the three others lost approximately $600, $700, and $1,000 a month of their pensions. All of the workers retired in 2008.

- **NEW HAMPSHIRE:** Starting July 2011, New Hampshire localities may see public worker pension costs increase by 23%. The New Hampshire Municipal Association represents more than 250 local governments and school districts that are currently sponsoring a lawsuit against the state. The association claims it was unconstitutional for the legislators to lower state contributions to the public retirement system covering teachers, fire, police, and government employees from 35% to 30%. This left localities to cover the rest, which totals approximately $27 million.

- **NEW JERSEY:** New Jersey's governor has proposed skipping the entire $3 billion pension payment this year because the state has an $11 billion budget gap.

- The director of the New Jersey League, a lobbyist group for legal issues and training local officials, makes $191,580 and will receive a monthly retirement payout of $9,185. The director is not a government worker, but will still receive his retirement payout from taxpayers.
- As of October 2009, there were 406 retirees in New Jersey collection pensions of $100K or more. Meanwhile, the pension is underfunded by approximately $34 billion.

- **NEW YORK:** Approximately 6,000 school employees in New York will be able to start collecting their retirement earlier than previously allowed, as long as they have served at least 25 to 30 years, and are between 55 and 62 years of age. The new retirement program will cost state taxpayers $15.8 million per year.
  - By 2012, the cost of state worker pensions and health benefits are estimated to reach $7.9 billion per year. If benefits expenditures reach nearly $8 billion, the cost of benefits for the average state employee will come out to be about 62% of their base salary.
  - Currently, the total cost of the average state worker is $91,724, where $63,750 comes from salary while the other $27,974 is spent on pensions and benefits. By 2012, the total cost per state worker could reach $114,000, with $43,000 of that accounting for benefits.
  - More than 300 police and firefighters that retired in Yonkers within the last decade get pensions exceeding their base pay. One former Yonkers detective receives a pension of $140,727, which is 75% higher than his base pay. One Yonkers detective, who was stripped of pay for 40 days for violating overtime policies, was still able to work $124,336 in overtime during his last year. He now receives a pension of $133,661.
  - New York City spends a total of $13.6 billion on public retirement and benefits for municipal employees.

Approximately $6.7 billion go towards the five retirement systems, while $6.9 billion is spent on employee health insurance and other benefits.

- Overtime increased 500% in 4 years among Buffalo firefighters, growing from $2.2 million in 2004 to $10.6 million in 2008, leading to a 50% increase in the average firefighter pension. One specific example is a retired chief who earned a base salary of $62,136 in 2007, overtime of $102,998 and a pension of $84,950.

- Police officers in Tonawanda, NY are guaranteed an additional 17 days of overtime in the year preceding their retirement, thereby giving them a considerably higher pension. 17 days at time-and-a half equals 25½ days normal pay, or about a 10% "raise" in the last year of service.

- In New York City, a railroad car repairman with a base salary of $62,976 managed to earn a total compensation of $283,373 (an extra $220,397 primarily from overtime.) A road car inspector earned a total of $278,746 including $165,867 in overtime and $41,284 in unused vacation and sick days cashed in at retirement; he now receives a pension check of $10,122 per month.

- **OREGON:** Of the 63,298 Oregon retirees from the Public Employee Retirement System (PERS) between 1990 and 2008, about 5,000 had pensions GREATER than their final salary. 5% of 2008 retirees, or about 300, also had pensions GREATER than 100% of their final salary.

- **PENNSYLVANIA:** The pension for government employees in Pittsburgh, PA is approximately 34% funded, with an unfunded liability of $989.5 million. To avoid a state takeover, the city is attempting to up that level to 50%, partly by leasing its parking garages and meters to a private company for a one-time lump sum around $200 million.
  - Homeowners in PA will pay an additional $558 per year just to fund previously granted pension increases.

- In 2001, lawmakers gave themselves a 50% pension boost and gave a 25% raise to 340,000 state and school workers.
- Philadelphia raised the sales tax from 7% to 8% in order to raise money for pension contributions.
- **RHODE ISLAND:** In Rhode Island, public labor unions are joining forces to file a lawsuit against the state for implementing pension reform in June in order to save state taxpayers millions. One of the provisions of this new reform is the retirement age, now raised to age 62.
  - The RI governor proposed unpaid "government shut-down days" that would save the state an estimated $57.6 million. According to the *Providence Journal* on March 7, 2010, a business-backed organization found that "state taxpayer contributions to those pensions nearly tripled over the last decade, jumping from $79.9 million in 2001 to a projected $218 million in the coming year."
  - The RI legislature faces a "budget hole of $220 million in the current year and another $437 million in the next.
  - Overall, state personnel expenditures will consume $1.7 billion in the coming year." They also reported on March 7, 2010 that "Rhode Island cannot afford the system that currently promises lifetime pension benefits to 19,733 retired public school teachers and state workers."
- **TENNESSEE:** In Tennessee, more than 700 state workers each racked up over $10,000 in overtime during the 2008 fiscal year, with nearly 300 workers increasing their salaries by 50% through overtime and 16 actually doubling their salaries.
- **TEXAS:** Despite losing 15.7% or $255 million last year, the staff of the $1.9 billion Houston municipal pension fund are awarding themselves a raise plan which will increase payroll by 6%.
  - Of the 23 Fort Worth city retirees receiving pensions over $100,000, 13 are former police and fire department employees.

- Eighty-two Texas pension funds have unfunded liabilities of over $23 billion.
- In Corpus Christi, Texas, 35 municipal workers made 50% or more of their total pay through overtime in fiscal year 2008.

- **UTAH:** Utah's public employee retirement fund has almost a $3 billion shortfall. The plan covers 156,000 past and present workers. The state law actually encourages double dipping by requiring new employers to pay their 401(k) in the same amount that the previous employer gave to the fund. This policy may be unique to Utah and costs the state between $10 and $17 million annually.
  - Another Utah problem is that after only 20 years, police and firefighters can retire with a full pension, but many of them return to work.

- **VERMONT:** The teachers pension system of Vermont may be in trouble due to some of the benefits including lifetime health care, pensions equal to 50% of their last pay and retiring at age 62 or after 30 years. The state's obligation currently stands at $73.5 million in payouts, and is expected to increase to $105 million in 2011.
  - The state of Vermont has been forced to increase its contribution to the state pension system by 70% over the last five years, up from $24.4 million to $41.5 million this year. In 2010, that amount is expected to increase yet again to $63.5 million, while the state faces an $85 million revenue loss.

- **WASHINGTON:** The chief executive of the Valley Medical Center collected a retirement payoff of $1.73 million this year even though he is still working at the facility, raking in a salary of $900,000 in 2008. The $1.73 million payout is separate from the guaranteed pension he'll receive when he actually does retire.

- **WEST VIRGINIA:** Teacher pensions in West Virginia are in trouble, facing an unfunded liability of $4 billion. In addition, the retiree health care system for public employees is unfunded by $7.8 billion.
  - Unions have made a suggestion on how taxpayers can cover the liability. They want a payment of $150 million per year, and an additional 2%, every year, for 19 years. The unions also want taxpayers to contribute $359 million for the first year, which will reach $1.9 billion by year 20.

What's the largest public sector pension we could find? It's $509,000 a year (increasing every year for cost of living!) paid by California's CalPERS to a former city manager. There are now 9,000 public sector retirees in California with pensions exceeding $100,000 a year.

You are probably wondering, "How can all this have happened, and why didn't I know about it?" **There's a simple explanation: public sector entities don't WANT you to know what they're doing with your tax dollars.** They have unbelievably creative ways of hiding the truth from you, as you'll learn in the next chapter.

*"It is true that U.S. fiscal policy is **unsustainable**..."*

—Dr. Douglas Holtz-Eakin, former director
Congressional Budget Office. Spring 2008

_____ Chapter Four _____

Hiding Costs from Taxpayers

How do they do it? How can federal and local governments and school districts provide such lavish pay and benefits and incur such huge debt and unfunded liabilities without taxpayers knowing about it? It's called "off the balance sheet accounting."

Public sector entities are not held to the same standards of accounting and reporting that are required of businesses in the private sector. The result is that many, if not all, public sector entities maintain several sets of books that make it impossible for taxpayers to determine exactly where their tax dollars are going or the long-term liabilities that exist in connection with these compensation, benefits and entitlement programs. The compensation, benefits and unfunded liabilities associated with these early retirement and entitlement programs are generally either not disclosed to taxpayers or are presented by using accounting practices and actuarial assumptions that would not be allowed in the private sector.

> The result of the failure to fairly and fully disclose the true elements of the cost of government and public education has been to create a generally unseen and definitely **unsustainable** financial burden on the employers and employees in the private sector. Each year as a bit more

of the emerging iceberg of hidden costs becomes visible, there are budget shortfalls and the need for even more deficit spending and/or the creation of more debt.

We cannot blame any politician or political party for creating what has now become a full-blown national financial crisis. Perhaps Pogo was right when he said, "We have met the enemy, and he is us." America's habit of engaging in "short-term thinking in a long-term world" has resulted in trading-off a nasty union negotiation or a pay raise today in return for providing more pay and benefits tomorrow.

Over the past decades, it has resulted in the creation of almost unbelievable unfunded financial obligation that is required to meet promises made to civil servants and those in public education. By refusing to identify and acknowledge these future obligations as debt in their financial reporting, the public sector has hidden trillions of dollars of promised future benefits (often to themselves) from the taxpaying public. It has often appeared cheaper to promise something tomorrow instead of paying something today. Those charged with the responsibility of managing the public sector bureaucracies have acted with reckless abandon for the last 40 years, but they really went off the tracks beginning in 1985.

The Beginning of the Divergence of Accounting Disclosure

1985 was the beginning of a huge divergence between public and private sector accounting practices. In the private sector, the Federal Accounting Standards Board (FASB) recognized that corporations had pension plans (usually known as defined benefit plans) that carried with them significant liabilities that were not shown on corporate balance sheets. This allowed corporations to appear far healthier, financially, than they really were, because the unfunded costs of future promised pensions were not shown to investors on the audited financial statements. Huge industrial corporations, heavily unionized, routinely promised increased pension benefits in the future in order to save payroll costs in the short-term. These future liabilities would pose a huge financial strain on these corporations in future years, a fact that wasn't readily discernible to investors.

FASB changed the game when it issued the *Statement of Financial Accounting Standards (SFAS) 87*, labeled "Employers' Accounting for Pensions" which required corporations to show the funding status of future pension liabilities as a standard part of corporate accounting and reporting. It was the beginning of the end for large corporations like General Motors who had enormous previously undisclosed liabilities connected with its union contracts. And it was also the beginning of the end for defined benefit pension plans in the private sector.

The SFAS 87 requirement to show the unfunded liabilities, usually defined as the unfunded excess of accrued liability over the value of the pension fund assets, was the ultimate game changer in the private sector. For the first time, investors saw the current financial implications of the cost of future benefits that had been promised by corporations–and they didn't like what they saw. There was a significant hue and cry from corporations opposing this disclosure, as the long-term liabilities and the present costs of funding them made many corporations with pension plans look a lot worse financially. Many would be, once these obligations were reported, technically insolvent.

Most corporations quickly vested their current employees, terminated their pension plans and went to 401(k) plans instead. The new 401(k) plans offered several attractive benefits to businesses and their employees. To businesses, it allowed the cost of the plan to be seen and fixed each year. There was no additional unfunded future liability. It was also attractive to both employers and employees because the workforce needed a new kind of retirement plan. The U.S. workforce had become very mobile, and traditional pension plans were not regarded as a significant benefit by younger workers because they did not stay with any given employer long enough to gain a significant benefit. One in five workers changed jobs each year, which meant the average job tenure was only five years. The old defined benefit plans were not portable, and had little or no value to an employee that would not be staying for a long-term career. The 401(k) plans were fully portable, and could be taken by employees from job to job. They appeared to be a "win-win" for employers and employees.

The corporations that had union-negotiated pension plans couldn't terminate them and were stuck with the consequences. They could no longer hide the fact that they had made promises that would be impossible to keep in the future. One by one, the large national unionized companies failed. First came some major airlines, then the steel industry, the mining industry, and the automotive industry. Once it became known that these large corporations had negotiated enormous future obligations in return for short-term payroll cost savings or to avoid a work stoppage, the true financial position of these companies became known and their destiny was determined. The question was not "if" but "when" they would crumble under the burden of the financially unsustainable promises they had made. Hindsight is always 20/20, but it now appears that if the company was large and couldn't terminate or dramatically reduce its pension plan because of union contracts in 1985, it doesn't exist today. That means that entire industries and huge corporations, and the jobs that they created, are no longer in operation.

Government Made Up Its Own Rules

But those FASB accounting and disclosure rules didn't apply to the public sector. Just a year earlier, in 1984, the Government Accounting Standards Board (GASB) had been created. GASB created its own rules, very different from FASB requirements. Its rules recognized that government entities are not subject to IRS regulations related to funding and disclosure. They are not bound by the requirements of the Employee Retirement Income Security Act (ERISA) nor regulated by the Department of Labor. In 1985, the public sector did not follow FASB's lead and did not require that private-sector accounting, reporting and disclosure standards be employed. Their enormous pension liabilities would continue to be off the balance sheet.

GASB rules are based on the premise that public sector entities are different. GASB has always argued that government does not have assets in the same way private companies do. It owns national parks, state capitol buildings, etc. that belong to the taxpayers and have no real value as they are not properties that can be sold. GASB has always held that normal corporate accounting of assets and liabilities wouldn't make sense to use.

In the past couple of years, things have changed. Public sector entities are selling assets and/or are selling long-term leases on public assets, like parking garages, toll roads, parking meters and state buildings. Chapter Nine will outline how some governments have been selling or leasing assets to get a "quick fix" of cash by selling or long-term leasing of the people's assets just to get enough money to perpetuate their unbridled spending for another year or two. This demonstrates that the GASB theory that "governments need different accounting rules" because "government assets are different" no longer holds water.

GASB argues that the same justification can be applied to profit and loss (P&L) statements. Public sector entities don't have profits or losses. Its income is not based on selling a product in competition with others, as it has a monopoly. Its product cannot become obsolete, sent offshore or be defeated in the marketplace by a competitor. Public entities very rarely go bankrupt (at least until now.) **So the public sector says that it needs DIFFERENT accounting rules. And therein lies the rub. Acceptance of that premise by taxpayers means that public sector entities are free to make up ALL of their own rules, accounting standards and disclosure requirements.**

The most significant departure from private sector practices involves the way public sector entities are allowed to account for the liabilities associated with pension plans, and the fact that there was no requirement at all until 2009 to recognize the liability associated with the continuation of health insurance and other benefits after retirement. **The fact that they have been allowed to "play by their own rules" is bankrupting America.**

Some people in the public sector believe that government shouldn't even bother defining the present value of the future liability or identifying an unfunded liability at all. They think governments should just promise whatever they want, and pay the benefits out of current revenues when people retire. That's like you or me saying, "I'm going to send my daughter to college in 15 years at a cost of $20,000 a year, but I'll just pay it out of my current income when the time comes." And then, since it doesn't "cost" anything right now, saying, "As a matter of fact, I'll send yours, and yours, and yours to college, too, out of my current income when the time comes."

The Pension Liability Ponzi Scheme

Governments do calculate unfunded liabilities, but the way most of them do it is the greatest Ponzi scheme of all time. These liabilities are always kept off the balance sheet, and are most often presented in horribly misleading ways.

Let's use a hypothetical example to illustrate the way many of these public sector pension scams really work:

Let's say that you are the Manager of a very small town. You are the only employee. You are 25 years old and want the citizens to give you a pension plan. You're only earning $35,000 a year, but want to make a career there, and want to retire at age 55 (30 years from now) as most other government workers in other cities do. Your first step is to go to a pension consultant or actuary and ask them to create a pension plan proposal for the city council to approve.

You tell the consultant that you want to retire at age 55 at 50% of your pay, with 2% cost of living raises after retirement. He'll ask you two important questions. The first is an estimate of what your raises will be each year. You'll probably tell him to estimate 3%. Sounds reasonable and fair.

He'll then ask you how much interest you want to assume you'll earn on the money the town puts into your pension plan funding each year. That's a tough question. You'll probably say, "I don't know, but I want to be absolutely positive that the money will be there when I'm 55. They are guaranteeing this pension to me and they will want to be sure that we don't create a liability 30 years from now that they don't have the money to pay for."

Your consultant will probably advise that you use the most conservative investments possible. You won't make a huge amount of interest earnings because you'll be using the safest investments you can find. "That's great," you'll say, "as long as I, and the town, can be sure the money will be there." You'll probably settle on about 3.5%. That's conservative. (Although many people today wish they could earn an absolutely safe 3.5%.) Even with a conservative assumption, there are still no guarantees. Depressions and all kinds of things can happen to negatively impact on a 3.5% assumption. But it is probably a reasonable approach.

The actuary will return with your proposal for the city council. It will show that you are projected to be earning $84,000 a year 30 years from now when you retire. It will show that to provide your pension, the plan will need to accumulate $862,000 by the time you are 55. They will have to put $15,854 a year into your pension fund if they want "level" funding. Or, if they want to just put in a percentage of your pay, they can put in 30% of your pay each year. And, they will have an "unfunded liability" today of $307,000, which is the present value of the $862,000 that they need 30 years from now. It is "off the balance sheet" in their accounting reports, and doesn't count as debt in the way they keep their books, but they will have to show the taxpayers this number in a separate report. Some taxpayers are smart enough to know that this really IS debt that they have to pay off.

"Holy smokes! They'll never buy that," you'll say. "There is no way they'll contribute 30% of my pay to a pension plan. They don't have anything like that themselves!"

The consultant will say, "Well, we can make it look like it costs less. We can change our assumptions. For example, if we assume that you'll earn 5% on these funds before and after retirement, the numbers reduce a lot." He'll show you that if you assume a 5% return, you only need to accumulate $716,000. The "level" deposit needed to fund your pension plan reduces to only $10,129 a year, or they can put in 20% of your pay each year. And the current unfunded liability reduces to only $165,000. But, he'll caution you, "In order to earn 5% compounded, you'll have to take higher risk with your investments. That means the risk that the money WON'T be there in 30 years increases." "Still too much", you say. "No way are the taxpayers going to put in a level $10,000 a year for my pension, or 20% of my pay every year."

Your friendly consultant will say, "I thought you might say that, so I took the liberty of doing an 8% assumption. Assuming you'll earn 8% compounded, you'll only have to put in $4,192 a year if you use "level" funding, or only 8% of your pay if you want to fund on a "percentage of pay" basis. You'll only need to accumulate $516,000 in 30 years, and your unfunded liability drops all the way down to $51,373."

"Can I DO that?" you ask, probably with some level of astonishment. "Yes, you can," he'll tell you. "Government accounting standards, GASB, permits you to use any cockamamie interest rate assumption you want to." "Wonderful", you'll say. "I can sell this pension plan to the council. It only costs 8% of my pay!"

"But," your consultant cautions you, "the chances of your earning 8% compounded, without fail, for the 30 years before you retire and the expected 25 years you'll live after you retire, a total period of 55 years, are very, very remote. There will have to be a very aggressive investment approach taken, and with such aggressive approaches come very high risks. I don't know anyone who has earned 8%, compounded, for 55 years. The town will have to pay you a pension of $42,000 a year, increasing at 2% a year, whether there is money in the plan or not. They may be smart enough not accept an 8% assumption. And remember," he'll say, "the REAL unfunded liability that we arrived at when we did our first calculations is $307,000, not the $51,000 you'll be showing them. The difference between the two is 600%! You might ask, "But we don't have to show them that, do we?" He'll answer, "No, you don't."

Your consultant will add, "You should recognize that if they should give you bigger than 3% average annual raises, or if you should work overtime or cash in unused sick and vacation days in your last year of employment, it will increase your pay in the last year, and increase the amount of your pension. You won't have funded for that at all." You might ask again, "We don't have to tell them that detail, do we?" He'll answer, "No, we don't."

He'll show you that if you should, for example, work $10,000 in overtime in your last year, and cash in $40,000 of unused vacation and sick pay, your actual compensation when you are age 55 will be $134,000 that year and the town will owe you a pension of $67,000 a year, not the $42,000 amount that they had projected. That means that the "real" unfunded liability today if we built-in these revised assumptions, would be $453,000 today, not the $53,000 you're showing them. That's 9 TIMES larger than it appears to be."

He might add that you're also proposing that the town provide you with free health insurance for you and your wife after you retire. Currently, that costs the town $1,200 a month. Even if we assume that health insurance only goes up 5% a year for the next 30 years, the premium when you retire will be $62,000 a year and growing at 5%. The present value of that $1.3 million future liability is another $420,000 or so, today." He'll add, "Fortunately, we don't have to tell them about that, and you don't have to fund for it. It is a liability that is completely invisible to the taxpayer. But we know that between the pension plan and the health insurance plan, the town will have a liability 30 years from now of about $2.4 million for you, with a present value of unfunded liability being about $850,000+ today, and they're only going to be putting $4,000 a year into the pension plan. There's just no way that $4,000 a year, for 30 years, can do all that."

"You're right," you'll say. "In 5-10 or 15 years, the town will find out and get really upset with this, and maybe they'll even try to cancel it." "Well," the expert will say, "Not really. You see, the government accounting standards allow you to continue to report and pay-down the original $51,000 unfunded liability that was based on our original assumptions, and to report that the funding level is adequate, no matter how much is REALLY in the pension account. Of course, the town will need $2.4 million 30 years from now that they won't have. But that isn't our problem, is it? They will have to pay you, anyway, because they are guaranteeing these benefits to you. It's a bit misleading to the taxpayers, but it's not my job to write accounting rules. I only follow them." He'll also say, "What we are doing is completely by the book, and you can't be criticized for any wrongdoing and neither can I. But if you have any smart, analytical councilmen or women, you might have a problem here."

"Don't worry," you'll say, "they won't have a clue. I'll only show them your last 8% proposal, and we don't have to talk about health insurance. I can truthfully say that an expert designed this pension plan. It meets all approved actuarial and accounting standards. It is consistent with what other government plans are doing. It is fair and reasonable, and it only produces a $52,000 unfunded liability with a requirement that they contribute either $4,000 a year or 8% of my pay a year to my pension plan. They'll buy that! Besides, these council people won't be around 30 years from now, anyway."

So, that's how a $2.4 MILLION future liability, with a present value liability of $850,000 is expressed to taxpayers as a current $51,000 unfunded liability. This example is for ONE person, who will retire at $62,000 a year at age 55, with 2% cost of living raises, and with paid health insurance. This one person is a "middle of the road" example. We know that there are many thousands of people in public sector pension plans retiring with pension plan benefits like the one above, and that there are thousands upon thousands of public sector workers retiring at $100,000 a year or more, plus health insurance benefits. Even those with lower pensions usually have paid or highly subsidized health insurance that can actually cost more than their pensions. How much is the REAL unknown liability to the American taxpayer for the pensions and health insurance of the 18 million people in the public sector who have such plans? Several experts have calculated the combined unfunded liabilities for these pension and health insurance plans to be about $3.5 trillion. That is all off the balance sheet debt that must be collected in taxes.

> Public sector pension plans, unions and GASB will HATE this book. They will line up experts 'til the cows come home. They will fight like wounded lions defending the practices that we are exposing in this book. They have great credentials. They will amass economists, actuaries and pension experts. They can't admit their complicity with a practice of deception. They absolutely must continue defending a lying, cheating, hideously irresponsible practice of deception from the American taxpayer. To do otherwise would expose what they have done—committed one of the greatest and certainly the most financially devastating accounting frauds in history.

Getting to the Real Numbers

There is no more important subject to American taxpayers than the scope of the debt and unfunded liabilities that have been incurred by our governments at every level, and hidden from the taxpayer. **It has put our entire economy on the brink of collapse, and has impoverished the private sector and enriched the public sector. It must be corrected, and corrected immediately, if our nation is to**

survive as a free enterprise republic. Unfortunately, it is a complex issue, and one that is rarely, if ever, explained by the media. Also unfortunately, very few people understand the intricacies of pension valuations or accounting practices.

This chapter must suffice as a "cram course" for anyone who refuses to be buffaloed by lots of guys and gals in suits with initials after their names, paid for by your government or school board with your tax dollars, who will try to buffalo you into believing the absolute BS they are shoveling out. (The last chapter in this book provides you with a surefire way to find out what the true numbers are. You must require your elected officials to hire independent actuaries and to follow the guidelines we set forth. If you decide to do this, and see the real numbers, brace yourself!)

> There is no more important subject to American taxpayers than the scope of the debt and unfunded liabilities that have been incurred by our governments at every level, and hidden from the taxpayer.

There is no "school" for elected officials to teach them how to read a balance sheet, P&L, a public sector financial statement or budget. There is no class to explain what an "actuarial valuation" for a pension plan is, or how to read and understand one. Elected officials must rely on the reporting standards and processes that were in place before they got there. They must also rely, for current financial information, on the professional unelected management of the bureaucracy or bureaucracies they are charged with directing. In many cases, these unelected bureaucrats actually receive the same lavish benefits for themselves that they so generously agree to provide for their employees. Most of all, the elected officials must rely on the financial reporting and disclosure to be an accurate portrayal of the financial condition of the entity they are elected to control and direct.

Unfortunately, most elected officials lack the training to understand and question the financial reports or actuarial valuations presented to them and are faced (perhaps opposed) by an armada of bureaucrats, officials, accountants, actuaries and "accounting standards" that appear to assure that the numbers presented are an accurate reflection of the financial status of the public sector entity. And, according to GASB rules, they usually are. Nowhere does this create a larger problem than in accounting for pension and other post-retirement benefits costs.

Public sector pension plans generally do not buy annuities for retirees. That would require cash, and they don't have it. Rather, they calculate how much they must set aside each year in order to accumulate enough money to pay out the pensioner for his or her remaining lifetime when the employee reaches his or her retirement date. The fund accumulates the money, and the fund pays it out. If adequate assets are not available to meet the payout requirements, the governmental entity has to pay its pensioners anyway, since virtually all government and school district pension plans are guaranteed.

As we saw in our previous example, misleading assumptions related to salary increases and interest rates often mask the magnitude of the problem. Actually, the situation with public sector pensions is even worse than simple interest rate and earnings growth assumption gamesmanship. There are many other important provisions and assumptions you must make in a pension plan. Each of them requires someone to make assumptions as to their impact on plan costs. Other elements involve increases in pension benefits after retirement, bigger benefits to disabled retirees or providing retirement benefits based on only 5 or 10 years of service. They also include survivor benefits, so that if a retiree dies, benefits will be paid to the beneficiary.

> The earlier the retirement benefit is to begin, the longer it will be paid and the less time is available to accumulate the necessary funds. It's a double-edged sword…less time to accumulate more money.

Each of these benefits will increase the cost of the pension plan, and the assumptions intended to recognize them will be included in the actuarial calculation of the amount needed to fund the plan. Public sector plans tend to "assume low" and "give high." Every time reality differs from assumptions, the costs go up.

As every actuary knows, early retirement costs a fortune. The earlier the retirement benefit is to begin, the longer it will be paid and the less time is available to accumulate the necessary funds. It's a double-edged sword…less time to accumulate more money. If you hired someone at age 21, and your plan's normal retirement age was 65, you'd have 44 years to save enough to pay him for 17 years. If you decided to have retirement benefits begin at age 55, you'd have only 34 years to save enough to pay him for 27 years. That's 25% less time to come up with 60% more money. And if you compound the problem by assuming that employees will get smaller raises than they actually do, or you'll earn more interest that you can actually make, you'll have created a financial quagmire from which you cannot escape.

Here are a couple of quick examples on the cost of providing early retirement benefits.

- Let's look at someone who makes a large pension rather quickly, like a law enforcement officer. Let's say you hire him at age 21 with a salary of $30,000 per year. He retires with a pension of $75,000 per year after 25 years. You'll need to accumulate $1.9 million for his pension during his working service years, or a contribution of about $45,000 a year.

- In the case of one of those larger pensions we've shown you, let's look at a civil servant. The civil servant retires at age 51 with 30 years of service at a $260,000 annual pension. This would require the accumulation of $5.8 million dollars, or an annual contribution of $108,000 a year for the 30 working years. That's why you and I can't retire at $260,000 a year at age 51. We'd have to earn about $175,000 a year before taxes, just to clear enough to make our own pension plan contribution!

Pension investment assumptions can always be adjusted to make the numbers look better. Unfortunately, the true cost of the pension plans is based on actual results, not assumptions. Using high interest return assumptions can disguise the true cost of what is being promised, but time will ultimately catch up but not for a while. Public sector officials can take comfort in thinking: "We won't be here then. We'll be retired and collecting our generous and guaranteed pensions before anyone finds out. That problem is for the taxpayer 30 years from now to deal with." And taxpayers are facing the consequences of those decisions every day.

Exposing Flawed Accounting Practices

In a *Wall Street Journal* editorial "Pension Bomb Ticks Louder," appearing April 27, 2010, it was reported that Stanford University's Institute of Economic Policy Research had released a study "suggesting a $500 billion unfunded liability for California's three biggest pension funds... This shortfall is about six times the size of this years' California state budget and seven times more than the voter-approved general obligations bonds." Stanford had used a 4.14% interest assumption rather than the 7.5%, 7.75% and 8% assumptions used by the three funds. "This year, $5.5 billion was diverted from other programs, such as higher education and parks, to cover the shortfall," says the *Wall Street Journal.*

New Jersey has staggering financial problems, too. New Jerseys' Governor Chris Christie has been trying to deal with a $90 BILLION unfunded liability for pensions and benefits. The state already has the highest property taxes in the nation and an 8.95% income tax rate. He's having a hard time with the unions. While he wanted teachers to forgo raises for one year and pay 1.5% (that is one point five percent!) of their health insurance costs, they REFUSED, preferring to push tax increases on individuals and small businesses, from 8.95% to 10.75%, which is a 17% increase.

In the public sector, retirement under defined benefits pension plans at ages ranging from 40 to 55 is commonplace. Most of these pensions are guaranteed. That is why virtually all economists agree that pension assets should be invested in a way that assures the money will be there for retirees by using low risk investment portfolios. Assuming 7%, 8% or 9% on a compounded basis requires that investment managers create high-risk investment portfolios to achieve such gains. With high risk comes the potential for big losses, as every investor learned in 2001 and again in 2008. Public sector pension plans were no exception. They took risks to achieve gains necessary to match their own assumptions, and they lost…big time. Huge pension assets, assumed to be growing at an assumed 7–9% per year lost 30%–40% of their value. But the pension fund reporting shows that those assets are still there, and still growing at 7–9%. The results were predictable. Public sector plans had to continue to take high risk and big chances because they had told the taxpayer that the cost of promised pensions would be satisfied by big investment gains. They lost.

With no DOL (Department of Labor), no IRS (Internal Revenue Service), and no FASB (Financial Accounting Standards Board) rules nor non-compliance penalties to direct them or punish them if they stray, actuaries comply with existing GASB (Government Accounting Standards Board) standards and requirements of the entity that hires them. And the public sector entity that hires them does NOT want the actuary to explain why their actuarial assumptions are unreasonable.

> The basic GASB standard is based on a premise that is frightening to contemplate. In essence, it says, "We do not need to follow the rules that apply to the private sector. They can go out of business, while we are here forever. They can fail, but we can't. They cannot control their future income, but we can. We will always be here, and we can always get the money we need via taxes. Therefore, we do not need to fund for future benefits the same way they do. There is no risk of our going out of business, while private sector companies do face that risk. While they must remain current in funding the present value of their future promised benefits, we don't need to. There-

fore the funding level requirements that are applied to private companies do not apply to us."

That's how the State of New Jersey justified making NO contributions to their pension plan for 6 years, and why they are facing unfunded liabilities of $90 billion. The deficit that they admit to is determined by GASB standards! If they used private sector accounting standards, the world would see the truth, and the truth would be that New Jersey is out of business...put there by their own pension plans.

Each of the 2,500+ public sector pension plans is different. Each has different benefits provisions, retirement formulas and inherent assumptions. It is impossible for this author to delve into the actuarial valuations, or the accuracy of the inherent assumptions in order to find out how far-removed from reality their pension reporting is. Dealing with interest rate assumptions is easier, as there is quite a bit of statistical data that summarizes average public sector pension assets and interest rate assumptions. It is not uncommon for the public sector entities to assume that they will earn 8% compounded forever. Even when actual results are far lower these underlying assumptions don't get changed. The plan funding requirements are based (and reported to taxpayers) on these unattainable investment returns.

Public sector plans use a convenient device called "smoothing." It is based on the premise that the public sector entity will be here forever and an assumption of an average return of 8% over an infinite timeframe is reasonable and shouldn't be adjusted based on short-term (even a decade or more) of actual results. Even when public sector entities had huge pension shortfalls in the 2001 "tech bubble" and even when they got crushed again in the 2008 financial market collapse, their pension calculations are based on the fact that they are earning, and have earned, 8% during the past decade, while their actual earnings have been 3% or less.

Public Sector Pension Assumptions Are Not Realistic

These spurious assumptions allow public sector plans to report funding levels that are far removed from reality and hide the fact that the public sector entities have made promises that they cannot possibly afford to keep.

> The liabilities are so staggering that GASB and public sector entities cannot possibly admit they have been wrong and that their reports have created a financial debacle. To do so would create the recognition of liabilities that would show that virtually every public sector entity that has a defined benefit pension plan is hopelessly bankrupt. The numbers reported to taxpayers are so far removed from reality that virtually everyone that looks at them (except GASB) has agreed that these pension plans are "unsustainable." The dictionary definition of "unsustainable" is: *cannot be continued.*

In a June 2009 report entitled "The Need for Transparency in Public Sector Pensions," members of the British-North American Committee (BNAC) compared the occupational public pension funding and disclosure requirements of public sector entities in Great Britain, Canada and the United States. They concluded that these plans are using unreasonably high interest rate assumptions (discount rates) that are far higher than their own sovereign (market-based) interest rates. They calculated that the total U.S. occupational public sector net liability (liability minus current assets) would be $1.7 trillion larger than currently admitted if more prudent interest assumptions were used, but pointed out that they did not have complete data on municipal plans and that, "...we are likely to underestimate the scale of public pension sector in the U.S., and therefore also underestimate the true headline net liability." They concluded that, as of the end of 2007, the net liability was at least $3.8 trillion.

The report stated that that employee pension plans "suffer from a strong element of wishful thinking in their choice of discount rates to calculate liabilities." They strongly recommended that the U.S's own sovereign interest rates be used, and noted that such practice would be in accordance with rules of the International Accounting Standards Board, Standard 25. They also noted "...Governments should consider very carefully whether they should continue to accrue unfunded pension liabilities...We think that for the public sector, all intergenerational transfers should be represented by explicit Government debt. Debt is transparent and understood by the electorate. Other liabilities are not."

In a completely separate and independent report, The Free Enterprise Nation, Inc. commissioned a similar evaluation by Andrew Biggs, a resident scholar at the American Enterprise Institute and former principal deputy commissioner and deputy commissioner for policy at the Social Security Administration. In his study, "Truth in Accounting: Calculating the Market Value of Unfunded Obligations in State and Local Government Pension Plans," Biggs used an interest assumption of 3.27%, the average municipal bond rate, and applied this more prudent assumption to the plans he evaluated. He reported that as of 2006, although the stated unfunded liability of nonfederal public sector pension plans was $400 billion, it would really have been $3.5 trillion, a $3.1 trillion difference, if his more prudent and realistic interest assumptions were utilized. In essence, the actual unfunded liability of nonfederal public sector pension plans would be 8.5 TIMES what they say it is.

Another report, published in the *Journal of Economic Perspectives* by Robert Novy-Marx and Joshua Rauh, determined that the underfunding of these government pensions is now $3.2 trillion. "The value of pension promises already made by U.S. state governments will grow to approximately $7.9 trillion in 15 years...Insuring both taxpayers against funding deficits and plan participants against benefit reductions would cost almost $2 trillion today, even though governments portray state pensions as almost fully funded."

All three of the reports were done independently. All were trying to determine what the REAL unfunded obligations of public sector pension plans are. All are guesses, since none were able to review all 2,547 different plans, and none were able to investigate any OTHER aspects of plan valuations, such as pay increase assumptions, spiking, disability provisions, cost-of-living raises or numerous other factors on which actual plan obligations and assumptions are based. As a result, there is a strong likelihood that their calculations actually UNDERSTATE the real unfunded liability.

Whether you use Biggs's $3.5 trillion, BNAC's $3.8 trillion, or Novy-Marx/Rauh's $3.2 trillion estimates, the recognition of this unfunded liability as debt would sink virtually every public sector entity in the United States. The average of the three studies is a $3.5 trillion unfunded liability, or approximately 8 TIMES what is reported to the public. How significant is that number? At the end of 2008, the professed debt of all nonfederal public sector entities was $2.2 trillion, plus $400 billion off the balance sheet in unfunded liabilities, for a total of $2.6 trillion. If we add $3 trillion more, based on the three reports cited above, their total debt is more than DOUBLE what they say it is, and that does not include the unfunded liabilities for health insurance!

> The impact of the current misleading accounting and reporting practices is that public sector entities are actually paying out money each year as if the underlying funds were there. Since they are not, there is a budget "shortfall" every year, requiring even more debt, more taxes, or another reduction in services.

The editorial entitled "The Government Pay Boom," which appeared in the *Wall Street Journal* on March, 26, 2010, says the State of Illinois had to "issue $3.5 billion in bonds merely to meet its mandatory contribution to the worker retirement program..." and "...near bankrupt New Jersey would have to pay $7 billion a year if it properly accounted for its pension and health benefits."

The Time to Challenge is Long Overdue

The fact that the public sector allows retirement as young as age 40, and public sector retirement at age 55 is commonplace, has generally not been challenged by the private sector taxpayer, or by the elected officials who represent them. Until recently, there was no organization representing the interests of the private sector at all. **No one has said, "If the Social Security Administration has to keep pushing back the retirement age for me, why aren't we doing the same thing in the public sector?** Why do 21 million public sector employees get to retire at age 50 or 55 (paid for by me!) when I can't retire myself?"

This public sector pension crisis has been enabled by an accounting system and reporting standards that have allowed public sector entities to completely mislead voters. Each time public sector salaries have increased (and they have increased dramatically in the last decade), and each time the size of government has grown, the cost of the pensions that are based on these salaries, has gone up accordingly.

> By pretending that the pension funds have been earning 7%–9%, thus creating absolutely mythical statements of funding adequacy, the public sector hides the true costs of these plans from the taxpayer. They continue to raise taxes to meet the costs (new money for old promises). In the outside world, this is known as a Ponzi scheme.

Governments know that as long as enough new money is coming in, they can hide the fact that they don't have enough money to keep past promises. With the public sector pension Ponzi scheme, as with every other Ponzi scheme, there comes a day when there isn't enough money coming in to meet the promises that have been made. For decades, that day was tomorrow. For taxpayers in 2010, that day is today.

To compound the problem for taxpayers, every state operates on a "cash" budget and is required to balance the budget each year.

While one set of books deals with pensions and the funding status of these plans, the state budget presents a completely different set of numbers. State budgets are concerned only with "cash in" and "cash out" each year. They show the actual amounts paid to pensioners and do not concern themselves with what amounts will be paid next year or the year after that. They may know (as a Florida legislator recently told me) that "we're anticipating a $5.2 billion shortfall next year, but this year, we're dealing with the $3.2 billion shortage." Their job is to balance the budget this year, which they will accomplish by asking for federal stimulus funds or cutting programs and services, and increasing taxes. It is for next year's legislature to figure out how to solve the $5.2 billion problem.

The Hidden Costs of Free and Subsidized Health Insurance

Public sector retirees also get free or subsidized health insurance. What does that cost? The Pew Center on the States, in a report entitled "The Trillion Dollar Gap" estimates the liability for retiree coverage under nonfederal health insurance plans to be $587 billion, of which $555 billion is unfunded. If that estimate is correct, the liability is larger than what the public sector entities say their total pension unfunded liabilities are! What are the REAL unfunded retiree health insurance liabilities? Once again, the answer is, "No one knows" because there is no private sector type of uniform accounting and reporting standard that would provide an accurate number that taxpayers can rely on.

Until recently, GASB did not require reporting or disclosure of unfunded retiree health care liability at all. In 2009, GASB said that it was time that this expensive benefit, and the unfunded liabilities of these benefits, should be accounted for and disclosed to taxpayers. After all, it is another type of pension plan, and its costs go up dramatically every year. For example, in Florida the state health insurance plan costs $1,400 a month in 2009 for family coverage, and the state pays 90% for 96,000 of its active employees, and 100% of it for 25,000 employees. The cost to continue health insurance after retirement at age 50 or 55 is huge and can in many cases be worth more than the pension benefit itself. Annual health insurance rate increases can be 10% to 30%.

Putting this liability out there for all to see for the first time will be a real shocker. GASB decided to make things a bit easier. **It decided that this "shock to the system" should be alleviated and declared that in 2009, only 1/30th of the estimated unfunded liability should be reported and amortized.** The next year, 2/30th would be included, and each year thereafter, 1/30th should be added in. In 30 years, the real numbers will be there for all to see. In the meantime, 1/30th of a growing unfunded liability will appear as if by magic each year, to be added to the funding and amortization requirements in public sector accounting. Isn't transparency wonderful?

The failure to account for health insurance benefits for retirees, and the underfunding of public pension plans is not only due to their unique style of cooking the books. Politics also plays a role. As Thomas Firey from the Cato Institute explains:

> *"New York Times reporter Mary Williams Walsh nicely summarizes the dynamic that creates this liability: '[Public pension plans] are governed by boards that often include municipal labor leaders, whose duty to represent their workers' interests can easily conflict with their fiduciary duty to represent the plan itself. And even the most exemplary pension boards can be overruled, in many cases, by politicians whose priorities may be incompatible with sound financial management.'...Between then and now, I suppose we'll hide under some coats and hope that somehow everything will work out."*

Who is on the hook for this? If city, state and local pension benefit promises are to be kept, it will be up to taxpayers to come up with the money—either through higher taxes or lower service levels.

Because of bookkeeping and accounting trickery, the public sector entity always needs more money than it has to meet the current demands of its pension and continued health insurance plans. No matter what they do, they can't find enough services to cut, people to fire or taxes to increase. Somehow, they need more cash…and quickly.

Over the years, the quick solution has often been to issue "Pension Obligation Bonds" (POB's). In most cases, they are incurring very long term debt in order to have enough money to pay one or two years' worth of obligations. That's like taking out a 20 year loan in order to make this month's house payment. How long can that continue? Other public sector plans have issued POB's on the premise that "we can borrow at 4%, invest it at 8% and make the difference." Unfortunately, some hard lessons were learned when long-term bonds were issued and the money quickly shrank when the market tanked. The result is that those public sector plans dramatically INCREASED the pension costs to taxpayers.

The problem is that the benefits of many public sector pension plans are **guaranteed by taxpayers.** Unlike Social Security benefits, which are not guaranteed by law and which can be reduced, benefits in state and local pension plans are usually guaranteed by the state and local governments.

Andrew Biggs points out that it's rather unlikely the powerful government unions would permit any changes to pension benefits already accrued, but there are options for changing this unsustainable path in the future:

> "… While accrued benefits are virtually sacrosanct, governments do have the ability to alter the terms of which future benefits are earned. Employee contributions can be increased, and the benefit formula made less generous going forward. While government employees will understandably be upset, it is worth noting that state and local pension benefits are generally significantly more generous than pensions paid by Social Security and private sector defined benefit or defined contribution retirement programs. As the costs of an aging population come to bear, these costs should be shared proportionately between taxpayers and beneficiaries."

We can't afford to keep providing one class of citizens, our public servants, with retirement benefits that are 4 to 10 times what private sector employees get from Social Security, paid 10-25 years earlier. We cannot allow Ponzi-style bookkeeping to continue to mislead taxpayers into thinking their money is being prudently spent, and that public sector accounting is transparent, accurate and truthful. It isn't.

*"Even after economic and financial conditions have returned to normal, in the absence of further policy actions, the federal budget appears set to remain on an **unsustainable** path."*

—Ben Bernanke, Chairman
of the Federal Reserve Board,
April 27, 2010

Chapter Five

Creating a Dependency— The "Nanny State"

The term "nanny state" has been widely used to describe government attempts to determine what is best for all of us. It is a most unfortunate term, because it is so benign and sounds only like a minor irritant. Nannies are those selected and paid by parents to assist in the caregiving of their child or children. They are entrusted to represent the parents and are carefully chosen and monitored by the parents. They are hired, fired and rewarded by the parents. They serve directly under the control of the parents. The control is with the parents. The nanny's pay, working hours and conditions of employment are established by the parents. Most importantly, the rules enforced by the nanny are the rules established by the parents, not those of the nanny's own making.

In no way does the term nanny state properly describe the abridgment of individual rights that occur when our government assumes power over us expressly prohibited by the Constitution. The federal government has assumed the power to require your employer to take taxes out of your paycheck before you are even paid, and to immediately remit payment to them, although income taxes are not due until the end of the year. The government not only

TAKES from your paycheck, it takes the tax too early and does not pay interest on the "loan" it has forcibly taken from you. Even if your circumstances are such that no income taxes are ultimately payable, it simply refunds the money the following year, by which time it has forcibly taken taxes from several months of your income in that year, as well. The central government not only can take whatever it wants and redistribute it to whomever it wants, but it has assumed the power to make you adhere to ITS rules of comportment and behavior. That isn't a nanny state, it is the definition of a tyrannical state: one that exercises direct control over virtually every aspect of individual lives and individual freedom.

> Government imposed behavior can result in an absolutely insane and conflicting array of laws. My intent is not to favor one side or the other or to judge which of the opposing views is correct but to demonstrate that no matter which side you are on, the rules imposed by government do not stand up under the scrutiny of a universally-employed and common moral imperative.

Let's examine just a few of the rules of behavior that governments have established.

- The treatment of gambling is probably the most hypocritical behavior. Most states treat gambling as a crime but then sponsor their own lotteries (formerly known as the numbers racket.) Many allow pari-mutuel horse and/or dog racing. The reason, of course, is that governments often employ "the ends justify the means" to disguise their hypocrisy on the grounds that what they are doing is for the common good. "It's for the SCHOOLS!" enables the government to make astonishing profits from gambling activities that are banned as bad for you, immoral, or regressive, if done by anyone else.

- In another example, how about the recent national publicity exposing the fact that a 16 year old girl in Washington was provided a free abortion by her school clinic under the condition that she not tell her parents about it? The state had determined that the 16 year old child had the right to privacy from her own parents. What if something had gone horribly wrong with the abortion? What if she had died? Does anyone think it is right to send a 16 year old, without parents, to some clinic where strangers put her in a hospital gown and roll her in for the procedure? Can you imagine the fear this young girl must have felt? The result of that school-run abortion program is that the young girl learned that the school or state, not her parents, would determine what was good for her, and would protect her rights against her own parents. What if the parents knew something that the school clinic didn't know? Perhaps the young girl had other emotional or developmental problems of which the school was unaware? If they knew that their 16 year old daughter became pregnant, perhaps it would cause the parents to re-examine their own roles in parenting. Perhaps they would want to be involved in counseling that might take place. What impact would the pregnancy/abortion have on her siblings in the same family? Would the brothers and sisters know about it all? Or if they were told, would they join in a conspiracy of silence against the parents? Don't these school clinics receive state, and by extension, federal funding? Doesn't current law prohibit the use of taxpayer dollars to provide abortion? Where does the school board, state or federal government have the right to establish a financial dependency, a moral authority and to share secrets with our own children?

- How about the states that can't figure out whether unborn children have rights or not? The national press covered the case of the man in California who murdered his pregnant wife. He was found guilty of the first-degree murder of his wife, and manslaughter of the unborn child. How can the same state that permits abortions on the grounds that an unborn child has no legal rights then find a man guilty of manslaughter for killing an unborn child?

- What about the states that ban smoking **unless** it's marijuana?

- How about the cities and states that will boycott ANOTHER STATE of the union, because they don't like the laws the citizens of the other state implemented? (Did I just write what I just wrote, or am I having a bizarre Orwellian nightmare?)

- Or what about the drive to "eliminate fat people," especially fat children? Can you imagine the pain inflicted on a child when he or she is targeted by government for being fat? One government has banned putting toys in "Happy Meals." Will they require removing jelly from jelly donuts next? Or Alfredo sauce from pasta? Or bacon at breakfast? Just how far can our governments go to control individual behavior? Does any government have the right to decide how much people should weigh, and therefore what they are allowed to eat? Is a ban on Twinkies and milkshakes next on the horizon?

- Now that government is in the health "care" business, shouldn't it ban all activities that involve very high risk? After all WE have to pay for it when people are injured or killed. Isn't it logical that Black Diamond ski slopes should be outlawed, as should be sky diving, auto and motorcycle racing, rock climbing, scuba diving and bungee jumping? These do not serve the public good, and expose our government to having to pay the costs of this reckless behavior. And running 26 miles just for the fun of it should definitely be banned, shouldn't it? After all, two people DIED in the last major national marathon. If government does allow running, don't you think they should require a permit and a health examination first? Why should we allow those OLD FAT PEOPLE to run?

It is clear that when government starts to interpret what your rights are, it must also give itself the legal authority to determine what is right or wrong. Leaders of the party in a one-party rule environment, with the help of a compliant Supreme Court, can do virtually anything they want to. They could decide that, in addition to your right to health insurance (even if they force you to pay for it) you have the right to food, clothing and shelter. Should it be determined that these are rights, as opposed to basic needs, the government may just decide to take them from you and provide them to someone else. That was the general idea that created communism in the first place.

In the recent debates about federal government policies, particularly those related to health care reform legislation, we've heard more and more references to socialism and capitalism. Right-wingers often call liberals the term socialists, while left-wingers attack right-wingers as capitalist pigs. And we've heard the term communist thrown into the mix, too. Let's agree to use *American Heritage Dictionary* definitions:

> **Socialism.** *Any of the various theories or systems of social organizations in which the means of producing and distributing goods is owned collectively or by a centralized government that often plans and controls the economy.*

> **Communism.** *1. A theoretical economic system characterized by the collective ownership of property and by the organization of labor for common advantage to all members. 2. A system of government in which the state plans and controls the economy and a single, often authoritarian party holds power, claiming to make progress toward a higher social order...*

> **Capitalism.** *An economic system in which the means of production and distribution are privately or corporately owned and development is proportionate to the accumulation and reinvestment of profits gained in a free market.*

If you search the words free enterprise on the internet, you are automatically directed to capitalism. Enough said.

Free Enterprise and Socialism Don't Mix

The private sector has always been the jobs creator of our nation. Individual freedom, self-determination and risk-taking in order to achieve one's own version of success have always been essential ingredients in the growth of the American economy.

One of the first settlements, in Jamestown, Virginia, was actually a capitalist risk-taking venture by backers of The Virginia Company, based in London. Free-enterprisers participated in the Oklahoma land rush and the San Francisco gold rush, and free-enterprisers were among the farmers who settled in the Midwest and among the cattle barons of Texas. The transcontinental railroad, the airline industry, the computer industry, the telephone, radio and television industries were all created under a free enterprise system that enabled risk-taking, accepted failure and allowed rewards to be achieved by the intrepid few that persevered.

Virtually everything we see around us, and virtually all of the jobs needed to support it, was created by free enterprise. In a few hundred years, the United States of America has grown from practically nothing but raw land and promise, to the richest, most successful and most powerful nation (both economically and militarily) in the history of the world. It did so because it was different. It had a tolerance for diverse backgrounds and nationalities, endless individual opportunity and an unquenchable demand for liberty and personal freedom. America was built on free enterprise capitalism.

Few people call themselves socialists. Even fewer call themselves capitalists. What are we then? Republicans? Democrats? Independents? Libertarians? What do these terms mean, anyway? A common stereotype is that Democrats are liberals and socialists and atheists, pro-choice and anti-war. Republicans are capitalists, dominated by greed, overzealous Christians, and are pro-life and pro-war. We all know, instinctively that the stereotypes aren't valid. But they are convenient. How can we define ourselves since apparently no one wants to bear the stereotypical mantle of liberal, communist, socialist or capitalist? People are coming up with new terms to define themselves, apparently hoping that a different label will wear better on them.

We've been hearing more and more people say, "I'm a social liberal, but a fiscal conservative." What does THAT mean? Does it mean we should have lots of social welfare and entitlement programs but not pay for them? Or does it mean, "I support every social welfare and entitlement program, but I want YOU to pay for them?" I have never heard anyone say, "I am a social conservative, but a fiscal liberal," have you?

> As Congressman Jack Kemp pointed out when he conducted his presidential primary campaign in 1988, we really do have two economies in the United States, a socialist one and a capitalist one. Those who work in the public sector are actually living in a very socialistic economy. Government owns the "business" and the buildings and the equipment. Government and public education workers are paid by the government, receive health care and vacations provided by the government, and they retire with government-provided pay. They have great job security and excellent workplace rules. They are generally unaffected by economic downturns. They will generally not be rewarded for individual performance but know that the longer they stay in service, the better things will be.

Public Sector Unions

The impact of unionization of the public sector has gone largely unnoticed in recent decades. What is astonishing is that public sector unions are allowed to exist in the first place. **The taxpayers in the private sector have given a monopoly to our elected governments and public school districts.** Once we have given them their monopoly, we have no choice but to use their services. A competitive free market does not exist. If they want to make us wait in line for 2 hours to get a license plate, we have no choice but to endure it. We also give them the right to tax us. **Why on earth would taxpayers create a monopoly, then give that monopoly a right to tax us for what they need, and then allow centralized unions to dictate to US how much they will be paid, and to control every other condition of employment?** Sound crazy? We all know that it is.

Since most workers in the public sector are in traditionally white collar jobs, it would appear, at first glance, that unionization wouldn't be an attractive fit for those workers. Unions were formed originally to represent the interests of tradesmen (trade unions) and laborers (labor unions) whose work often consisted of similar work and/or of repetitive production-line processes. Individual achievement was difficult, if not impossible, to measure for a person who was one of hundreds who worked on a production line doing virtually the same thing as all the others. The idea of creating identical pay based on the specific skill set or on the identical work process for all workers was a seemingly logical way to arrive at pay scales and working conditions for each of them. Unionization was the means by which all workers could collectively achieve higher pay and better benefits for themselves in an environment that couldn't recognize or reward individual productivity.

In the past 40 years, the idea of unionization has carried over to white-collar jobs in the public sector, although these workers have usually been in jobs in which they were able to distinguish themselves by doing more or better work than their colleagues. The result of increased unionization in the public sector is that these workers have become trapped in one size fits all pay and benefits arrangements. While some choose not to enter public service because of this drawback and others are forced to live with it because there is no other way to pursue their vocation, others have sought it out as a means of receiving pay and benefits that are perhaps superior to those that they could achieve based on their personal performance in the private sector. Whatever the reason, public sector workers are now the most highly unionized segment of the American workforce, and they have used their bargaining power to enhance their pay and benefits to those well beyond levels provided in the private sector.

The "New Socialism" and a Growing Dependency

> Life is good in the public sector, the socialist part of our economy, because someone else is paying for it. **Our socialist economy lives because the capitalist (free enterprise) workers are taxed to pay for it.** The voters in the free enterprise economy told the public service economy, "You can take what you need from me. I'll give you the right to tax me for it." The result is that the public sector has taken VERY good care of itself. They've promised themselves all kinds of things that the poor taxpayer in the private sector has to pay for that he will never have for himself.

Ironically, the most heavily unionized part of our economy includes those in public education who teach our children. Some, perhaps most, of those in public education love their socialistic world, because there is great control over working conditions, the pay is good, the job (once seniority has been established) is secure, the work-year is 9 to 9½ months and retirement usually begins at 55 or earlier. Is it any wonder that those in our heavily-unionized educational system, from kindergarten all the way through college, tend to lean towards the socialist economic system that serves them so well?

In a book published in 1994 entitled *The New Unionism in the New Society,* Dr. Leo Troy, Distinguished Professor of Economics at Rutgers University, discusses a different way of looking at socialism. He pointed out that under "old socialism," government controlled the means of production, but under "new socialism" government doesn't need to own the means of production...they just need to control the money that comes from it! He states:

"The essence of new socialism is government ownership of an increasing share of the national income, not the means of production. The core of new socialism is the socialism of income." He continues by quoting Nobel Laureate Dr. Milton Freidman, who had written in 1989, using the "old" definition of socialism, "All means of production in the United States-people, land, machines, buildings, etc. produce our national income. By that test, government owns 45% of the means of production that produce national income. The U.S. is now 45% socialist."

Whether you use the term socialist, communist, progressive or liberal to describe it, the concept of government control of the economy, whether by ownership of the means of production or control of the income that comes from it, **is in direct competition with free enterprise.** You can't have it both ways. So let's admit it. Some want government to control the economy, and some don't. It isn't a conservative or a liberal issue, and it's not a Republican or a Democrat issue. It is a right of self-advancement and right of self-determination issue. It is a personal freedom issue.

The inherent problem with the concept of government control of the economy, and the attendant death of free enterprise, is that in order to achieve a redistributive economy government will have to destroy the goose that lays the golden egg. The public sector, or socialist part of our economy, only has it so good because it is entirely supported by the private sector, by free enterprise capitalists. **If the private sector goes under, so does the good life in the public sector.**

And it IS going under. In 2009, there were 1.5 million fewer workers in the private sector than there were 10 years earlier. During that same period, 20 million new jobs needed to be added just to keep up with population growth. That means that in 2009, 21.5 MILLION fewer jobs exist than were currently required. Add 2 million more jobs in 2010, and another 2 million jobs in 2011 and continue to carry it forward. Where will all these jobs come from? (How long can our kids stay in graduate school?) Each year, we have fewer companies and fewer private sector workers that must support more and more public sector workers, with hugely escalating pay and benefits costs. How can that work? It can't. It's unsustainable. That's why everyone, in both the public and private sectors, has a vested interest in keeping free enterprise alive, healthy and growing. **The public sector needs the private sector to pay the bills. The private sector needs the public sector to provide security and teach our children. We need each other.**

Those that want the government to control the entire economy must oppose free enterprise in favor of a redistributive, socialist society. Are there really those would take such a position? Actually, a lot of people would. In general, those who see themselves as receivers from the government would favor such an idea. Those who would be the ones taken from, would oppose it. Unless the Supreme Court decides to protect the rights that each of us is guaranteed in the constitution, the side that wins is the side that can get the most votes. If the redistributive government side wins enough to gain effectively one-party rule, that's enough, even if only temporarily, to achieve the needed changes to put government in charge of everything.

As we've seen with Social Security, Medicare and the establishment of new government bureaucracies, once they are established they are almost impossible to undo. The key for the establishment of a permanent redistributive government—a social welfare state—is to establish a systemic wealth transfer until those who are left with anything to take from are easily outvoted by those who want more.

How can government (including state and local governments) create a redistributive state? The simple answer is to create an alliance of all of those who benefit from redistribution. The redistribution alliance is composed of those who believe that government should take from others and give to them either through direct handouts or via compensation as employees of the government. Establishment of an elected redistributive government requires a large number of voters who have a dependency on government. The more who become dependent on government, the larger the potential alliance becomes.

The problem is that in order to accomplish a large dependency, a significant portion of the nation's wealth must be transferred to a growing pool of those who are dependent on government. Since the United States is a democracy, and those from whom wealth will be taken can vote, that would appear to be quite difficult to accomplish. It would seem likely that the majority of citizens would resist attempts by governments to extract tax dollars from them in order to bestow significant financial rewards to government dependents. After all, the private sector still represents the majority of voters who would presumably vote against those who would take from them and give to others. **But it is simple to accomplish if governments hide what they are doing from the private sector electorate.**

If government promises pay, job security and benefits to its own employees and then hides the true costs from the private sector taxpayers, voters won't know until it is too late exactly what took place. And if government promises critically needed benefits to more and more citizens, even including many of those in the private sector, those citizens will also voluntarily or involuntarily become part of the redistribution alliance.

> The key to the creation of a permanent redistributive state is to build a large and growing constituency of dependents by hiding the continuing reallocation of tax dollars from the private sector to the public/dependency sector. Then make even more commitments, incurring even greater future obligations that are so massive that virtually all citizens will be forced to rely on the government for their own financial survival, making them all dependents.

In addition to government and public education employees, there are many millions of voters who are now dependent on government. Government is giving down payments for home purchasing, bailing out those underwater on home mortgages, accepting and guaranteeing mortgages from people who don't really qualify for mortgages, adding even more dependents to the system. To appease the masses, Government even provides handouts to anyone, regardless of income, as they did with the "Cash for Clunkers" program that gave a total of $4 billion to anyone who wanted to trade in an inefficient car for a newer, better one. (The $4 billion was debt, to be repaid by future taxpayers, of course.) **Generally not reported during the press frenzy surrounding the "Cash for Clunkers" program was the fact that the government had approved a January 1, 2009 cost of living raise of 3.9% to all federal employees, costing the taxpayer another $4 billion (also in the form of debt to be repaid by taxpayers.)**

Two recently signed laws affecting our children are the best examples of government creation of a new dependent class. The first is the student loan industry, which has just been nationalized, or taken over by the federal government. The government will now loan money to our children directly for college tuition. The children will depend on the government for the money they need, and the government will give it to them. They will rely on the government being generous in dealing with any difficulties to pay the money back. Even better, the government tells these students that if they go to work for ANY public sector entity and stay for ten years (while making minimal payments), the government will entirely forgive the outstanding balance, tax-free. For a young student with a law or graduate degree, student loans of $100,000 are not uncommon. If they go to work for the public sector, they will effectively receive a $10,000 per year tax-free supplement to their pay, compliments of the private sector taxpayer (many of whom are trying to take enough of their paychecks home to pay for loans they took to send their OWN children to college.) After 10 years, they will now be well entrenched in the public sector system, making great pay and receiving great benefits. What are the chances that they will move to the private sector? Meanwhile, the person with huge student loans who went to work in the private sector will spend most of his or her career trying to pay off those student loans.

The health care "reform" bill provided an additional great benefit to our children. Imagine this conversation between two of the framers of the new legislation: "To make insurance affordable, we'll have to charge older people a little less and younger people much more. The premiums for young people will go through the roof! Young voters between 18 and 24, OUR CONSTITUENCY, will go berserk!" The answer? "Not to worry. We'll say in the new legislation that all insurers must cover children under their parents' policies until they are 26 years old. Terrific! We'll keep our non-taxpaying student constituency very happy. We'll lend them gobs of money, and then forgive it if they come to work for us. And we'll be sure they never have to pay a significant health insurance premium at all if they join the public sector. We have FABULOUS benefits, and we require very low contributions. Their votes are 'in the bag.' Brilliant!"

Can the government make an entire generation of young people, including millions of college graduates, dependent on them financially? Of course they can. But someone has to pay. Insurance isn't free just because people under 26 are added to mom and dad's policies. The price of family coverage has to go up. (Years ago, young people became independent of their parents at a much younger age. If we are going to treat people up to age 26 as dependents, perhaps we should have them wait until they are 27 to vote?) It also isn't "free" when the federal government forgives a $100,000 student loan. The money was given to the student. He or she used the money to buy a car, rent an apartment or even pay tuition and books. The cash was given to the student by the government. When the loan is forgiven, someone has to pay for it. It is, of course, the companies and workers in the private sector.

The process of building huge new dependencies is well underway. Public sector entities at every level have built enormous dependencies. They have successfully hidden from the private sector the transfer of wealth from the private sector to the public sector. They pay public sector employees more, provide more benefits, offer job security based on tenure not talent, bestow early and generous retirement programs and provide other entitlement programs on which millions of Americans have become dependent. Government has interfered with, or taken over, the relationship that parents have with their own children by establishing the fact that government will provide our children with their own rights to privacy, will counsel them on sex and abortion, will provide financial support and will determine what is morally right or wrong.

Governments have built huge dependencies, especially from government workers, by promising pay and benefits that they do not have the money to pay for. It has simply passed the financial burden on to those who must pay tomorrow when the bills come due. It has hidden this from the private sector taxpayers by using accounting and bookkeeping trickery allowing the accumulation of massive undisclosed debt.

Virtually all of this has occurred while private sector workers and businesses have operated under the assumption that elected officials have generally represented their best interests, and have always represented the facts fully and completely to voters. This trust has been misplaced, as the true extent of the transfer of wealth from private sector taxpayers to public sector employees, and the nearly incalculable accrued unfunded liabilities associated with them, have never been fully and clearly disclosed.

Two Kinds of Taxpayers

One of the inherent problems in dealing with uncontrolled government spending, debt and waste is that those addressing the subject usually deal with the impact on "the taxpayer." But the identification of the taxpayer as the party bearing the burden of big government is, as we've seen, overly simplistic. There are two categories of taxpayers, private sector taxpayers and public sector taxpayers. On the surface, it would appear that all taxpayers would have a clear and common interest and that all taxpayers would react more or less similarly to issues related to government spending and tax increases. **But since public sector taxpayers are themselves paid with tax dollars, they would naturally be inclined to support higher taxes if they are the direct beneficiaries of these tax payments.**

For example, it would be expected that most public school teachers would vote in favor of a general tax increase designed to increase the pay and benefits of public school teachers. Similarly, government employees would vote for larger government or more government spending because it is likely that they will be the direct beneficiary of the tax increase, and that their individual gain would be more than their individual tax payment. To the extent that such voting behavior is likely, it behooves those in the private sector who are being required to fund more or bigger government to know where their tax dollars are going, and ultimately how much debt will be required to be paid back.

The lines used to separate the private sector from the public sector have become blurry recently as government has wrested control of much of the insurance, financial services, automobile, student loan and home mortgage industries. We also know that government spending to rebuild infrastructure and create jobs will create an enormous additional dependency on government because it will use borrowed tax dollars to pay contractors to rebuild infrastructure (as long as they are fully unionized), taking even more from the private sector, and adding even more to its list of dependents.

How big is the current government dependency? No one knows for sure. Some guesswork can roughly approximate the percentage of the electorate that is likely to vote in favor of a redistributive government. There are 89,000 public sector entities in the United States supported by the taxpayer, either directly via tax payments or indirectly via tolls, fees and licenses. This sector employs an estimated 22 million. One would expect them to be inclined toward redistribution of tax dollars to themselves. There are 150 million income tax filers, of whom 47%, or about 70 million, either pay no taxes or get a refund of taxes they never paid. They would be expected to be inclined toward redistribution, too, since tax increases have no negative impact on them. Public higher education employs another 1.5 million. They live in a socialist-like environment, and would be expected to lean toward getting more from others. In addition, according to the U.S. Department of Health and Human Services, 15% of our population, or about 43 million people, are receiving some kind of welfare from government. They have defined two categories of welfare recipients, "beneficiaries" and "dependents." Beneficiaries receive some welfare support, and dependents rely on welfare for more than half of their total income. In the beneficiary category are the 43 million Americans who receive either Aid to Families with Dependent Children, Temporary Assistance for Needy Families, food stamps (the average monthly benefit is $133.00 per individual) or Supplemental Security Income. The "dependent" category represents ¼th of all of those who receive any form of welfare, or about 11 million Americans. Many if not most of this group of 43 million beneficiaries and dependents are children who cannot yet vote. It is probably safe to guess that 20% are of voting age, which represents about 9 million voters.

Add to this an estimated 14 million voters between the ages of 18 and 24, most of whom do not support themselves (pay no income taxes) but do have the ability to vote for more tax payments from others. Although firm statistics concerning the voting results for the 18–24 age group are not available, the participation in the last presidential election by those aged 18–29 is estimated at 24 million (nearly 20% of all voters) of which 66% voted for President Obama. It was the second-largest young voter turnout is U.S. history. In a survey by *Declare Yourself*, 42% of young voters identified themselves as Democrats and 24% as Republicans, a nearly 2–1 ratio.

Based on the above, there appears to be a large pool of voters who would be predisposed to bigger, more generous government. The above numbers add up to more than 110 million, but that is certainly not a useful number, as many of the groups overlap. There are undoubtedly private sector workers who pay no taxes, and students who do pay taxes. But the constituency that would be expected to favor redistribution is obviously quite large. Let's eliminate 40% (taking a wild guess to estimate overlap) and that would give us about 65 million voters who might lean strongly toward redistribution. That equals about ½ of all the voters in the last presidential election. Certainly, they don't all vote the same way. And many don't vote at all. It appears reasonable to surmise that there would be a strong tendency for this group, who either is paid with tax dollars or pays no taxes, or both, to support the premise that someone else should pay more taxes for government to redistribute to them.

> Based on the premise that there is a difference between public and private sector taxpayers, one might expect that political candidates and elected officials would have recognized the differences and addressed the obvious issues. It is far more expedient, and much less dangerous, to lump together the taxpayers as a group and develop a political campaign accordingly. What candidate or elected official wants to take on the unified and organized unions representing the public sector if he or she cannot rely on the strong support of an equally unified and well-financed private sector? **Since the private sector is not organized, not unified, and has little or no financial muscle, it is no wonder that it has been squeezed nearly to death by the financial demands of the public sector unions.**

The voter in the private sector would generally be expected to have a predisposition toward voting against more taxes and against more redistribution, as there is rarely a direct benefit to the private sector taxpayer when taxes are increased. But the voter in this sector is commonly confronted by appeals from the "holy trinity" of taxpayer motivation—police, firefighters and public education. It is the rare taxpayer in the private sector who can bring himself to oppose more spending on law enforcement, fire protection or education of our children. When confronted with threats from government or public education that they will be forced to reduce the numbers or quality of these critical resources, the average taxpayer will grudgingly concede to supporting the tax increase as a good citizen.

We first heard the term "Washington Monument Ploy" used by The Tax Foundation, a non-partisan think tank in Washington, D.C. In dealing with the cost of government and public education at every level, all taxpayers must understand the hugely significant impact of this method of getting taxpayers to approve higher taxes and/or more debt. According to The Tax Foundation, the "Washington Monument Ploy" was created when public officials, faced with the possibility of spending cuts, responded by threatening to end the most popular and sympathetic program under their control–the National Park Service threatened to close the Washington Monument if its budget was cut. The tactic is a favorite of bureaucrats and politicians. The hope is that when lawmakers and the general public learn of the beloved programs that would be completely eliminated, the talk of spending cuts will quickly disappear, and it often works.

> The voter is commonly confronted by appeals from the "holy trinity" of taxpayer motivation–police, firefighters and public education.

Unfortunately, the cute-sounding term "Washington Monument Ploy" lightens the impact of the devastating tactic that is employed routinely by virtually every level of government. It might better be characterized as "legalized extortion" by our public sector monopolies, and we have all seen it in use.

Here's how it works:

First you must recognize that the public sector entity is a MONOPOLY. If they don't provide the service we require of them, we can't get it elsewhere. They are our public schools, policemen, firefighters, court systems and other vital services.

A budget crisis occurs. There is a budget shortfall brought about by the HUGE costs of public sector pay, benefits and unfunded liabilities. (You have seen some of the examples in earlier chapters and will see more horrific examples in later chapters.) There simply isn't enough money to pay all the gold-plated benefits and retirement plans that have been provided (and hidden) from taxpayers.

The public school, or city, county or state needs more money because there is a "tax shortfall" or necessary increases due to inflation and public needs, they say. Taxpayers and elected officials balk at raising taxes even further.

The public sector entity then says, "If you don't give me more money I will have no choice but to close schools early, release prisoners from prison, reduce police protection or reduce the number of firefighters we need to protect you."

Never disclosed to taxpayers: the fact that the actual reason there is a need for more taxes is caused directly by indefensibly generous pay and pensions to these constituencies. The taxpayer is faced with a "Hobson's Choice," that is pay more or suffer. **The public sector entity now RULES the taxpayer by virtue of the fact that it has a monopoly on a critical service,** and can deny the taxpayer these very services and protections that it was hired to provide in the first place.

Now we come to the "need" to increase taxes. Who will vote in favor of these increases? That's pretty easy to predict: The voters who prefer redistribution because they directly benefit will vote for those who would increase taxes and spending, because they don't pay taxes or are paid by taxes in the first place. In addition, usually because of the "holy trinity" and "Washington Monument Ploy" appeals, a significant portion of the private sector voters will also support those candidates who want to tax more. The beauty of this voter math is that if you already have 35% of voters in the tank, you only have to win 25% of the remaining voters to carry the day. That means that 75% of private sector voters can vote against redistribution and lose in the election. If that isn't a situation that calls for organization and unity by the private sector, I don't know what is.

The elements of the private sector have never been unified. Large corporations have Political Action Committees (PACs), lobbyists and individual political connections that are utilized to advance their own company's interests. Often, the interests of these large corporations find a niche helpful to themselves but harmful to the private sector as a whole. Who can forget the CEO of General Electric proclaiming, "We're all Democrats now!" when he saw the billions his company could make by embracing proposed "Cap and Trade" taxes and other "climate change" opportunities?

We've seen entire industries support the unpopular health care reform legislation in order to protect their own business interests. Large corporations spend their money on specific and limited interests. Small companies and America's 5 million tiny entrepreneurial businesses lack the resources to fund PACs or lobbyists and rarely have direct political connections with politicians. Ditto for the workers in the private sector.

Even though there are 108 million workers in the private sector, and 5 million employers, their interests are totally ignored because they are not and have never been a unified force. It is getting more and more commonplace to see private sector workers join the fray in demonizing large corporations, although they are themselves paid by those same companies. Why do they join in, or tolerate, the demonization of their own employers? I believe it is because corporations have done a very poor job of educating and unifying their own employees. The corporations have not fought back, thus lending credibility to the detractors when they complain about corporate greed and corporate excess.

Getting private sector employers and employees on the same page and working together to protect free enterprise is an absolute necessity. Corporations can't vote, but their employees can. Once they combine forces to protect free enterprise, they'll become a powerhouse that can significantly impact taxes and public policy.

*"At current projections, the federal government will go into **unsustainable** debt if it is to meet its Social Security, Medicaid and Medicare obligations to baby boomer retirees and others."*

—The Dallas Morning News,
September 21, 2008

Chapter Six

Social Security: A Crisis within a Crisis

The impact of baby boomers on Social Security has been discussed for decades. Begun in 1935, Social Security is a redistributive process, charging active workers and their employers to pay for those who are currently receiving Social Security retirement benefits. It was assumed back in 1935 that there would always be more workers than retirees. Not contemplated was the fact that life expectancy would increase from 68 to 80 over the next 75 years and that as people lived longer, the burden of payment would increase accordingly. Also not contemplated back in 1935 was that population growth, and job growth, might not grow evenly. As time went by, these problems with the system have been tinkered with by making small adjustments in Social Security payroll taxes and benefits.

It has long been known that the transfer system would work only if there were considerably more active workers paying Social Security taxes than there were retirees receiving benefits. In the early years, whenever tax collections exceeded payout requirements, the excess was allocated to a Social Security Trust Fund, which resulted in the creation of another government Ponzi scheme, as we shall see. When the system began, there were eight active workers providing benefits for every retiree. In the early 1980s, it became apparent that a baby boom had occurred between 1946 and 1961 and that population growth had slowed considerably since then. A huge growth bulge had occurred, and these workers would reach age 65 from 2011 to 2026. Numbering an estimated 77 million Americans, about 25% of our entire population, the attainment of age 65 will entitle them all to Social Security.

A slower population growth since 1961 and increases in life expectancy would mean that fewer and fewer workers would be available to provide retirement income to an increasing base of retirees.

> With new beneficiaries becoming entitled to Social Security at a rate of approximately 5 million a year beginning in 2011, it became clear that the beneficiaries would overpower the workforce to the extent that for every retiree, there would be only two, not eight, workers to support them. The financial strain on active workers to fund these retirees would become so large that enormous increases in payroll taxes would have to be made in order to avoid the necessity of cancelling or reducing Social Security benefits.

There was a crisis looming, and government decided to deal with it by vastly increasing the Social Security Trust Fund. This would be accomplished by increasing Social Security payroll taxes in order to pre-fund at least some of the oncoming financial burden.

Social Security taxes were increased dramatically in 1983, and during the next 25 years, the government collected $2.5 trillion MORE than required to support current retirees. In effect, workers during that period (and employers who were required to pay an amount equal to employee contributions) **paid twice**, once to provide benefits to existing retirees and a second time to pre-fund a significant portion of their own future retirement benefits. **This $2.5 trillion in excess Social Security taxes became a windfall to support increased government spending and entitlements.**

This was quite easy to do. **Here's how it worked:**

> The government deposited U.S. Treasuries, not real money, into a trust fund. Treasuries are IOUs. The government uses treasuries to borrow money from us, and from countries like China, Saudi Arabia, etc. It pays us interest and promises to pay us our original investment back when it matures. Government decided, "Why not borrow from ourselves." By putting U.S. Treasuries in the trust fund it had cash to spend. **This has allowed Congress to behave recklessly and irresponsibly for decades.**
>
> It spent the Social Security trust fund, knowing that virtually nothing would be there but IOUs when the funds were needed. It knew that at some future date, Congress would have to deal with any funding shortfall by eliminating or reducing benefits, or by getting even more tax money from active workers, or both. But that was in the future and not for the government to worry about now.

> Congress spent the Social Security trust fund knowing that virtually nothing would be there but IOUs when the funds were needed.

The windfall of revenues coming in from dramatically increased payroll taxes and the use of this money to fund other government operations made it appear that government was doing a great job balancing the budget. At one State of the Union speech, President Clinton beamed as he announced that the federal deficit that year was "exactly zero." The timing was great, as the unseen off the balance sheet Social Security debt was piling up, and all of the payroll taxes were being spent as fast as they came in. It appeared that President Clinton had worked a miracle by balancing the budget.

The Baby Boomer Nightmare

The federal government has never guaranteed Social Security benefits. The obligation to provide these future benefits has never been recognized by the federal government as debt, because it can cancel or reduce Social Security benefits if it so chooses. Unfortunately, most American workers have assumed that Social Security will always be there, and they depend on Social Security to fund all or a substantial part of their needed retirement income. This is particularly true of baby boomers, many of whom consider Social Security the only dependable retirement income they can count on. That's due to the fact that virtually all of the other sources of potential retirement income have shrunken dramatically or disappeared in recent years.

Most baby boomers in the private sector don't have a fixed income pension plan, known as a defined benefit plan. Defined benefit pensions were terminated by most private sector employers in favor of 401(k) plans in the late 1980s and into the 1990s as accounting rules required disclosure of the huge liability that loomed ahead if defined benefit plans were not properly funded. The cost to adequately fund these programs was so high that these plans were virtually killed off in the private sector. But the public sector faced no such requirement with its own pension plans and with other entitlement programs. They were allowed to continue making promises they knew they could not hope to keep. They did this by tricking the taxpayers with bookkeeping and reporting practices, explained in Chapter Four. The result is an enormous disparity between public sector and private sector employees when it comes to retirement income.

Back in the 1980s when private sector pension plans began to disappear, the popular consensus was that Social Security represented only one leg of a four-legged stool on which retirement security should be based. The other three legs would be 401(k) plans, personal savings and home ownership. The possibility of having a home that was fully paid for thus reducing costs in retirement, or the possibility of selling the house, moving into a smaller home and investing the profits for retirement income was seen as the fourth leg. It sounded sensible in the 1980s, and baby boomers were dependent on the long-term success of the theory.

As noted earlier, baby boomers entered the private sector work-force between 1964 and 1983. When pensions started to disappear in the late 1980s, the oldest had 20-25 years in the workforce and the newest boomers had just started working. That's about when they started to pay (and their employers started to pay) increased payroll taxes in order to pay for those already retired, and to pre-fund for their own Social Security benefits via deposits to the trust fund. Private sector boomers were now betting their financial future that their four-legged retirement stool would be there when they needed it.

Back in the 1980s, it was assumed that the new 401(k) plan would allow the magic of compounding interest to accrue to the benefit of the private sector worker. Everyone saw exhibits showing that if you put $X into your 401(k) for 30 or 40 years, the magic of compound interest would provide you with a comfortable nest egg by age 65. But not long after the 401(k) became the basis on which most retirement plans depended, assumptions of compounding long-term interest returns began to look shaky.

The first problem with the 401(k) occurred when it morphed into a savings account that could be tapped for certain needs, like education, medical expenses, house improvements, etc. **In a page taken from the government's own book of idiotic financial prac-tices, you could get that new pool or deck for the backyard or pay Jimmy's college expenses with your 401(k) plan.** Just borrow from the 401(k), and pay yourself back later. Maybe the 401(k) could have delivered on its heady expectations if these plans had locked up money for retirement and didn't allow any early withdrawals, and if markets and compound interest had worked the way they were supposed to. But they didn't.

Soon after the 401(k) was implemented, all of the assumptions concerning compound interest and average returns fell apart. Many boomers increased debt during the same period by buying a more expensive home, or by borrowing home equity for other spending. Then real estate values collapsed and the stock market crashed.

That meant retirement at age 65 for private sector baby boomers was now becoming almost impossible.

The year 1991 started the beginning of market and financial turmoil that in the next decade would virtually "saw off" three of the legs of the retirement chair. The "tech bubble" wiped out a large percentage of assets in many 401(k) plans. During the ensuing seven years the Dow (Dow Jones Industrial Average) was relatively flat, and little or nothing was earned in average investment gains. Real estate looked to be a wonderful investment as huge gains were almost guaranteed. Then in 2008, the real estate collapse hit (brought on by Congress when it mandated that banks must follow idiotic lending practices to unqualified home buyers), wiping out both the gains that appeared to exist in real estate and forcing another hit to stock market and 401(k) values. Even worse, many Americans had INCREASED their mortgages to take advantage of much lower rates providing easy access to cash for other things like new cars, vacation homes or credit card debt.

When stock markets and real estate values plunged, people got very conservative with their investment portfolios, moving to cash and bonds to preserve what they could. That meant preserving some principal at the expense of interest earnings or stock appreciation when and if the market improved. Many employers began reducing or eliminating matching 401(k) contributions. The wheels had come off of 401(k) plans. As the tsunami of baby boomers gets closer and closer to planned retirement at age 65 (beginning with about 5 million people in 2011 and adding 5 million more each year), their plans for retirement income that had been made in the 1980s and early 1990s have fallen apart.

Dashed Expectations for 80 Million Americans

The problem is (as is the case in public sector pension plans) the undependability of achieving desired and projected compound interest returns on investments. Let's take a look at how compound interest is SUPPOSED to work, and what can happen in reality:

Assume that in 1990, you were a responsible 40 year-old worker and decided to put away the maximum that your employer would match in your 401(k) plan. At a salary of $82,000 a year, you could put 3%, or $2,500, into your 401(k). That meant a total of $5,000 a year would go into the plan for 25 years. You expected to earn a compounded investment gain of 7%. Based on those assumptions, in 2015 you'd have $365,000.

Assuming a 4% annual drawdown after retirement (nicely conservative), you'd have an income of about $15,000 a year when you reached 65. With Social Security of $24,000 a year, you'd have a total income of about $39,000 a year. Your house would be paid for, so living expenses would be low. Sounds like decent planning.

But let's say you put the $5,000 away for 25 years, and some horrific events happened in the interim. The "tech bubble" happened, the real estate crash and financial sector meltdown happened. By 2001, you had earned 7% compounded (no mean feat!) and had accumulated $95,000. But you lost 30% in the 2001 "tech bubble," leaving you with $66,000. You kept making your $5,000 annual contributions, but your portfolio was flat as the Dow gained virtually nothing for a decade. You had $116,000 in 2007.

Then the market tanked again in 2008, and you lost 30%. Your assets at the end of the year were $81,000. Nineteen years after starting, you had $81,000 in your 401(k). If you kept your job, and kept making your $5,000 annual contribution, and are able to earn 7% compounded for the next six years, you'll only have about $125,000 at age 65. A 4% drawdown will only produce an income of $5,000 a year, much less than half of what you had planned for.

Even worse, the house is no way near being paid off. It's worth less than it was when purchased in 2005, and property taxes will eat up a huge part of total retirement income. It's a situation of "can't afford to sell it, and can't afford to keep it." There's nothing to look forward to in retirement income but Social Security. Living expenses, including house payments and taxes, are far more than Social Security will provide.

To complicate matters (unknown to most people when they become eligible for Social Security and Medicare) you will have to PAY for Part B of Medicare, and this payment will be deducted directly from your Social Security check. Based on retirement income from all sources, individuals will be charged a minimum of $110.00 per person per month to a current maximum of $353.60. The federal government is already planning to increase these charges and will certainly continue to do so in the decades ahead, thus reducing the actual benefit that Social Security provides to retirees. For you and many private sector boomers, as seen in this scenario, retirement seems impossible. And that is where many baby boomers will find themselves as they reach retirement age between 2011 and 2026. That's one-fourth of our population. It's about us, and about our moms and dads.

As boomers survey the wreckage in 2010, many recognize that their home mortgage won't be paid off when they reach retirement age. As a matter of fact, mortgages often exceed the value of the home. Investments (even if religiously made) and 401(k) plans have not grown as expected over the past 10 years. The 401(k) plan balances are a fraction of the estimates that had been projected when they enrolled in them. Retirement is NOT on the horizon, and if the current job is lost, financial failure becomes an increasingly imminent threat.

What does that all mean to private sector baby boomers who will reach age 65 in the next 15 years? How many people will be impacted by the loss of three legs of their retirement stool? We can begin with the oft-quoted estimate of 77 million baby boomers (born between 1946 and 1961) who will reach age 65 in the next 15 years. A person born in 1946 (the first baby boomer) would reach retirement age in 2011. That's why we see the reference to "77 million Americans first becoming eligible for Social Security in 2011." But we need to look closer at that assumption.

Public sector entities are not required to participate in Social Security, and many don't. Most public sector entities that do elect to participate in Social Security also have additional pension benefits.

Let's look at what that means. The first baby boomers were born in 1946. They began entering the workforce in 1964 at age 18. The last baby boomers would have been born in 1961, and if they went to college for four years, they would have entered the workforce in 1983. So we can bracket the years in which baby boomers entered the workforce: 1964–1983.

The war in Vietnam and the draft meant that many young men were required to serve in the military. That meant many baby boomers served in the military during the war period from about 1964 until the war ended in 1975. In virtually all public sector pension plans, time served in the military counts as years of service in their own pension plans. Those who made a career in the military could retire in 20 years, meaning there were baby boomer military retirees as early as 1984. And that means that those who began work in the public sector from 1964 on, or subsequent to that with credit for military service, were eligible for public sector pensions. Most public sector pension plans allow retirement after 30 years of service, if not sooner. That means that most baby boomers that began work in 1964 and worked in the public sector for 30 years began to be eligible to retire in 1994. Even the LAST baby boomers that entered the workforce in 1983 after going to college would be eligible to retire in 2013. This means that virtually all baby boomers who worked in the public sector will already have retired just at the time that private sector workers begin reaching Social Security retirement age in 2011. Who is paying these public sector workers? It has to be the private sector workers who paid, and are paying, taxes to support them.

The problem is that there are a limited number of private sector workers and employers who pay for the retirement benefits for others. While the federal government thinks only about Social Security, the private sector taxpayers have not only been paying for the other person's Social Security benefits, but they are ALSO paying for the pensions for all of the estimated 17 million public sector workers who have plans in addition to Social Security. They pay payroll taxes for Social Security, but they also pay property taxes, sales taxes, income taxes and a myriad of other taxes to pay for the additional public sector retirees plans.

"GenX" Public Sector Retirees Add to the Burden

A further complication arises when the post-baby boom generation is added to the mix. Known as "GenX," these Americans were born from 1961 to 1976. They began entering the workforce from 1979 to 1994. If they went to work in the public sector, they began retiring as early as 1999! Assuming 30 years of service, all GenX public sector workers will have already retired by 2024, before the last private sector baby boomers reach Social Security retirement age and receive their benefits.

> The private sector employees and employers will have spent a working lifetime paying taxes to support the Social Security pensions of those who were already retired, plus taxes to pre-fund $2.5 trillion of their own benefits (100% of which was spent on other things by Congress), and for the additional pensions of all public sector workers. And don't forget, many public entities are not required to participate in Social Security.

We don't know exactly how many public sector baby boomers and GenXers have become eligible for retirement. Since about 12%–15% of the workforce is employed in the public sector, we might make a decent guess by saying that 12% of baby boomers are or were eligible for retirement prior to the age of 65. Based on that guess, about 12% of 77 million, or approximately 9 million, are or were public sector employees. If this guesstimate is correct, then 9 million public sector baby boomers have already retired, and some GenX public sector workers have ALSO already entered paid retirement years, and the rest will join them in the next 15 crisis years as private sector baby boomers also become eligible for Social Security.

> The problem is that everyone focuses on Social Security, but there are about 20 million public sector workers who get MORE than Social Security. Higher pensions and benefits, payable earlier, compliments of the private sector worker. And there are fewer and fewer private sector workers every day.

The recession has resulted in high levels of unemployment, reducing the amount of people in the private sector workforce. Those baby boomers left in the workforce are increasingly demonstrating that, even with Social Security, they can't afford to retire. A recent survey from AARP found that nearly two-thirds (65%) of surveyed workers age 45 or older said that, barring significant economic improvements, they would be delaying their retirements and working longer. The impact of baby boomer public sector employees retiring BEFORE 2011, joined by Gen X public sector workers who began retiring in 1999, creates a financial burden on private sector taxpayers that has not been recognized.

The federal government deals with federal retirees and Social Security, and charges taxpayers to support it, while state and local governments deal with other public sector pensions and charge taxpayers to support them. **The private sector taxpayer must pay taxes to support them all.** The result is that the often discussed Social Security crisis is actually significantly understated.

The private sector taxpayer pays to support school board, city, county and state retirees, plus federal and military retirees PLUS Social Security retirees, all while being unable to retire himself. It is a disparity not only in timing but in amount. While the private sector boomer has a Social Security check of about $1,500 per month to look forward to, he has paid to provide his "public servants" with benefits of $3,000, $4,000, $10,000, $20,000, even $40,000 per month.

We have a looming crisis that will affect a huge number of Americans, the likes of which have not been seen since the Great Depression. Simply put, many of our citizens who are at or close to retirement years will be in serious financial difficulty. They will be unable to afford to retire, and many will not be able to keep their jobs or find new ones when needed. Many private sector baby boomers will not be able to live on their average $1,200-$1,500 per month Social Security pension. Most will have no choice but to remain in the workforce indefinitely. While they remain in the workforce, they and the rest of private sector workers will be paying taxes to support public sector workers who retired years ago, at multiples of Social Security benefits.

The public sector retirees will be in the large homes, with vacation cottages, boats and motor homes. Private sector retirees will be generally destitute. Churchill, seeing this, might have said, "Never was so much owed by so few to so many."

Two Classes of Retirees—Rich Public Sector and Poor Private Sector

We are already beginning to see two classes of retirees, the well-to-do public sector retirees and the private sector retiree on life-support. That trend will become magnified in the next decade as huge differences in pension checks drive private sector retirees to stay at work until they are forced to live with their children or to live in group homes.

To the private sector worker, the unfunded liability of Social Security is a double-edged sword. Congress will find itself forced to either dramatically increase taxes or reduce benefits, or both. In most cases, since the general disappearance of defined benefit pension plans in the private sector since the 1980s, private sector workers have come to rely on Social Security as their ONLY means of retirement survival. **States, local governments or school boards guarantee most public sector retirement plans. Since Social Security is NOT guaranteed, Congress will be tempted to reduce these benefits.**

Congress is already discussing moving back the retirement age again, instituting "means testing" for Social Security eligibility, and is routinely increasing Medicare Part B premiums beyond the current maximum of $353.60 per month per person. Meanwhile, benefits for public sector retirees cannot be reduced, requiring ever-increasing taxation to support unsustainable levels of promised benefits. This will have a devastating impact on private sector workers who are currently retired, on baby boomers retiring in 2011 and thereafter, and on the private sector employers and employees who must pay taxes to support this.

If the current unemployment rate continues, the Social Security deficit in 2009 and 2010 may approach $20 billion. These deficits will be made up from the illusory trust fund, allowing Congress to continue to pay Social Security benefits even when the transfer payments from active workers to fund retired workers isn't adequate. That means the fictitious trust fund will go broke sooner rather than later. When that happens, Congress will have "no choice" but to reduce benefits, dramatically increase taxes or both.

As Michael Tanner, Director of the Cato Institute's Project on Social Security Choice stated:

> *"Social Security benefits are not guaranteed. They are not guaranteed legally because workers have no contractual or property rights to any benefits whatsoever. In two landmark cases, Flemming v. Nestor and Helvering v. Davis, the U.S. Supreme Court ruled that Social Security taxes are not contributions or savings, but simply taxes, and that Social Security benefits are simply a government spending program, no different than, say, farm price supports. Congress and the President may change, reduce, or even eliminate benefits at any time. As a result, retirees must depend on the goodwill of 535 politicians to determine how much they will*

receive in retirement. And what could be less guaranteed than a politician's promise? In fact, Congress has voted to reduce Social Security benefits in the past. For example, in 1983, Congress raised the retirement age."

In 2009, for the first time since Social Security began in 1935, the government paid more in Social Security benefits than it received from payroll taxes. Even if the economy recovers, and millions of workers begin once again paying payroll taxes, Social Security will run at a deficit beginning in 2016.

The Social Security Administration estimated in May 2009 that after adjusting for inflation, Social Security deficits would reach $68 billion in 2020, $170 billion in 2030 and $293 billion in 2035. However, since then, the picture has worsened. A projected surplus in 2009 turned into a $9 billion deficit, just a few months after the surplus estimate was made. It is now clear that the deficits will be larger, and will come sooner, than the Social Security Administration predicted in May 2009.

There is no doubt that Congress will meddle with Social Security as it deals with unsustainable deficits and debt. Discussions on Capitol Hill already include: yet another set-back of the retirement age; increasing the charge for Medicare Part B (which is deducted from Social Security checks); "means testing" of recipients, so that benefits are not paid for those who don't "need" them; increasing taxes on benefits; charging more to workers and corporations in payroll taxes; and even inventing new kinds of taxes to fill in the bottomless financial hole they have dug for us.

Baby boomers have paid twice for their Social Security benefits, once for those who were already retired, and again to pre-fund their own Social Security benefits. The money was squandered by Congress, and America is in trouble because of it. Tragically, even if the government pays boomers their benefits in full as promised, the benefits levels are inadequate to sustain life for many, if not most, boomers. With three legs of the four-legged retirement stool gone, a national catastrophe will be faced as 70 million enter their sunset years with little or no hope of independence and real fear of financial ruin. Congress MUST honor our nation's obligation to the private sector workers who paid, and paid, and paid, and who are now potentially relegated to financial ruin.

Experts have agreed that there are three ways to fix Social Security:

1. reduce benefits;

2. increase taxes; or

3. both of the above.

None of those remedies is appropriate for those that are within 15 years of retirement. There simply isn't time for them to find an alternative. We have to draw a line, probably applying to those currently below age 50. For those over 50, we must shift the off the balance sheet obligation of Social Security to the debt column, recognize it and fund for it. We cannot tolerate the disenfranchisement of 77 million baby boomers from the benefits they have depended on, and **paid for twice,** during their entire working careers. But we can devise a public/private retirement plan for those under 50 that would shift from a redistribution system to a prepaid system. For the next 15 or 20 years, the burden would be high, but tolerable. The alternatives are not.

*"We cannot allow ourselves to be in a situation where the debt continues to rise," Federal Reserve Board chairman Ben Bernanke told Congress. "That means more and more interest payments, which swell the deficit, which leads to an **unsustainable** situation."*

— Newark Star-Ledger.
June 28, 2009

_____ Chapter Seven _____

The Health Care "Reform" Debacle

With the passage of the recent health care reform legislation, the United States Congress passed legislation that is both unconstitutional and financially unsustainable. There is an ongoing and significant effort to either get the Supreme Court to declare the new law unconstitutional or to get Congress to repeal it. We believe that there is a distinct possibility that The Patient Protection and Affordable Care Act will be repealed in the next session of Congress, or that the Supreme Court will find the act unconstitutional. If either should occur, the debate will start again as to what should be done by Congress, if anything, to solve the national health insurance problems. This chapter contains a brief history of how we got to this point in our current health care/health insurance debacle.

Government has had a lot to do with creating many of the problems that confront us today. It will be impossible to solve the enormous problems through legislation without an understanding of what government has done to get us here in the first place. We must understand what should be undone in order to move forward in a way to benefit all Americans.

There is historical precedent in both the passage and the repeal of an act that mandates health care. Congress passed the Medicare

Catastrophic Care Act of 1988, intending to mandate a solution to the problems faced by some seniors with very large claims. It provided prescription drug coverage and a large array of new benefits. What was significant, however, is that a majority of seniors had their own private insurance and therefore did not need more Medicare coverage, and they certainly didn't like the fact that they would face an increase in Medicare premiums to pay for it. The national furor among seniors led to the passage of the Medicare Catastrophic Coverage **Repeal** Act of 1989.

If repeal efforts on the current health care reform act fail, there will undoubtedly be continuing efforts to make significant modifications before it is fully implemented in 2014. Health care reform, and the taxes required to support it, will serve as pivotal issues in Congressional elections in 2010 and 2012 and in the Presidential election in 2012.

There will likely be challenges as to the constitutionality of its provisions brought before the Supreme Court. Twenty states have joined together to file a suit against the federal government on the premise that Congress has exceeded its constitutional authority. Their complaint begins:

> *"The Act represents an unprecedented encroachment on the liberty of individuals living in the Plaintiff's respective states, by mandating that all citizens and legal residents have qualifying health care coverage or pay a tax penalty. The Constitution nowhere authorizes the United States to mandate, either directly or under threat of penalty, that all citizens and legal residents have qualifying health care coverage. By imposing such a mandate, the Act exceeds the powers of the United States under Article 1 of the Constitution and violates the Tenth Amendment to the Constitution." It adds, "The Act also represents an unprecedented encroachment on the sovereignty of the States..."*

At the root of health care reform legislation are significant legitimate problems with health care costs, health insurance and the massive deficits that exist in order to fund previously passed government programs, Medicare and Medicaid. The debate and resulting legislation has involved a confusing array of facts (and fallacies) that were used to support its passage. The cry that "50 million Americans don't have health care" was inaccurate, but effective.

Claims of the flaws in our current health care system revolved around the argument that the U.S. "has the highest costs but ranks 38th in life expectancy," appearing to prove the ineffectiveness and wastefulness of our current system. Receiving scant publicity were those who pointed out that **if you removed deaths caused by homicide and auto accidents, the U.S. has the highest life expectancy in the world.**

But comparing national mortality statistics can be misleading for other reasons, as well. The U.S. leads the world in teen pregnancies and in the resultant low birth weight babies. These "preemies" are provided with huge and expensive medical resources. Some other countries' infant mortality statistics don't include births of less than a specified weight or body length. While in the U.S. hundreds of thousands or even millions of dollars might be spent on a very low birth weight child, other countries wouldn't even consider them, statistically, as live births.

Shouldn't we factor in that U.S. teens have the highest pregnancy rate in the world and teens have by far the highest rate of low-birth weight (under 5 pounds 8 ounces) and very low-birth weight (under 3 pounds 5 ounces) babies? One in three teenage girls in the U.S. gets pregnant before she reaches the age of 20, of which 81% are unmarried. In 2008, there were 750,000 teen pregnancies, with 215,000 ending in abortion and 535,000 resulting in live births, a huge number of which were low birth weight and required significant health care costs. Shouldn't we factor in both the health care costs and the effect on mortality rates that are caused by a societal problem that is virtually unique to the United States? It seems fair to say that there appears to be no scientific basis for comparing the effectiveness of one country's entire health care system against another's in a way that its impact on overall mortality can be accurately assessed.

When specific diagnosis mortality results measure U.S. outcomes against those of other countries, the U.S. health care system is the clear winner. For example, the U.S. leads the world in survival rates for breast cancer at 84%, and prostate cancer at 92%. Meanwhile, in the national health care environment, figures can be frightening. In the United Kingdom, the survival rate for breast cancer is 70% and for prostate cancer it is 51%. We're talking about survival. Life itself.

If we are to compare the U.S. medical care delivery system with other countries using life expectancy as a measure, shouldn't we take into consideration that we save tens of thousands of low birth weight babies (at huge cost) and that large numbers of gunshot wounds, homicides and traffic accidents just don't happen in other countries? To what extent does all this both increase medical costs and increase the rate of mortality? Should we be examining the overall statistics that compare U.S. life expectancy with other countries that have virtually no homicides, few traffic accidents and low rates of teen pregnancies and "preemies?" Of course we shouldn't.

Is the Problem "Health Care" or "Health Insurance"?

Congress really misled the American people when it started saying that "50 million have no health care," when it was referring to statistics concerning health insurance coverage. Is "health care" the same as "health insurance?" One might think so, if you listen to some members of Congress. The two terms have been used loosely and interchangeably in Congress over the past few years. We are also often told by some of the leaders in Congress that we have a "right" to "health care." According to Speaker of the House Nancy Pelosi:

> "...the American people have been exploited by the insurance industry. We can't walk away from this. So I have faith in them that they value what this is—health care as a right, not a privilege."

Was she talking about health care or health insurance? Does the insurance industry provide health care? She actually said that the health insurance industry has "exploited the American people." She damned an entire industry and got away with it. No one said, "Wait a minute! That is untrue and unfair! How do you DARE to make such an unsupported and prejudicial statement?" Where does it say in our Constitution that we have a right to health care or health insurance? Do we have a right to car insurance, homeowners insurance and life insurance? Do we have a right to credit cards? Savings accounts? Speaker Pelosi, what ARE you talking about?

Further, is she saying that there is ANY American who cannot get health care? Hospitals must treat, for free, anyone who seeks care, whether they can pay or not. That is the law. Medicaid provides for the indigent. That's another law. Any American is free to call a doctor of his own choosing, make an appointment and go see him. Who, exactly, is denied health care?

Defining the "Uninsured"

Congress's definition of uninsured includes nearly 18 million Americans with a household income of $50,000 or more per year but who have no health insurance. It also defines the indigent (many of whom are eligible for Medicaid) as uninsured. Even worse, it defined those as uninsured (and thus needing government help) all those who chose NOT to enroll in their own employer's highly subsidized health insurance plans. I have personal experience with this. When I was president of a company with 1,000 employees, we paid 80% of the employee health insurance premium. About 15% chose not to participate because they didn't feel they needed it. Congress defined these people as uninsured and in need of government help.

This disingenuous approach of defining those who had no health care was clearly intended to dramatize and justify an emergency approach to pass legislation without fully exploring all of the specific problem areas and seeking solutions on a selective basis.

We all have basic needs for food, clothing and shelter. Certainly without these, health care becomes less significant. Are these rights, too? Does that require our government to provide them to us? If so, how does it decide who gets how much food, clothing or shelter? Who pays for it? Do we follow Lenin's advice and let the government decide for each of us, following the axiom, "From each according to his ability, and to each according to his needs?"

> The new Patient Protection and Affordable Care Act represents one of the most serious abridgments of human rights that the U.S. government has ever attempted.

What, exactly, is the role of government in providing us with health care, or health insurance, or food, clothing and shelter?

Most would agree that society (all of us) should help those who are in dire need and who cannot help themselves. Thousands of organizations provide such assistance every day. What role should the government play? When did we decide that government should step in to help us even when we don't want or need its help? Who is in charge here, anyway?

The Constitutionality Issue

Congress clearly does NOT have the right to dictate what and how much insurance Americans must buy, and to fine them or tax them if they fail to comply. Congress also does NOT have the right to force employers to purchase insurance for their employees. And Congress does NOT have the right to force states to pay to provide health insurance to those the Congress tells them to provide it to.

The new legislation also seriously abridges the right of individual free choice of physicians. It limits the treatment that a doctor or hospital may provide, and what equipment the hospital may maintain. It eliminates the fundamental rights we all have, of liberty, free choice and self-determination. It also eliminates personal responsibility. It will fine employers for failing to pay for health insurance in addition to the compensation they provide to employees, thus limiting the creation of jobs, limiting resources available for the compensation of employees and limiting employees' rights to use compensation as they feel is in their best personal interest or the interests of their own family members.

The new Patient Protection and Affordable Care Act represents one of the most serious abridgments of human rights that the U.S. government has ever attempted.

> If the American voter allows Congress to dictate that insurance must be purchased and the coverage that must be provided, one of the most fundamental of all American rights will be taken away: **personal freedom.**

Congress Needs to Get Its Priorities Straight

Current financial problems in the United States are staggering. Moody's bond rating service has a "negative outlook" on every municipality in the nation. The federal debt now approaches our gross domestic product (GDP), and it is projected to increase for the next decade. Because of federal bookkeeping madness, the unfunded liability of current entitlement programs is not included as debt. This liability is estimated to exceed $100 trillion! We are at war in two faraway countries, and our armed forces are stretched to the breaking point. Unemployment is at historic levels, and is predicted to remain high for years to come. Medicare and Medicaid are financially unsustainable. Social Security is financially unsustainable. The Postal Service is financially unsustainable. Fannie Mae and Freddie Mac have been taken over by the government and are incurring enormous losses and accruing staggering new and irresponsible levels of debt.

During the long months that the 111th Congress has been in session, it has paid scant attention to these staggering problems. Instead,

Congress has concentrated on health care reform, including scandalous deal-making with every major special-interest group imaginable and with very special appropriations given to recalcitrant politicians. The taxpayer will pay dearly for those votes for decades to come.

Congress developed its health care reform package without input from the American people. Leaders of the majority party in Congress met with representatives of various special interest groups, including the pharmaceutical industry, the insurance industry, the American Medical Association, unions, the AARP and various other special interest players. But just whom were these groups representing? The AMA represents only 15% of physicians and earns $70 million to $100 million a year selling medical treatment coding **to the federal government.** AARP purports to represent 40 million Americans over the age of 50, but earns about $1 billion a year selling supplemental health insurance ... a business certain to grow as government takes over the health "care" industry. And what about the "coincidence" that the pharmaceutical industry increased prices 10% to all of us, then promised the government rebates on Medicare prescriptions, and then supported the health care "reform" legislation? And Senators unabashedly and openly "sold" their votes to get pork to bring home in return for supporting "health reform." The unions got a special tax exemption so that their members wouldn't have to pay taxes on their own gold-plated health plans, but everyone else would pay taxes on theirs, and they, too, supported the "reform" measures.

Each of these special interests was apparently more concerned with their own survival and prosperity in the event of a federal government takeover of our health care system than it was with the plight of the vast majority of private businesses and employees—in other words, our economy and nation. These private sector businesses and employees will bear the brunt of the costs of this government plundering, and they weren't even invited to participate. In upper social circles there's a saying, "If you aren't invited to the dinner, you're on the menu." We provided quite a feast!

Simply put, they carved up the turf just like Roosevelt, Stalin and Churchill carved-up Europe after WWII. We were supposed to be viewing this live on TV, remember? Perhaps they thought we were dumb enough to take it lying down. As a friend of mine asked when Congress passed the health care "reform" bill, "Do they think we are THAT stupid?" Of course they do.

Health care reform legislation could be the harbinger of many more intrusions into the life of the average American citizen than the U.S. Constitution permits. Should our government be determining exactly what level of health care benefits will be provided to those who cannot or will not pay or the appropriate levels of the rationing of medical treatment? What additional steps will Congress deem necessary to keep health care costs under control? What other individual rights will be abridged by Congress in the name of serving the people?

Under the new law, the government will dictate what medical treatments will be provided and what the appropriate payment level is. Most experts agree that this will result in a severe shortage of physicians who will be willing to treat elderly patients. Currently, those over the age of 50 represent nearly one-third of the United States population. As this segment of the population ages, the government will

> Health care reform legislation could be the harbinger of many more intrusions into the life of the average American citizen than the U.S. Constitution permits.

be faced with a vastly increased number of Americans entering the years during which their health care needs are the greatest. Government will now determine the scope and quality of health care, while facing enormous self-inflicted debt and deficits in other areas. It is likely that government will say it has no choice but to further curtail payment levels and treatment methods in order to keep costs under control. The combination of fewer physicians, more patients, lower payments and rationing of health care treatment will have a devastating impact on Americans over the age of fifty, all 100 million of them!

Government Meddling Caused the Problem in the First Place

Why has government interfered for so many years in the field of health care and health insurance? And in doing so, did it create a problem so big that it cannot be fixed?

One of my favorite stories involves a spring training baseball game. The coach sends a rookie out to play left field. A long fly ball is hit directly at the rookie. The rookie gets under the ball, and the ball hits the heel of the glove and bounces out. The coach yells encouragement, "That's OK, rookie, we all make mistakes. Just keep your eye on the ball…you'll be fine." Another sharp hit to left field lines toward the rookie. The ball takes a bounce over the head of the rookie. The manager becomes a bit more impatient, "Aw, for cryin' out loud, rookie! You can do better than that. Concentrate!" Another towering ball flies out to left field. The rookie moves under it. The ball hits the webbing of the glove and glances off. Now the manager is fed up. "That's it! I've had enough. I'll SHOW you how this position should be played!" He storms out to left field, sending the rookie back to the dugout. The manager waits out in left field. A fly ball heads his way. He confidently lopes under the ball, and nonchalantly holds up his glove. The ball hits the heel and bounces out. The manager runs, screaming, into the dugout, throwing his glove at the ground in front of the rookie. "ROOKIE," he yells, "YOU'VE GOT LEFT FIELD SO FOULED UP, **NO ONE** CAN PLAY IT!"

Government has health care and health insurance so fouled up that it may be true that "no one can play it." Its solution, in the health care reform legislation, has been to say, "It's so bad, that we need to do more of it." Say, what?

Health care and health insurance began to get completely screwed up when the government decided to allow a tax deduction to companies to provide health insurance for their employees who would receive these benefits on a tax-free basis. No taxes were paid by employees on the compensation they received if it was in the form of health insurance. This was a double win. Employers could get tax-free compensation to their employees and the employer didn't need to pay payroll taxes on the amount of the premiums they paid on behalf of employees.

Nonsensically, Congress did not allow a self-employed person to purchase his or her own health insurance on a tax-favored basis. The tax deductibility and tax-free benefit to employees encouraged employers to extol the value of these fringe benefits to their employees and to look for ways to increase the things that would be covered under health insurance plans. It was a no brainer to provide as many of these benefits as possible, in lieu of compensation. Unions negotiated for these benefits to be enriched and to be provided to employees after retirement, even if retirement was at age 40 or 45 or 50. To most employers, there was no requirement to recognize the current liabilities involved with promising these future benefits. It was free on a short-term basis.

Because these employee benefits were tax-deductible to the employer and tax-free to the employee, it was smart tax practice to provide as much under health insurance as possible. **Health insurance morphed from something intended to protect against a future unforeseeable loss, to something that could provide immediate short-term benefits, i.e. reimbursement of relatively small and routine health care expenses.**

Because of tax policy, and the resulting practice of employers and insurers to expand the definition of covered expenses, what we define as health insurance today is not really insurance at all. True insurance is intended to cover unforeseen and catastrophic losses. But health insurance today is usually defined by most of us by its coverage, meaning which medical expenses will be paid for by someone else. And it seems that almost everyone wants ALL medical expenses paid by someone else.

What if Homeowner's Insurance Worked Like Health Insurance?

Imagine that homeowners insurance worked the way health insurance works today. The homeowner's policy would cover lawn mowing, tree trimming, house painting, roof replacement, appliance repairs and every other expense that might be faced by a property owner. And, oh yes, by the way, it would also pay for catastrophic losses in the event of fire, hurricanes, floods and the like.

How might this play out if homeowners insurance worked like health insurance? Let's live in a dream world of such insurance. You notice that your air conditioning unit is squeaking. You call the AC people who immediately send a repairman. The repairman looks it over and reports, "It looks like the main bearings are going, so we're replacing the unit with a new one. And, while we were here, we noticed that the other AC unit was about the same age, and probably will go soon, too, so we're replacing that. Please give me $20 for your "co-pay" for the visit. The insurance company will take care of the rest." Similarly, when the roof leaks, or the dishwasher breaks, or the garbage disposal goes on the blink, you call the vendor, the vendor charges you a pittance, and the insurer pays the rest. You wouldn't care if you really needed a new AC unit, or what it cost. Someone else was paying the bill. The insurer, if they tried to deny or reduce a claim, would be demonized for it. Legislators would "fix" the problem by saying insurers couldn't deny a claim.

The insurance company would obviously have to charge more and more over the years. New replacement AC units would be much better and at far higher cost than the originals. If you bought a new house in disrepair, you'd call the vendors and say, "Fix it. Here's your $20. The insurance company will pick up the rest." Every time you called a vendor, they'd have a new AC or other appliance, at higher and higher costs. Who cares? You're not paying for it.

Insurers would, of course, raise prices to cover claims. Once again, legislators would stop the outrage of insurers raising their prices, by preventing the insurer from raising prices. They'd pass laws setting premium limitations. They'd tell insurers, "You have to buy 50 year roofs," or "You have to pay for foliage replacement when bad weather causes a loss." Predictably, most insurers would go broke, or stop selling homeowners insurance. Those who remained in business would find another way to reduce claims. What they'd have to do is change their policies to require you to use vendors with whom they have special heavily discounted pricing arrangements and strict rules as to when the vendor could replace an old AC unit with a new one. Eventually, the insurer's rules would say, "Even if the AC unit is a rusting hulk, you can't replace it if you can find any way to keep it running." The AC repairman would have a big problem. If you REALLY needed a new unit, he'd be unable to provide it. The insurer is now in charge of what you can, and cannot, have. The AC repairman would have another problem. His contract with the insurance company pays him so much less than his real "costs" of providing services, that he has to charge his other customers, who are not insured by that carrier, more and more to make up the difference. He would hate the system but if he said that he would only serve the people who don't have deals with insurance companies, he'd lose half of his customers and go out of business. He'd have no choice but to take what the insurance company paid, and charge everyone else a lot more. Now compare that with health insurance today.

Health insurance is the most difficult of all forms of insurance to underwrite. In addition to being expected to pay for expenses that do not fit the true definition of "insurable events" (unpredictable and catastrophic), it operates in a world of rapidly changing treatments, technologies and pharmaceuticals. And the worst part of health insurance is that if the insurer pays a bundle to keep you alive, you live to have another claim on another day. Death is cheap to health insurance carriers. Life is expensive. Think about that when you contemplate what government will do with the health insurance coverage it provides when it has budget problems. We can all see it coming: "We're sorry, we just can't afford to place all these elderly people in intensive care facilities and provide expensive surgical procedures. They are going to die soon, anyway."

Health insurance is different, not only because it is expected to pay for predictable and/or non-catastrophic events, but because it has no defined maximum claim. Life insurance has a set amount. Car insurance is based on the depreciated value of the car at time of loss, with a maximum set amount. The same is true for homeowners and virtually every other kind of insurance. But with health insurance, the total potential risk is unknown. The amount and cost of each treatment is unknown, and the total claim that might be incurred is also unknown. If a person gets cancer, no one knows what the treatment costs will be.

Unlike a car or a house insurer that has a total loss maximum, the health insurer can't just total you and send your next of kin a pre-defined and fixed market value of what it insured. With health insurance there is an unknown risk for the insurer and a fixed premium to provide for it. Health insurance claims are unpredictable for many reasons. New drugs and treatments are unveiled almost every day. Each time one of these new drugs or procedures is introduced, totally unforeseen costs appear as if by magic.

In the 1980s, AIDS appeared. Those expenses weren't in anyone's forecasts. New illnesses and conditions have been discovered, requiring treatment. Who had ever heard of ADD or ADHD? Is dyslexia an illness requiring treatment? To make it even more complex, pharmaceutical companies are now advertising widely, telling us to "ask your doctor" for a prescription if your leg falls asleep too often, or if you have a ringing in your ears, or if you want to prevent plaque build-up in your arteries, or if you want to experience the unlikely possibility of a 4 hour erection. Prescription claims are now driven by television advertising as often as they are by a person going to the doctor with a complaint. If you have a problem you don't consider serious enough to take to the doctor, the ads tell you, "Go see your doctor. Incur a visit charge. Get a prescription." If the doctor prescribes the medication (often forever) the insurance company will be expected to pay for it, forever.

Health insurers must undertake the most complex guesswork in order to arrive at adequate premium rate estimates. In the early days of health insurance, they used morbidity tables that told them what percent of any given age group would have what kind of illness in a given year. Other data included the cost of treating that illness in that locale. By considering the demographics of a group, these morbidity and cost statistics allowed insurers to estimate what their claims would be and to price their insurance accordingly. In the cases of individuals seeking health insurance, they would underwrite the health history of the individual. If there was no ongoing illness that pre-existed the onset of insurance, they'd establish a premium, take the risk and cross their fingers that they got it right. Almost no one ever got it right!

As a health insurance underwriter told me many years ago, "When you set a health insurance premium to insure someone for $200 a month, it can only be $200 to the good, but it can be infinitely bad."

An inherent problem with health insurance is that there are many potential treatments and providers and many different philosophies concerning treatment methods and the extent to which experimental, unproven or questionable treatments should be utilized. If a physician recommends a potential life-saving surgery or treatment that has never been done before, or has been done with mixed results, should the insurer have to pay for it? If so, to what limit?

Who Should "Ration" Health Care?

Emotion and politics always play a great part in dealing with health insurance. If an experimental procedure, costing $1,000,000 might save your life or the life of your child, should the insurer pay for it? If they don't, you or your child might, and probably will, die. Providers won't undertake the treatment for free. They want to get paid. If the insurer does pay for it, where is the line drawn the next time another new procedure might be utilized on another person? And how is the insurer supposed to pay for this? Should they charge everyone else, to the point that insurance becomes unaffordable for most people? Who should set the outer limits of what an insurer must pay for? Where does it end?

That gets to the question of rationing. **Do you think health care should be rationed?** Before you answer, consider this scenario: A 101-year-old person is dying. He can be kept alive for 10 more minutes if we provide a treatment that will cost $1 million. Should we do it? Of course not. So we can agree that we now both believe in rationing.

The next question is a lot tougher: **What should be rationed and who should make the rationing decisions?** We'll never agree on that one, because we each want to maintain our right to determine for ourselves what the appropriate course of treatment should be for ourselves. Some people will willingly pay more for health insurance coverage that will apply virtually unlimited resources to preserve their own life, or the life of their child, even at very high cost. Others might be a bit more fatalistic and be inclined to select an insurance policy with limitations. That is a choice that each of us should be free to make. Actually, according to our Constitution, that is a choice that each of us IS free to make.

Many of us have living wills, but not many of us would say "let the insurance company decide when to pull the plug" or "let the government decide when to pull the plug." We want to make those decisions for ourselves or let a loved and trusted next-of-kin make that decision. Certainly not someone who has to pay to keep us plugged in and who saves a bundle if the plug is pulled!

How Government Created the Health Insurance/Health Care Mess

How did we get into this health insurance mess? It all started so innocently! **In the early years, group health insurance was sold based on the concepts of cost savings, tax advantages and as an employee benefit, never thinking that it would become an absolute entitlement and that every employee would expect an employer to provide payment for virtually every medical bill of every kind.**

I entered the group health insurance business just as Medicare was passed. At the time, Dr. Edward Annis, president of the

American Medical Association (AMA), had fought as an eloquent spokesman against the passage of Medicare. The AMA wasn't against providing health care for the needy or elderly. It was against making it a forced and totally unfunded entitlement program, transferring medical costs from those over age 65 to current workers. He said that government would ultimately determine the scope and quality of treatment for everyone over 65, taking away the right of self-determination from patients as well as the right of the doctor to treat his or her patient as he or she saw fit. He also opposed the concept of transferring the obligation to pay for health insurance from those who were over age 65 to those in the workforce. **He argued that such a system was unsustainable,** and that costs would be far higher than Congress predicted it would be. He argued that it made no sense to "solve" a problem that wasn't there.

Most people over age 65 had health insurance and were willing to pay for it. He asked, in one example of what Medicare could do, "Why should the government tax the little guy to provide health insurance for a millionaire?" He lost. Congress passed Medicare. In the following decade, by 1975, the cost of Medicare was TEN TIMES higher than the government had estimated it would be—as predicted by Dr. Annis and the AMA. And during that decade, "cost shifting" became a way of life in health care.

Medicare had massive problems almost immediately. It was never funded. Instead, it was a transfer of payments from workers, via payroll taxes, to provide benefits for retirees. As more and more people over the age of 65 began using more and more services, costs escalated alarmingly. As had been predicted, the tax burden being placed on workers to fund for the costs for those over 65 became increasingly difficult to bear. Medicare had to cut its costs. But it couldn't take away benefits. It was now seen as an entitlement.

And this is when the great departure took place—a departure that would doom the health care and health insurance industries. The federal government did something it had never done before, and hasn't done since, except in health care. It demanded (commanded) that it would pay arbitrary amounts that were well below the actual charges made by providers.

Usually, when governments buy things, bids are requested and received, and the government (supposedly) attempts to select the most cost-effective proposal. Inherent in federal government contracts is the premise that the provider of services must be paid fairly. These days, the government will require accounting to show that profit isn't more than 17% of the contract. But Medicare behaved quite differently. It said to health care providers, "You will accept my fees. You must agree to accept them if you want to treat anyone over 65."

Hospitals and doctors went along grudgingly with the new government policy. No one said, "You can't do that. It's unconstitutional. I have equal rights." Medicare used their awesome power to control costs. It was now firmly established as the major player in the cost shifting game. Medicare would pay less, and everyone else would pay more.

Over the years, Medicare started to dictate which procedures it would or would not pay for, as well as how much it would pay. The more Medicare reduced what it would pay, the more would have to be charged to everyone else. But that was not Medicare's problem. It was "saving money."

No one at the time took great issue with the fact that the government was paying less than the actual costs that were required, and therefore it was transferring the real underlying cost to everybody that wasn't covered by Medicare. It was also rationing health care treatment. Its refusal to pay actual costs was actually a "tax," charged to all other payers, but nobody recognized it, and nobody complained about it. As the years went by, Medicare paid less and less, forcing the providers to charge more and more to those who did not have Medicare coverage. Medicaid, established to provide money to states for treatment of the poor, followed suit.

Cost shifting from Medicare and Medicaid pushed up charges for everyone else. Insurance premiums began to skyrocket.

Insurers were being faced with increasing costs and their premiums jumped to cover them. Insurers began to behave very stupidly, because competition required it. They began offering unlimited maximum major medical coverage and they'd pay a lot of up-front costs and then 100% of all charges after the insured had paid $500 to $1,000 out of pocket. Deductibles of $100 per year were standard. A $100 deductible had been significant in 1965, but it was an ever-easier threshold to pass as inflation and health care costs increased. Insurers were paying more and more each year as "nickel and dime" claims became payable under major medical plans. Insurance policies that had been designed to protect against unforeseen and catastrophic risk were now paying for almost everything. Even worse, they were paying 80% and 100% of rapidly escalating charges.

> A key and seminal event was taking place in the 1970s, and no one really noticed. Health insurance was no longer insurance…it had become an obligation for someone else to pay virtually all of one's health care costs.

Of course premiums began to go through the roof. Insurers were facing cost shifting from Medicare and Medicaid, and providers were increasing charges to everyone else. Why not? Someone else was going to pay the costs, whatever they were. A crisis in health insurance costs ensued, and the industry moved to find a way to reduce unnecessary claims. Cost containment became the buzzwords of the health insurance field. Insurers began to implement requirements that a second surgical opinion be sought before surgery would be paid for. They began to require advanced determination before hospital admission would be permitted. They began to eliminate Friday or weekend admissions unless it was a case of a dire emergency. They had some small impact, but nothing seemed to stem the gusher of red ink hitting insurance companies.

Of course Congress felt it should step in and fix things again. Its premise? "If we can keep people healthy, we'll save money later because they won't have those huge claims." It sounded logical…of course if you encouraged people to get annual physicals and routine tests, you could prevent or intervene earlier to forestall the big claims later on. The idea had sex appeal.

But pros in the insurance industry asked the big question: "How can we pay what we're paying now, plus the built-in increases, PLUS all the "nickel and dime" preventive/diagnostic claims? It would cost more. How could we do that?"

Congress Strikes Again

Congress's answer to containing health care costs was the coercion of businesses to employ a relatively new concept called a Health Maintenance Organization (HMO). There had been a few, like Kaiser Permanente in California, that were not experiencing the same huge premium rate escalations. Maybe that concept could be employed nationally? The theory was that if an organization were formed that would provide ALL medical treatment needed by a patient, that organization would have a vested interest in keeping people healthy so that they wouldn't have bigger costs later on.

Some people asked, "How can you treat all the people that are sick, and will get sick, and then also pay for well baby care, annual physicals, shots and routine visits, too?" Some even asked, "Should we be doing this? Isn't there some level of individual responsibility involved here?" But their voices were lost in the noise. The accepted rationale was that the HMO would manage the treatment of each patient, and it would provide virtually every service needed. HMOs would be owned and operated mostly by physicians. The business models often didn't include any need for people who understood health insurance.

To those in the insurance industry it was clear that an HMO could not do both. It could not pay the same amount of money that other carriers were paying for medical claims and also include well baby care, full payment for maternity expenses, etc. They argued that it didn't make sense. How could you pay for more things and charge less? But Congress didn't know anything at all about health insurance. Knowing anything has never been a prerequisite for being elected to Congress, it seems.

HMOs sounded like such a great idea that Congress decided to make sure that many were started and that everyone had access to one. They passed the HMO Act of 1973, providing federal money including tax advantages and provisions mandating that every employer had to offer HMOs to their employees.

Almost overnight, HMOs were formed by the thousands. HMOs began springing up everywhere. There was one on nearly every corner. It was a gold rush for federal subsidies and mandated access to employers. What could be better? The government gives me money, I start an HMO, and then employers HAVE to let me pitch their employees in groups, during normal business hours.

It would be like "taking candy from a baby." The concept was simple—Create a panel of doctors and link up with a clinic or hospital. Design plans that pay for routine physicals, well baby care and full 100% coverage for maternity. Include provisions that if anything really serious happens, you must use our hospital and our physicians. We have contracts with the hospital and physicians that control their treatment practices and their fees. If we don't have a hospital of our own, we'll establish a discount arrangement with a nearby hospital and send our people there when needed. Our coverage will say, "If you want to go outside our HMO, we will provide very limited coverage," forcing our insured parties to stay within our system for all of their treatment. Then hire good-looking young gals to present these plans to groups of employees. Send a letter to the employers mandating that they allow us to pitch their employees. Give the "HMO girls" a nice slide show presentation and turn them loose.

Employers with more than 25 employees, if they had a group health insurance plan, had to allow an HMO to come in and solicit their employees to drop out of the group insurance plan provided by the employer and participate in the HMO instead. And that became the death-knell for health insurance as we knew it. The basic concept of underwriting the risk of a group became impossible.

Health insurance underwriting is based on a spread of the risk, with insurance companies basing rates on group demographics and actuarial tables. Over time, the group's own claims history would be used to predict next year's claims and the premium rates necessary to support them. Smaller groups would be pooled with other small groups to create a larger group with statistical reliability. It was very difficult to do, but they got rather close to it most of the time.

When the HMO Act was passed, local HMOs were allowed to selectively remove a certain portion of employees from the group plan and switch them to HMO coverage instead. This wrecked any chance that the group insurance carrier had of predicting claims. The insurance carrier had based their rates on the demographics and claims history of the ENTIRE group. They knew they had some young people and some old people, and some healthy people and some sick people. But they knew they had them all, and the insurer had some degree of predictability of claims costs by spreading the risk among the entire employee population. As HMOs siphoned off the youngest employees, the group insurer was left with an older and sicker group.

Here's how it usually worked:

A typical employer of, say, 100 employees would be approached by an HMO and told that there was a government mandate that allowed the HMO to solicit employees. The employer was compelled to pay the HMO the same portion of the premium that the employer was paying towards their selected health insurance plan.

HMOs relished the idea that they could seek enrollment from only the youngest and healthiest employees of the group, and not the oldest and most likely to incur significant claims. So they designed their plans to have a lot of free "nickel and dime" benefits for routine care, physicals, maternity expenses and for well-baby care. That's what younger employees cared about.

HMO benefits (and usually the "HMO girls" who presented them) were extremely attractive to the younger employees. Young employees generally weren't concerned with heart disease, cancer or other serious illnesses. They were concerned with what they would get for free. Full maternity! Full payment for routine care! Sign me up!

The expected and predictable happened, of course. The HMOs enrolled the youngest members of the group, who withdrew from the group health insurance plan that was sponsored by the employer and enrolled instead in the HMO to get their preventive care, well baby care and routine bills paid. The older employees of the group elected to stay with their health insurance carrier because they really didn't need full maternity or well baby coverage. They knew that in the event they had a serious illness (likely at their age), they wanted to be afforded the opportunity to seek treatment with any doctor or any hospital that they felt was most competent to serve their needs.

The HMO Act wrecked any real hope of survival by health insurance carriers. The health insurance carrier who had started the year with 100 employees covered and a reasonable spread of risk found itself at the end of the year having lost the 25 youngest employees of the group to an HMO, or to several HMOs, and now was left with the older and sicker portion of the group. In a textbook case of adverse selection, young members of the group who had significant illnesses stayed in the insured plan, while the young healthy ones went to an HMO. The insurer got to keep the old and the sick. The claims results, relative to premiums paid, were a disaster. Rates had to go up…way up. As rates went up for the insured plans because they had the older employees and the larger claims, HMO rates stayed lower. Employers began paying the lower of the costs between the HMO and the insured plan. More and more people elected the free or cheaper HMO, leaving only the oldest and sickest remaining covered by insurance carriers. Few recognized that the 'death spiral" for health insurance carriers had begun. Insurers began to lose astronomical amounts of money, and had to look for other ways to stay in business. Meanwhile, Medicare was solving its own problems by paying even less, shifting more and more to the health insurance providers.

Insurance Carriers Adapt

The next move by the insurance industry (those remaining few who were trying to stay alive), was to invent a new concept called managed care. They decided that if an HMO can manage the care of an insured, they could, too. This was a revolutionary approach wherein the health insurance carrier would actually take over the management of the scope, quality and amount of treatment that would be afforded to their insured parties. They also realized that they couldn't survive if Medicare, Medicaid, HMOs and Blue Cross plans (who also had huge discount arrangements with hospitals) were allowed to obtain discounts from hospitals and doctors while they weren't. They wanted the discounts, too!

It was typical for a hospital or doctor to make a charge for a service that wasn't really the amount they expected to be paid by Medicare, Medicaid, Blue Cross or an HMO. They knew that the charge was a mythical one, paid only by someone who didn't have a special discount arrangement. Perhaps they would show a charge of $120, knowing that they would actually only be paid $60 by Medicare, and perhaps only $65 by Blue Cross. The insurance carriers and the uninsured would pay full list prices, and these prices were much higher than they should be, because the costs were being shifted to them. The larger the discounts, or the lower the pre-arranged set fees that doctors and hospitals made to some payers, the more they had to increase their billed charges to those who had no special payment arrangement.

Insurers and many physicians started forming Preferred Provider Organizations (PPO). Doctors, or groups of doctors, would agree that if Insurer X sent them patients, they would adhere to certain treatment limitations and would charge less. The insurer would steer patients to PPOs by telling their insureds that the plan would pay much less if the insured did NOT go to the preferred provider. The AMA fought this idea, recognizing that this could lead to the formation of monopolies, but the Federal Trade Commission (FTC) said that this arrangement was not in restraint of trade, because it was reducing health insurance costs. It was doing nothing of the sort. It was legalizing a practice that was patently illegal (for very good reasons) in every other industry, and would lead to the formation of the very monopolies that the AMA had warned about. That would become justification for Congress to meddle again in the health care/health insurance industries when it decided to pass health care reform legislation in 2010.

Monopolies, Market Power and Restraint of Trade

Restraint of trade laws are designed to prevent illegal monopolies from forming. They follow a rule of reason that says if a firm has "market power," they cannot use this power to decrease competition. But large insurers began to obtain "most favored nation" contracts from hospitals, which did give them a cost advantage over their competitors. The contracts between insurers, who used their "market power" to obtain them, and hospitals that had no choice but to accept them, created discount arrangements or discounted fee schedules to be charged by the hospital. Only the largest insurers had a population large enough to command these discount arrangements. The FTC, on the premise of reducing health insurance costs, was permitting contractual arrangements that were clearly in restraint of trade. This was illegal in every other industry in America, and would undoubtedly create monopolies. Years later, Congress would decry that there were not enough insurance providers to provide a choice to the insured. No kidding.

Hospitals in an Untenable and Unthinkable Position

Typically, an insurance company with a large insured population in a city would approach each hospital and say, for example, "I am Ajax Insurance Company, and I have X of insured in this city. You can be a member hospital, or a non-member hospital. If you are a member hospital, my insureds will receive nearly full benefits should they choose to use your facility. If you are a non-member hospital, my members will only receive a portion of the benefits that would otherwise be payable. In effect I will "steer" my insured population to you if you accept my fee schedule. In order to be a member hospital, you have to agree to accept my preferred schedule of payments for virtually every procedure you perform. You also have to accept my rules regarding which procedures you may perform, and under what circumstances." The large insurer was now obtaining effectively the same deal that Medicare, Medicaid, Blue Cross and the HMO's had. Who would be left to pay the real costs?

The hospitals found themselves in an untenable position. They could either allow this large insurer a substantial discount, or they could lose a significant portion of the population as potential patients. Most took the offer.

The hospitals and doctors faced an increasingly serious accounting problem. If it cost $100 to perform a certain procedure (with overhead, salaries, expenses and profit built in), and Medicare and Medicaid and HMOs and Blue Cross, and now Ajax Insurance Company pay less than $100, they had to charge everyone else more than $100. That's the reason that doctor and hospital bills today are complete fiction. Few, if any, pay the charges that appear on the bill. The $30 aspirin doesn't really cost $30 and virtually no one actually pays $30. What, then, are health care costs?

The unlucky person who came to the hospital who did not have Medicare, Medicaid, Blue Cross, an HMO, Ajax Insurance or another insurer who had a "deal" is billed enough to cover the entire shortfall between actual costs and those that are paid by insurers. The result is that billed costs have increased ridiculously. The procedure that actually costs $200 is now billed at $1,000 or more.

The hospital billed charges that are and were a complete fiction. It is at best misleading and, at worst, fraudulent. And small health insurers and those without health insurance who don't have a special deal have to pay charges. The result was that the largest insurers paid less on claims, and put the smaller insurers (who lacked the power to get those discounts) out of business. The large insurers became virtual monopolies or "oligopolies" in most areas.

In the ensuing two decades virtually all major health insurance carriers left the health insurance business. (Some just went out of business entirely.) We should have learned that government cannot create successful private sector businesses but it CAN destroy them. Some of the huge multi-billion dollar insurers who provided group health insurance in 1985 but no longer do include:

Allstate Life Insurance Company

American Family Life Insurance Company of Columbus

American General Group Insurance Company

Bankers Assurance Company

Subsidiary/Bankers Life-Nebraska

Business Men's Assurance Company

The CNA Insurance Companies

Colonial Life & Accident

Confederation Life Insurance Company

Connecticut General, a Cigna Company

Crown Life Insurance Company

Educators Mutual Life Insurance Company

Equitable Group & Health Insurance Company, a division of The Equitable

First Continental Life & Accident Insurance Company

General American Life Insurance Company

The Great-West Life Assurance Company

Group Life & Health Insurance Company

GroupAmerica Insurance Company

The Hartford Insurance Group

Home Life Insurance Company of New York

John Alden Life Insurance Company

John Hancock Mutual Life Insurance Company

Life Insurance Company of North American, a Cigna Company

Life Insurance Company of The Southwest

Lincoln National Life Insurance Company

Massachusetts Mutual Life Insurance Company

Metropolitan Life Insurance Company

The Midland Mutual Life Insurance Company

MONY Financial Services

Mutual Benefit Life

Mutual of Omaha

The New England

New York Life Insurance Company

North Atlantic Life Insurance Company

Northwestern National Life Insurance Company

Pacific Mutual

The Paul Revere Life Insurance Company

Philadelphia American Life Insurance Company

Phoenix Mutual Life Insurance Company

Pilot Life Insurance Company

The Principal Financial Group

Protective Life Insurance Company

Provident Indemnity Life Insurance Company

Provident Life and Accident Insurance Company

Provident Mutual Life Insurance Company of Philadelphia

Prudential Insurance Company

Safeco Life

Security Life of Denver

Shenandoah Life Insurance Company

State Mutual Life Assurance Company

Transamerica Occidental Life Insurance Company

The Travelers Insurance Company

Union Labor Life Insurance Company

Unionmutual Life

United States Life Insurance Company

Congress Could Act, but Doesn't

While all of the cost shifting was going on, insurers had compliance problems with state laws. Insurers are regulated by the states, while the employers buying the insurance from them are regulated by the federal government. The two governments, federal and state, have created a bizarre world of overlapping and contradictory regulations that makes it almost impossible for any health insurer to survive.

It began in 1973 when the federal government passed the Employee Retirement Income Security Act (ERISA). (*Note:* **all public sector entities are exempt** from compliance with ERISA and the associated penalties.) Although primarily focused on pension plans, it described basic requirements concerning all employee benefits plans. It contained a provision saying that no state may regulate any employee benefits plan. That sounds pretty clear. But that isn't what happened.

States have the right and obligation to regulate insurance companies. The regulation of these companies is important. The foundation of most state insurance departments goes back to the Great Depression, when insurance companies went broke because they lacked the reserves to pay obligated claims. As a result, various states established rules and regulations governing the behavior of, and dealing with the financial solvency of, insurance companies doing business in their state.

States took on not only the right to determine if the insurance company was fiscally sound, but they actually assumed the right to determine what the insurance company would be allowed to sell and what they would be allowed to charge for services and products.

Although ERISA says that no state may regulate any employee benefit plan, the states took the position that their right to regulate insurance companies gave them the right to regulate the employee benefit plans sold by insurance companies. As a result, states began to dictate with great precision the exact coverage that must be offered, the conditions under which they must be offered and the premiums that could be charged. They didn't regulate what an employer could buy, they regulated what an insurer could sell!

Every state has different rules and different regulations. Often the rules and regulations will depend on the strength of special interest groups concerning coverage that is mandated. The result is 50 different and sometimes contradictory sets of rules and regulations, and ever-changing laws and mandates. This environment makes successful large-scale insurance company operations virtually impossible.

> In an almost incomprehensible failure, Congress did NOT apply its Constitutional authority to "regulate commerce between the states." Unbelievably, while Congress has used the commerce clause to interfere in areas that are clearly prohibited by our Constitution, it chose NOT to involve itself in an area that clearly DID require Congressional involvement! Congress allowed barriers to be established in every single state of the union, preventing commerce between the states.

In the latest iteration of idiotic statements made by leaders of Congress, they have complained that health insurers impose limitations for pre-existing conditions. **They are really saying to insurers, "You are refusing to insure burning ships! That's outrageous!"** In what other form of insurance would Congress insist that insurers pay for a claim that is happening right now? Insure a car AFTER it has had an accident? Sell life insurance AFTER the guy is dead?

Insure a house AFTER it has burned down? How on earth can Congress (and the president) look at supposedly smart Americans and demonize health insurance carriers for refusing to insure a known claim? But they do, and they do it with a straight face.

With all of this interference into free markets of health care and health insurance, governments have "fouled up left field so bad, that no one can play it." Their solution of taking it over so that they can fix it themselves is being implemented at exactly the same time that they admit that Medicare, their 1965 creation, is TRILLIONS of dollars in the hole, and there is no way out unless they dramatically cut costs or reduce benefits. What planet have they been living on?

No One Knows What Health Care "Costs" Really Are

Isn't it remarkable that in the entire debate concerning health care costs, little or nothing has been said about hospital, medical or pharmaceutical costs, or excessive compensation being provided to those who run those sectors or work there? Or about pay and benefits provided to hospital workers? Only the insurance carrier is responsible for the entire health care/health insurance debacle. But the health care business must be pretty good. Hospitals have taken to advertising on television that their hospital is better than another one. Most are non-profits but they're acting like they're selling cars. There must be a reason!

Just for fun I went to www.Guidestar.org. They provide access to Form 990 that must be filed by non-profit organizations. The IRS requires non-profits to file Form 990 and to make them publicly available. **They always make interesting reading, especially when you consider that these organizations don't have profits and pay no income taxes.** They MUST spend everything they make in order to avoid the appearance of making a profit. There's an easy solution to that. You can always spend it on yourself!

These non-profits are, in effect, taxpayer-supported because they don't pay sales, property or income taxes and we do, and they can directly or via their foundation receive tax-deductible contributions from people who ALSO avoid paying taxes. And...they can then pay the money to themselves! How cool!

Unscientific and Random Sampling—Yet Telling Examples

To do some random research, I considered names that I thought would lead me to random hospitals. I then looked at the Form 990 to see what their highest-paid people made. Certainly that is far from a scientific study, and all I could hope to learn was a glimpse of how much money was in the non-profit hospital business.

I first stumbled across Baptist St. Anthony's Hospital in Amarillo, Texas.

- The CEO was paid $945,000 plus $237,000 to a special deferred compensation plan.
- They have two doctors who serve as "VP-Staff Rel." One makes $599,000 and the other $562,000.
- The VP of Operations earns $562,000.
- The 7th highest-paid earns $436,000.

Then I found University Community Hospital in Tampa, FL.

- The CEO made $510,000 plus a $300,000 contribution to a supplemental retirement plan.
- The medical director earns $437,000.

Next, I found University Hospital in Cincinnati.

- The five highest-paid NON-officers were all nurses, averaging $179,000 each.
- The top officer earned $1,319,000 plus a $576,000 contribution to his benefit plan.
- The COO earned $961,000 and the SVPs averaged $562,000.

- I have no idea how much their average workers earn, or what their benefits are. But I'll bet they are at, or in excess of, public sector levels.

Why am I bringing this up? I bring it up because health care non-profits are BIG BUSINESS but they are not generally seen as such by the U.S. taxpayer. There is a lot of MONEY being made in the health care business! Yet that money does not have to support what the private taxpayers must support. Something is wrong with this picture.

On April 20, 2010, the *Wall Street Journal* ran an article reporting that the prices for brand-name pharmaceuticals jumped 9.1% last year, the largest increase in more than a decade, and it was occurring during one of the worst economic downturns in U.S. history. Industry spokespersons said it was purely coincidental that they had (a) supported the health care reform legislation and (b) agreed in negotiations with those writing the new bill to give rebates to Medicaid beginning next year.

Since every major payer only has to pay a predetermined amount that has absolutely nothing to do with the charges that appear on the bill, we have no idea what anything really and truly costs. **In reality, no one in America knows what real health care costs are.** A hospital may present a $10,000 bill for a two-day stay, showing aspirin at $80 each, and a unit of blood at $1,000, but it knows that nobody really pays that. Medicare doesn't pay that. Medicaid doesn't pay that. Ajax doesn't pay that. Blue Cross doesn't pay that. Nobody pays that, except for the poor sap that goes to the hospital with no insurance. He will get that full charge bill, and the hospital will chase him to the gates of hell to collect it. And if he can't or doesn't pay, those bogus billed charges will be written-off, either as uncollectable or as indigent care. The fact is that no one knows what health care costs really are, so how can we possibly attack or control them?

Maybe we'll be lucky enough to get a do-over. If the health care reform legislation is overturned by the Supreme Court or the next Congress, we'll have to take another hard look at the whole mess we're in. Before Congress can really learn what it takes to undo the great harm it has already done, it needs to recognize that there is a difference between health care and health insurance. It needs to determine exactly what the proper role of government should be, and it needs to get out of areas in which it has never belonged.

> There is a difference between health care and health insurance. It needs to determine exactly what the proper role of government should be, and it needs to get out of areas in which it has never belonged.

Can all of these health care and health insurance problems be solved? Of course they can if our free market can be allowed to operate and our citizens can be allowed to use their own judgment and determine their own risk tolerance. They are very smart consumers when they are permitted to make their own buying decisions.

Steps That We Must Take

There are a number of steps we must take.

FIRST, we must determine what health care costs actually are. We can do this by requiring that all payers must pay the same for any given procedure, and that the provider must charge the same amount for each procedure to every payer. The provider could charge whatever he or she wants to, but they would not be permitted to give discounts to third-party payers. That would end the false, misleading (and, in my opinion, fraudulent) practice of producing invoices that have no relationship to actual costs. We must say that the charge must be paid, whether by Medicare, Medicaid, any commercial carrier or anyone without insurance.

SECOND, we have to change tax policy. Benefits to employees should be considered compensation and taxed accordingly. Employers would have to pay payroll taxes on these amounts, and employees would have to pay income taxes on these amounts. I GUARANTEE that employees would want REAL insurance plans that cost a lot less, with high deductibles, less "nickel and dime" coverage, and much less taxable income charged to them. Additionally, the new true insurance plans would require an insured to pay a portion of the charges. This coinsurance would result in the person who incurs the charge actually CARING how much it is.

THIRD, we would require health care providers to publish their charges, so that consumers could know in advance which provider they would want to use.

FOURTH, Congress can say, "We meant it when we said no state may regulate any employee benefits plan. You may not, under the guise of regulating insurance companies, dictate what the specific coverage offered by those insurance or employee benefits plans will be." That would make it possible for large national insurers to achieve economies of scale by having policies that were the same everywhere. It would be possible for large organizations to have one large consistent plan that would cost much less to administer, as they would not have to deal with the complexity of insurance law variations in every single state of the union.

FIFTH, to assure that basic protection was contained in all policies, the Federal government could come up with a standard minimum approved plan, in much the same way that they set minimum safety standards for automobiles.

SIXTH, the federal government would have to find a way (perhaps via tax policy) to assure that **every public sector entity and union must follow the same rules.**

SEVENTH, all of the above would apply to pre-age 65 retiree plans.

If Medicaid is not providing adequate protection to the truly needy, it should be reviewed and changed. But Medicaid should not be used as a substitute for those who could, but choose not to, provide insurance for themselves. Medicaid would be required to pay the actual charges made by the provider. No discounts!

This doesn't solve the problem of the person who elects not to buy insurance, or who cannot obtain insurance. If the person decides to go without insurance, they should have to deal with the consequences, as they would if they did not insure their house or their automobile. For those truly uninsurable because of an ongoing claim or a pre-existing condition, a one-time window, allowing minimal catastrophic coverage to be obtained, could be afforded once, when the new world of health insurance is implemented. One-time, open enrollment, everyone can get in a plan. Then the window closes.

> These are relatively easy things to do as compared with the trillion dollar costs associated with a federal government takeover of one-sixth of the economy and, more importantly, a takeover in which government decides what is best for us. These changes would revolutionize the health care industry in the United States.

Tough Medicine to Take, but the Alternative is Unthinkable

There would be many opponents, no doubt...particularly the unions who have secured unbelievably rich health insurance plans, tax-free, for their members. Recommended changes would have far-reaching impact in many ways. Income taxes would go up for those individuals who have group health plans. Employers would face increases in payroll taxes. The true costs of Medicare and Medicaid would be seen, as these plans began to pay actual costs, not hugely discounted rates. **Congress would have to focus on paying for what has already been promised, instead of creating more entitlement programs that no one can afford.**

The costs of obtaining insurance plans would go way down, as insurance became true insurance. Insurers would compete on a level playing field, with not one of them getting lower prices than another. Claims would be reduced as "nickel and dime" claims were borne by those who incurred them, and the buyer of health services became knowledgeable about varying costs among different providers. Consumers would actually care what the costs were, and adjust their buying habits accordingly. Large insurers would establish nationwide plans and pools of insureds. Their compliance costs with 50 different state laws would be eliminated. Individuals would be able to buy the amount of protection they were willing to pay for. Riders allowing coverage for experimental procedures, or extremely high limits, could be purchased if the insured wanted to pay the appropriate price.

All this would be tough medicine to take. But the alternative is to cede to the government forever the right to control the scope, quality and amount of our medical care and treatment. It really shouldn't be a very tough choice to make.

*"The U.S. government is on a burning platform of **unsustainable** policies and practices."*

—David Walker,
Comptroller General
of the United States.
January 2, 2008

Chapter Eight

Unions: The Allies of Big Government

Marking the first 100 days of the Obama administration, Service Employees International Union (SEIU) President Andrew Stern proclaimed, "SEIU is on the field, it's in the White House, it's in the administration." Indeed it is. The SEIU spent $67 million on politics in 2008. Stern was listed at the most frequent visitor to the White House between inauguration day and the end of October 2009, with 22 visits.

Together with 16 other unions who gave at least 90% of all of their political contributions to Democratic candidates, unions are now getting their payback from local, state and federal government officials that they helped to put in office. The result is the use of federal and state government power and the use of taxpayer dollars to force unionization on government contractors, private sector workers and even more government employees.

At stake is the 1% to 2% of **compensation taken as union dues and used to support even more union organizers and union-friendly candidates and to extract even more pay and benefits concessions from unwitting taxpayers.** Some unions even maintain "anti-candidate" funds to be used against recalcitrant candidates or elected officials. **Unions contributed more than $300 million toward**

election campaigns in 2008, influencing elected officials to support legislation and regulations forcing union membership on workers.

According to the Center for Responsive Politics and its website OpenSecrets.org, union organizations represented 1/3rd of the total contributions on their "Heavy Hitters" list. This list represents total contributions of the 100 biggest givers in federal-level politics since 1989. Unions were heavily represented among the top 10 givers, including the American Federation of State, County & Municipal Employees (AFSCME); International Brotherhood of Electrical Workers; National Education Association; Laborers Union; Service Employees International Union; and Carpenters & Joiners Union.

A *Wall Street Journal* article pointed to Labor Department filings showing that SEIU International spent about 20% of its annual budget, or some $67 million, on politics in 2008. The AFSCME reported spending $63 million on politics in 2008, just under 1/3rd of its budget. Another $13 million went to politics from the International Brotherhood of Teamsters in 2008, and $11 million was channeled to politics by the United Auto Workers in the same year.

Unionization of the Public Sector

The unionization of the public sector has led to an attainment of pay and benefits that are significantly higher than those provided in the private sector. In earlier chapters, we've seen the pay and benefits disparity that exists, as well as how these levels of pay and benefits and the associated huge unfunded liabilities are hidden from the taxpayer. It "takes two to tango" and the blame for the scale of these indefensible practices lies with those who represented the taxpayer in negotiations. As we've seen, at virtually every level of public education and government, those who were charged with the responsibility of representing the taxpayer "gave away the store."

> An estimated 40% of all public sector workers are unionized, as compared with 7% of the private sector.

There are many that believe that public sector employees should not be allowed to unionize in the first place, including the states of Virginia and North Carolina that prohibit unionization of state employees. Even Franklin Roosevelt, who signed the National Labor Relations Act and other pro-union legislation, apparently did not believe that federal employees should be allowed to unionize, as they were excluded under provisions of the act. That seemed to make sense.

Public sector employees are hired by taxpayers, who give them a monopoly on the services that they are paid to provide. It creates an obvious conflict when taxpayers also allow public servants to unionize. If they are allowed to be a monopoly to provide an essential public service not available elsewhere, why should they be allowed to create their own independent leadership, and to create their own workplace rules and compensation? Why should they at the same time possess the power to "take what they want" in taxes from the private sector taxpayer while they have been given the monopoly through our taxes? That is exactly what the private sector has allowed.

In the U.S. we are witnessing the operation of a "money pump" or a perpetual motion political machine. **Our tax dollars go to public sector workers. About 1% of these tax dollars goes from public sector workers to unions as dues.** Unions use the dues income to provide enormous financial support to candidates and elected officials who support the union agenda, which is to unionize even more of the public sector. They also use their money to OPPOSE candidates and elected officials who do not conform to their agenda. The union agenda is to get MORE of our tax dollars so that they can justify the dues they charge to their members. **Taxpayers are actually paying to support efforts that are directly in opposition to their own interests!**

> There are important differences between private sector and public sector unions. Unlike private sector unions existing at companies that must survive in a competitive environment, public sector unions work in areas that are created by taxpayers as monopolies. Whether it is

firefighters, police, public education or drivers licensing offices, the public sector entity does not operate in a competitive environment, and taxpayers do not have a choice to buy from someone else. Taxpayers are not free to shop elsewhere if the price being charged becomes too high. They must pay the price whether they want to or not, and whether they actually use the service or not.

Compare this with General Motors and other large unionized private sector (well, they USED to be private sector!) companies. If they had a strike, you could buy a car from another manufacturer. If their payroll costs got too high, they would have to pass that along to car buyers who were free NOT to buy the car. If they made promises of huge future benefits that would increase their costs, they had to disclose this to investors and fund for these promises, again hurting their ability to sell cars in competition with others, and wreaking havoc with their stock price to boot. The unions had to negotiate with management of the company, who had a lot to lose if they gave away too much. If they raised current pay and benefits too much, or agreed to work hours and union featherbedding demands, the costs of their vehicles would go up, and they would suffer negative consequences in the marketplace.

Prior to 1985, private company management could promise future benefits without having to account for them on their balance sheet or fully disclose them to investors. But when the Federal Accounting Standards Board (FASB) began requiring on the balance sheet disclosure, the full extent of their promises was made known, and that game ended in 1985. (No such disclosure is required of public entities, as we have learned.) The public sector, playing by a different rulebook and hiding what they were doing from taxpayers, was just getting started. The next 25 years would be the "golden age" of redistribution from unwitting taxpayers to public sector workers.

Public sector unions are not inhibited by the same factors in the private sector:

- The unions bargain with bureaucrats who often get the same benefits they agree to give to the union.
- Public sector employers are not inhibited by a lack of revenue, as they can charge whatever tax they need.
- There is no requirement to put long-term promises on the balance sheet or even to adequately fund them.
- Long-term promises are the easiest to make, as the tax-payers won't know about them, and the problem of paying for them will occur long after the bureaucrats or elected officials who agreed to them are gone (and often enjoying those generous retirement or health insurance benefits themselves.)
- If the union chooses to strike, the taxpayer will be deprived of the service completely. That means, in many cases, there can be school closings, a shutdown of public transportation or no garbage pickup.
- Worst of all, public sector unions can use their dues (from private taxpayers) to finance campaigns for candidates and elected officials, and/or to advocate for public policy or tax increases that benefit themselves.

They can, in effect, elect the very same people that they will bargain with for more or better benefits. The result is that unions strongly support one party that has long championed bigger government and more power to unions—the Democratic Party.

There are numerous examples of the extraordinary influence that unions have on government and public policy. As reported by Chris Edwards, Director of Tax Policy Studies at the Cato Institute:

> *"In November, for example, transit workers in Philadelphia went on a six-day strike over disagreements regarding pay. The strike created chaos for the 800,000 residents of the city who rely on government subway and bus services, and it likely caused substantial damages to the local economy."*

The unions can do more than strike; they can spend tens of millions on politicians and political advocacy to further their own interests. Edwards reported that the two largest teachers unions, the National Education Association and the American Federation of Teachers, collect about $2 billion a year in member fees and dues, and that in 2008 public sector unions spent $165 million on campaigns and ballot measures.

A case in point is Florida. In the spring of 2010, the state legislature passed a bill making it easier to fire weak teachers, reward good ones and eliminate tenure for new hires. Florida grants tenure (a guaranteed job forever) after 3 years of satisfactory performance evaluations. Tenure? For a kindergarten teacher? Yup, that's Florida. The bill was strongly opposed by the Florida Education Association (FEA). It ran television commercials of a man sitting at the teacher's desk in a classroom. He spoke of the critical importance of educating our children. He said that the Florida Education Association opposed changes in the Class Size Amendment and other changes that would negatively impact our public education system. This was all about the quality of education that we were providing to our children...our hope for the future. It was really inspirational. These people really cared so much about our children that they ran television ads to protect their interests. Moving, isn't it?

Would the average viewer know that the Florida Education Association is a teacher's union? No. There were also a lot of radio ads opposing the legislation, run by No Tallahassee Takeover, Inc., saying that passage of Senate Bill 6 would allow the legislature in Tallahassee to take over our education system, cut money to schools and perhaps increase property taxes. Would the average voter know that the group is registered to an attorney who represents the Florida Education Association as both an attorney and lobbyist? No.

What appeared to be grass roots opposition to the bill was anything but. It was a highly organized and well-funded campaign to build voter support for stopping passage or enactment of a bill that would provide better benefits to the taxpayer. (And would have actually been quite good for the teachers and very good for our children.) After the bill was passed in spite of their campaign to stop it, the FEA went into "Veto mode." They needed to get the Governor to veto it. But the Governor was a Republican, and the majority in the state house and senate were Republicans. That looked like an impossible task.

It just so happened that the Governor was running for the U.S. Senate, and that he was getting creamed in the polls by his Republican primary opponent, Marco Rubio. Unions favor Democrats and the Governor was Republican. The unions put on an all-out campaign urging the Governor to veto it, and he did so. Not long after that, the FEA ran television ads featuring small children saying, "Thank you, Governor for helping me get a good education." A few days later, the Governor announced that he had decided to leave the Republican Party and run for the Senate as an Independent. Subsequently, the Florida Education Association announced (SURPRISE!) that it would support TWO OPPOSING candidates: Democrat Kendrick Meeks AND "Independent" Charlie Crist (who is still Governor until January 2011 and still able to lend some support to the union causes, don't you think?)

If the teachers union wants to convince the taxpayers to give them more pay, benefits or job security, shouldn't they have to tell us, "We are a teachers union, and what we are selling you is about our OWN interests?" Isn't it outrageous that they can present themselves as an education association that is running TV commercials about "the needs of our children" when they are really a UNION with an agenda that is about their own pay and benefits and job security?

In California, the California Teachers Association (CTA) is the largest campaign contributor and lobbyist in the state. It spent more than $200 million during the last 10 years. In February 2010 it spent $630,000 fighting to repeal newly approved tax breaks for corporations. It formed Taxpayers for Jobs and Against Corporate Handouts and is trying to get on the November ballot to repeal the breaks, claiming this will save the state $2.5 billion a year. Why is a teacher's union spending more than a half a million dollars of its membership dues fighting corporate tax breaks? **Because it wants the money, not because it is trying to do Californians a favor.**

On July 9, 2009, the General Counsel of the National Education Association (NEA) Bob Chanin explained at their convention why "big labor" is so powerful.

> "...it is not because of our creative ideas; it is not because of the merit of our positions; it is not because we care about children; and it is not because we have a vision of a great public school for every child... The NEA and its affiliates are effective advocates because we have power. And we have power because there are more than 3.2 million people who are willing to pay us hundreds of millions of dollars in dues each year because they believe that we are the union that can most effectively represent them; the union that can protect the rights and advance their interests as education employees."

The Service Employees International Union (SEIU) is the most notorious for unabashed political spending. In addition to huge spending on federal election campaigns, SEIU also gets into local politics. On January 7, 2009, Kris Maher reported in the *Wall Street Journal* that Mr. Stern had also supported Illinois Governor Rod Blagojevich's campaign. "The SEIU was the governor's biggest campaign contributor, contributing $1.8 million for his two campaigns for governor" and "shortly after being elected, Mr. Blagojevich signed an executive order that enabled SEIU to organize tens of thousands of workers who care for people in their homes and whose pay is subsidized by the state." In another *Wall Street Journal* article (May 13, 2009) Maher reported that **SEIU had spent $85 million** on the 2008 campaign and that its officials said it was well worth it. Maher went on to include a quote from Mr. Stern, "We maxed out the credit card and now we're paying it off....we couldn't say to Barack Obama, 'Excuse me, we can't run your ads because our locals were late in paying their per capita.'"

The SEIU story continued as Michelle Malkin reported on her blog, Creators.com. Mr. Stern was quoted in the *Las Vegas Sun* as saying, "We spent a fortune to elect Barack Obama—$60.7 million to be exact, and we're proud of it." Malkin wrote on her blog that "the SEIU scored not one but two cabinet appointees: Health and Human Services Secretary Kathleen Sebelius and Labor Secretary Hilda Solis." Malkin's revelation that "the two million member union, which represents both government and private service employees, proudly claimed that it had 'knocked on 1.87 million doors, made 4.4 million phone calls…and sent more than 2.5 million pieces of mail in support of Obama,'" showed what the power of a well-organized and funded union can do. Among numerous other appointees was SEIU chief lobbyist Patrick Gaspard who served as the Obama's campaign national political director and later the transition team deputy director of personnel. SEIU Secretary-Treasurer Anna Burger was appointed to the president's Economic Recovery Advisory Board. Oh yes…there was one more important appointment: SEIU president Andy Stern recently issued a press release stating, "I am honored to have been asked to serve on the National Commission on Fiscal Responsibility and Reform, and thank President Obama for ensuring that the voice of ordinary working Americans will be heard."

Within weeks of taking office, President Obama had signed three very union-friendly Executive Orders, covered later in this chapter. The president made Mr. Stern his most frequent guest in the White House. Then he made key political appointments. It is hard to comprehend why no one raised the issue of the "Buckley case," one of the most-referenced Supreme Court rulings, which said, **"To the extent that large contributions are given to secure a political quid pro quo from current or potential office holders, the integrity of our system of representative democracy is undermined."**

On the business law section of the American Bar Association's website, Jan Witold Baran writes "Under no circumstances may anyone provide a campaign contribution or anything else of value to a government official in exchange for an official act. That is a quid pro quo, or what the laws usually refer to as bribes and gratuities."

Stern's gleeful and public claims of SEIU influence, a political contributor who actually bragged about his huge campaign contributions leading to the election of the president of the United States, must have been discomforting to the president's office. Although not a registered lobbyist, Stern's 20+ visits to the White House and the three union-friendly Presidential Executive Orders signed almost immediately after Obama took office, certainly presented at least the appearance of a quid pro quo. This discomforting situation is apparently going unreported in the national media and unchallenged by our law enforcement agencies (perhaps because the president actually RUNS the law enforcement agencies.) It certainly appears that we can be sure the unions and the public sector's plea—"Please, sir, I want some more"—will be answered favorably in Washington.

> The enormous strength of public sector unions can only mean that any attempt to reduce or to bring public sector pay and benefits under control will be met by enormous and well-financed opposition.

Their work will be made a bit easier because those who promised the benefits in the first place are mostly gone from the scene, replaced with people who inherited the mess. The current array of bureaucrats and elected officials do not fear punishment by the voters, as they can truthfully say, "It's not my fault. I didn't do it." Most will say, "My hands are tied. I can't do anything about it. These benefits are guaranteed by contract." For those campaigning for office, it's a lot easier to go along with unions than to oppose them.

The Manhattan Institute's senior fellow, Steven Malanga, explains it this way:

> *"In the private sector, employers who are too generous with pay and benefits will be punished. In the public sector, more union members mean more voters. And more voters mean more dollars for political campaigns to elect sympathetic politicians who will enact higher taxes to foot the bill for the upward arc of government spending on workers."*

An excellent policy paper is found on the Cato Institute Website, written by Don Bellante, David Denholm and Ivan Osorio and entitled "Vallejo Con Dios: Why Public Sector Unionism is a Bad Deal for Taxpayers and Representative Government." Using the City of Vallejo, California as a spectacular example of how governments can get themselves into impossible financial straits, they make numerous valid points. Vallejo actually went bankrupt because pay, benefits, overtime and retiree costs for their police and firefighters consumed 74% of the city's budget. Some examples? A police captain could receive $306,000 in pay and benefits, a lieutenant $247,644, with the average for firefighters at $171,000 (with 21 earning over $200,000 including overtime). In 2007, 292 city employees made over $100,000. The city had been attempting to negotiate lower wages for several years, but "the unions retorted that those would endanger public safety and the safety of police and firefighters." The outcome of this remains in the courts.

Dealing with excessive pay and benefits for unionized public sector employees will be a tough fight. They are organized and have millions of dollars to spend. But as Bellante, Denholm and Osorio state,

> "As keepers of the public purse, legislators and local council members have an obligation to protect taxpayers' interests. By granting monopoly power to labor unions, over the supply of government labor, elected officials undermine their duty to taxpayers..." Voters in the private sector must remind all those seeking their votes of that fact.

Public sector unions are doing great, but it certainly would be useful to them if they could collect more dues and support from workers in the private sector. No problem for the unions. They will just convince elected officials to coerce private sector employers to become unionized.

Pro-Union Legislation and Presidential Executive Orders

The proposed Employee Free Choice Act, currently pending in Congress, and Executive Orders 13495, 13496 and 13502 signed by President Obama within weeks of his inauguration, represent clear and concerted efforts to force unionization on private and public sector workers.

Early in 2009, President Obama signed three Executive Orders that strongly favor the interests of organized labor and will affect many employers that enter into contracts to provide goods or services to the federal government.

Executive Orders (EOs) are legally binding orders given by the president to agencies of the federal government, explains Jeffrey C. Fox of Catawba College on the ThisNation.com website. EOs "are generally used to direct federal agencies and officials in their execution of congressionally-established laws or policies." **Congressional approval is not required for EOs to take effect, "but they have the same legal weight as laws passed by Congress."** Fox says EOs "are controversial because they allow the president to make major decisions, even law, without consent from Congress. This…runs against the general logic of our Constitution—that no one should have power to act unilaterally." Where are the checks and balances?

Executive Orders Coerce Unionization

EO 13495

President Obama signed Executive Order 13495 on January 30, 2009. This Executive Order affects a contractor's ability to hire employees of his or her choosing when a contract to provide services to the federal government expires and a new contract for the same services is awarded to a different contractor. Executive Order 13495 will generally require the new contractor to offer employment to employees who worked under the prior contract before the new contractor can hire new employees to perform the work. The practical impact of this EO is that federal contractors who generally hire non-union workers, and are awarded new services contracts, are more likely to be deemed "successors" to the prior contractor's bargaining relationship with a union representing the prior contractor's employees. The NLRA (National Labor Relations Act) stipulates that if the contractor is deemed a "successor," it is not bound by the predecessor's labor contract, but it is obligated to negotiate with the union over a new collective bargaining agreement.

EO 13496

Executive Order 13496 was signed by President Obama on January 30, 2009. According to Goodwin Procter LLP, "Executive Order 13496 states that economy and efficiency in federal government procurement is most easily achieved when employees are well informed of their rights under federal labor laws, such as their right to organize and engage in collective bargaining under the National Labor Relations Act. Executive Order 13496 will require most contractors (and their subcontractors) that enter into new contracts with the federal government to post a notice of employee rights under federal labor laws in conspicuous locations. The Order revokes Executive Order 13201, which required most contractors who entered into contracts with the federal government to post Beck Notices, which informed employees that they cannot be required to join a union as a condition of employment. EO 13496 does not prohibit employers from posting Beck Notices or require their removal. However, the provision requiring contractors to post Beck Notices will no longer appear in government contracts."

The Associated Builders and Contractors, Inc. made comments before the United States Department of Labor's Office of Labor Management about implementation of EO 13496. They describe how EO 13496 would seek to utilize the Procurement Act to regulate labor relations and/or to influence their outcome:

"Although EO 13496 does not expressly say so, it is clear that the model upon which it is based, i.e., the president's assertion of authority under the Procurement Act 'to ensure the economical and efficient administration and completion of Government contracts,' was EO 13201 (Beck Order), which EO 13496 expressly revoked. However, while there may arguably be a few similarities between the two executive orders, the substance and detail of EO

13496 and, in turn, the Department's proposed regulations to implement EO 13496, go well beyond the sum and substance of the Beck Order and seek to influence the outcome of labor management relations in a manner that exceeds the authority which the president and department assert under the Procurement Act and is also preempted by the National Labor Relations Act (NLRA)."

EO 13502

Executive Order 13502 was issued by President Obama on February 6, 2009. It allows and encourages federal agencies to require contractors to use Project Labor Agreements (PLA) on federal construction projects of $25 million or more. A PLA is a pre-hire collective-bargaining agreement—often involving multiple employers and multiple unions—designed to systemize labor relations at a construction site. According to the order, PLAs promote efficient and timely completion of large-scale construction projects and prevent many of the problems inherent in such construction.

> The premise used to justify Executive Order 13502 is that it prevents labor disputes on construction projects. A report by the Beacon Hill Institute proves this justification to be false. Indeed, the Beacon Hill Institute report examined nearly $57.3 billion in construction projects completed from 2001–2008 costing or exceeding $25 million and found NO disputes attributable to NOT having a PLA.

In actuality, Executive Order 13502 **seeks to force unionization on non-union construction** companies working on federal construction projects. The construction industry is an industry with a comparatively high union membership. Even so, union membership is only 16% of the construction industry workforce. This means that 84% of the construction industry prefers to work non-union.

Executive Order 13502 is a costly giveaway to the construction unions and provides no proven benefit to taxpayers. The Beacon Hill Institute report showed that **PLAs reduce competition and add costs to construction projects.** In fact, 70–98% of the non-union contractors responding to various surveys stated that they would be less likely to bid on projects requiring PLAs and that **PLAs increase the cost of construction projects by 12% to 18%.** Executive Order 13502 has already begun to be challenged in court as promoting a discriminatory practice.

Forced Unionization of Daycare Providers

The leading contributor to the Democratic Party during the last two decades, the American Federation of State, County and Municipal Employees, is a driving power behind the forced unionization of over 233,000 home-based daycare providers within fourteen states. Michelle Berry from Michigan is one of them. She owns and runs a private daycare service in Michigan. Although she owns her own business and contracts independently to provide daycare services, she was informed by the Michigan Department of Human Services that she is a government employee and union member. The agency deducts union dues from the subsidies it sends to Berry on behalf of her low-income clients. The dues are then sent to a public-employee union that claims to represent her. Ms. Berry never voted to be part of a union and does not want to be part of a union.

How did this happen? Patrick J. Wright and Michael D. Jahr of the Mackinac Center in Michigan described this process in the *Wall Street Journal*:

> *"Ms. Berry did not choose to be a union member. This decision was forced upon her. Indeed, a year ago in December, Ms. Berry and more than 40,000 other home-based daycare providers throughout Michigan were suddenly informed they were members of Child Care Providers Together Michigan—a union created in 2006 by the United Auto Workers and the American Federation of State, County and Municipal Employees. The union had won a certification election conducted by mail under the auspices of the Michigan Employment Relations Commission. In that election only 6,000 daycare providers voted. The pro-labor vote turned out.*

> *Michigan is just one of 14 states who have now enabled home-based day-care providers to be organized into public-employee unions, affecting about 233,000 people. And nine states have done so with home health care providers. It's telling that in several states that have gone down this road, state and federal subsidies are the source of the union dues. In Michigan, the scheme is essentially throwing a cash lifeline to unions like the UAW, which are hemorrhaging members."*

Governor O'Malley (MD) is ready to hand over power to the unions while the state is fiscally vulnerable, and taxpayers and families will pay the price. He recently approved collective bargaining for the family childcare providers that receive financial backing from the state. The SEIU Local 500 is now allowed rights to represent the childcare providers within the state and received the names and contact information for 4,942 providers to recruit dues-payers. But what is the need for unions in this business…there are no dangerous working condition and no difficult supervisors to deal with. The director of public policy for Maryland State and Family Child Care Association, Donna Fowler, is against this, citing that "low-income families could be dropped when the unions negotiates higher reimbursement for providers." Her assumption can be backed up by a *New York Daily News* article published on May 14, 2009 saying, "Under a deal brokered by the city, which will cost $80 million, the workers will get the raises owed since 2007. At the same time, more than 1,100 children of low-income parents who are either looking for jobs or can't work because of illness will lose child care."

As unions push to organize both public sector and private sector entities, they rely heavily on something called a "neutrality agreement." The National Right to Work Committee (NRTWC) website describes the agreement as "a contract between a union and an employer under which the employer agrees to support a union's attempt to organize its workforce." Following are some of the coercive components of a so-called neutrality agreement:

- As opposed to expecting employers to assume a neutral position, such agreements usually impose a **gag rule,** curtailing any speech that is negative toward the union, thereby giving employees a one-sided view.

- Neutrality agreements tend to have "card check" provisions, ensuring that **no secret ballot elections** are held. Employers agree to recognize the union, as long as a specified number of signed cards are presented, often leading to employees being misled into providing their signatures.

- The agreements often give unions **access to the premises** during work hours for the purpose of collecting signed union authorization cards.

- Neutrality agreements often expect the company to provide **access to personal information** on employees, including their addresses. This can lead to high-pressure home visits by union officials.

- The agreements may mandate that employees attend company-paid **captive audience speeches** promoting union sign-ups and sometimes implying a risk of job loss to those who are not supportive.

The NRTWC further explains that neutrality agreements could even require an employer "to impose the neutrality agreement on other companies with whom it affiliates" and that some state and local governments are requiring employers that want to do business with them to sign neutrality agreements, even though federal law prohibits such requirements. The NRTWC concludes, "The bottom line is this: employees rights of free choice are sacrificed and lost under so-called neutrality agreements."

Whether or not the neutrality agreement is signed, unions are using their strength gained by an increasing dues stream from public sector employees to increase their efforts to get more members in the private sector. **An example is David Bego.**

David Bego is all too familiar with the Service Employees International Union, aka, SEIU. He wrote a book about his ordeal with them entitled *The Devil at My Doorstep*. Bego is the owner of Executive Management Services (EMS), a commercial cleaning and facility maintenance business with nearly 5,000 employees in 33 states. Bego takes pride in furnishing his employees with above-average market pay for the work they do as well as health care and vacation benefit packages far superior to those of their unionized competitors. According to the National Right to Work Committee, in September 2006, SEIU threatened Bego with an ultimatum: either become unionized or expect to get hit hard. Because he refused to be intimidated by SEIU, Bego, along with his family, his employees, his business and their customers, were subjected to a relentless SEIU campaign of vilification and harassment. His company locations were picketed and customers were pressured to stop doing business with EMS. Finally, in November 2007, EMS was able to start fighting back and filed 33 separate unfair labor practice charges against SEIU leaders with the National Labor Relations Board (NLRB). The Indianapolis regional office of the NLRB filed a complaint based on those charges in April 2008. A month later, SEIU leaders agreed to stop picketing EMS and harassing customers.

Employee Free Choice Act (H.R. 1409)

The Employee Free Choice Act (EFCA) H.R. 1409, also known as the Card Check Bill, was proposed on March 10, 2009. The purpose of the act is "to amend the National Labor Relations Act to establish an efficient system to enable employees to form, join or assist labor organizations, to provide for mandatory injunctions for unfair labor practices during organizing efforts and for other purposes." Indeed, the bill's goal is to amend the National Labor Relations Act, which provides private sector workers the right to choose whether they wish to be represented by a union. **This bill is the number one legislative priority of major U.S. labor unions and its aim is to make it easier for unions to organize workplaces and halt the 40 year decline in private sector union membership.**

This act has two provisions. The **first provision** allows a union to substitute, at its option, a Card Check selection for a secret ballot election. This provision was eliminated from the act in July 2009 when several moderate Democrats came to realize the unconstitutionality of the provision. Indeed, the secretive and coercive nature of the Card Check system infringes on the ordinary rights of political association that are guaranteed to workers, and perhaps their employers, under the First Amendment protections of freedom of speech. Card Check (also called majority sign up) is a method of organizing workers into a labor union through the use of a public ballot. Under Card Check, if union organizers can persuade more than 50% of workers at a facility to sign cards, they win.

The election process established under the National Labor Relations Act is a secret ballot process, whereby votes are confidential. The aim of the secret ballot is to ensure the vote reflects a sincere choice by forestalling attempts to influence the voter by intimidation or bribery. The Card Check provides no such protections against intimidation and bribery in the attainment of signatures.

As a demonstration of the forced-unionization mindset at hand in the current administration, however, it is important to understand the terms of this original provision. **As Richard Epstein of the University of Chicago Law School describes in a Cato Institute publication:**

> *"The Card Check rules allow unions to collect the cards at any location in whatever manner they see fit. They may do so in secret, so as to avoid an employer anti-unionization campaign and any discussion among workers as to the desirability of accepting union representation. The EFCA contains no provision for National Labors Relations Board (NLRB) supervision of the Card Check— e.g., signatures before an NRLB representative or storage in neutral hands. Workers are NOT allowed to pull their cards (which are valid for six months) from the union and the employer is NOT allowed to challenge any card on the ground that it was obtained under duress, misrepresentation or false promises."*

In simple terms, the law allows union representatives to intimidate workers to get them to sign the cards and then provides employers no recourse to correct this injustice. The Employee Free Choice Act is frequently compared to George Orwell's *1984* due to the clear and undeniable unconstitutionality of the provision.

The **second provision** of EFCA is still intact. As Epstein continues, EFCA introduces "compulsory interest arbitration that authorizes a panel of arbitrators…to hash out an initial two-year contract binding on the parties, who have no recourse to judicial review. The EFCA establishes an impossibly rapid timetable for negotiations." The U.S. Chamber of Commerce warns that this measure will be harmful to U.S. competitiveness, particularly that of small businesses. **The impact on small businesses is not to be discounted since small businesses represent about 50% of the U.S. GDP and have historically been the growth engine that pulls the country out of distressed economic times.** Forced unionization measures such as those described below by the U.S. Chamber of Commerce on its website will only serve to increase current unemployment levels:

> "The binding arbitration section of EFCA has the obvious flaw of forcing the complex negotiation of a contract into a compressed time frame. But it also brings the federal government into contract talks, which was never intended under the National Labor Relations Act."

> "Far from leading to productive bargaining, as unions claim, binding arbitration is likely to cause just the opposite. If a union feels it's losing the edge in contract talks, it has every incentive to stonewall and wait for an arbitration panel to hand down a contract."

> "Binding arbitration would mean that both parties are likely to get stuck with a contract they don't like. From the union perspective, that's fine, they would prefer a bad contract to no contract. But for an employer, you could be stuck with a contract that [is] completely incompatible with your cost structure and your business model— and you would have to live with that contract for two years."

> *"Even worse, from a worker's perspective, binding arbitration would deny them the ability to vote on the pay, benefits and working conditions in their new contract. Since the contract handed down by the arbitrator is binding, workers would lose the opportunity to change provisions they thought were unfair."*

As described above, the purpose of the Employee Free Choice Act is to amend the National Labor Relations Act, which provides a worker the right to choose whether or not to be represented by a union. Comments made by union leaders following the modification of the Card Check provisions in July 2009 reveal their confidence that U.S. labor law is moving more pro-union. As reported in the *New York Times*, "One top union official, who insisted on anonymity... said, 'Even if Card Check is jettisoned to political realities, I don't think people should be despondent over that because labor law reform can take different shapes.'" Executive Orders 13495, 13496 and 13502, previously discussed, are examples of the actions being taken by the current administration to change U.S. labor law to be more pro-union.

> The Employee Free Choice Act should more accurately be called the "Employee No Choice Act" as it seeks to take away a worker's right to choose to be represented by a union. Additionally, the theme of "No Choice but the Union Choice" is echoed in Executive Orders 13495, 13496 and 13502. Through these Executive Orders, President Obama is implementing drastic changes to existing U.S. labor law. He is employing federal funds and contracts to coerce unionization, without public debate or the consent of Congress.

Pro-union Campaign Continues

Even with Executive Orders 13495, 13496 and 13502, and the proposed Employee Free Choice Act on the congressional agenda, unions have more changes planned for the upcoming year. There are six key issues likely to take the forefront in 2010. Terrence Scanlon, president of the Capital Research Center, highlighted these in his article in the *Washington Times*. They are described below:

1. **Card Check.** Unions want to replace private ballot elections with sign-up cards instead, a practice that tends to intimidate and manipulate workers. While this issue was shelved in 2009, it's likely we haven't heard the last of it.

2. **Binding Arbitration.** This provision of the proposed Employee Free Choice Act could set the stage for unworkable demands by either the union or the employer as both try to improve their deals via the arbitrator. The current incentive for negotiating contracts in good faith would be gone if the federal government sent in an arbitrator to impose a contract if a settlement wasn't reached within a specified time.

3. **Union Pension Bailout.** Inadequate funding threatens many of the multiemployer pension funds that unions manage, and the unions want the U.S. taxpayers to bail them out. Senator Robert Casey (D-PA) has proposed the Create Jobs and Save Benefits Act of 2010. He wants the taxpayer to take on the obligation of paying pensions to union members whose unions have drastically underfunded their own plans.

4. **Union Reporting Requirements.** The Bush Labor Department instituted rules requiring unions to disclose and itemize how they spend their money. Union leaders do not like this requirement because it sheds light on how union funds have and are being misspent. Under Obama, the Labor Department has pursued the reduction of these reporting requirements and has delayed or canceled the establishment of any new requirements.

5. **More Stimulus.** Congress will talk about another stimulus bill because the last one "worked so well." They gave billions upon billions of dollars to state government to pay their employees, public school teachers and pension contributions. A stimulus bill that allows the federal government to bail out the states with

the deepest needs will redistribute individual income tax dollars to the most profligate states. Similar to the earlier stimulus bill, it would likely focus on the preservation of heavily unionized government jobs and the provision of advantages to unionized contractors over non-unionized ones.

6. **National Labor Relations Board (NLRB).** The role of the NLRB is to interpret labor law and oversee unionization elections so many people are concerned about the Obama administration's appointments to the board. One appointee, Craig Becker, has served as associate counsel of SEIU and was instrumental in building the framework for Card Check legislation.

It's no secret that the current administration is seeking to promote a pro-union agenda and is seeking to achieve its objective through the use of legislation, regulation and the improper use of taxpayer dollars, including massive amounts of new debt that will burden taxpayers for generations.

Unions Represent All—Whether They Want It or Not

As we have seen, at last count about 40% of Americans working in the public sector are unionized. Many public sector employees do not join the union and they may actually oppose some of the union-negotiated working conditions. Many oppose the fact that their local or national union leadership uses dues to support policies and political candidates whose views are in opposition to their own. **In some states, unions have secured "free rider" legislation that can require employees to pay union dues even if they do not choose to join the union.** Unions have often successfully argued that these workers get the "benefit" of union representation (getting a "free ride") and should be forced to pay for it, whether they like it or not.

In some other public sector entities union membership is mandated as a condition of employment. In states that are not "Right to Work" states, employees can be compelled to join unions or to pay union dues even if they don't want to. Unions have gone beyond just obtaining more pay and benefits for members. In many cases, they have become the virtual "employer" controlling all work requirements and establishing all pay and benefits policies. In public education, they are actually dictating practically everything to the school board about their own job requirements, and go so far as to choose textbooks and establish the curriculum. In many cases, public sector management has allowed unions to wrest control of every aspect of the employer/employee relationship.

Imagine public education workers who work 9 months a year and get all of the national holidays and school breaks for Christmas, as well as winter and spring holidays, who then demand and get "vacation pay" for additional vacation time. In many cases this time is accumulated (who needs it?), and paid for in a lump sum at the time of termination or retirement, at a much-higher rate of pay than when it was earned. On top of this, almost every union has secured seniority or tenure agreements that make it virtually impossible to fire an ineffective teacher or administrator. Excellent new and dedicated teachers must wait in line behind those senior to them in tenure, and will not be promoted or rewarded for dedication to their jobs that involves working more than the required hours, or achieving significant results in educating their students.

> In practically every unionized element of the public sector seniority rules, and any attempt to identify and reward personal achievement is strongly contested by the unions.

In practically every unionized element of the public sector seniority rules, and any attempt to identify and reward personal achievement is strongly contested by the unions. When inevitable cutbacks occur, the youngest–perhaps the best and brightest in the public sector—are the first to be terminated. The strength of public sector unions has resulted in their takeover of the employee/

employer relationship and the control of almost every aspect of employees' jobs, whether the employee is a union member or not.

The solution would require that each public sector entity take back control of the employee/employer relationship. Employees would keep their jobs and earn promotions based on merit, not seniority. Public sector workers could decertify the existing union and form one of their own that truly represents their direct and local interests.

Members of a union can get out if they wish. The National Right to Work Legal Defense Foundation outlines public sector decertification and deauthorization laws on their website. Such decertification processes for state and local government employees differ from state to state. Another resource for the union decertification process is "Kicking Out Your Union" on the website Unionfacts.com. The site includes information for employees in the 28 states *without* "right to work" laws and those in the 22 states *with* "right to work" laws that say employees do *not* have to join unions and pay dues or fees to avoid unions. Those 22 states are Alabama, Arizona, Arkansas, Florida, Georgia, Idaho, Iowa, Kansas, Louisiana, Mississippi, Nebraska, Nevada, North Carolina, North Dakota, Oklahoma, South Carolina, South Dakota, Tennessee, Texas, Utah, Virginia and Wyoming.

Unions Should be Local and Independent

Few would argue with the right of employees to unionize should they choose to do so. But does a large national union have the right to come in and unionize a group in order to make them a participant in a much larger national organization? If a group of schoolteachers in a Texas school district wish to unionize, for instance, or the employees of a private company wish to unionize, they have the right to hold meetings, choose leaders, vote on whether they wish to join the union and agree to pay dues. Their grievances would be unique to the working conditions in which they find themselves.

They would be represented by their leaders in dealing with the private or public sector entity that employs them.

But what happens when an outside organization with independent leadership comes in to that school district or private company and organizes the workforce to join ITS union? Outside funds (taken from union dues-payers in other states) are utilized to finance the teams of organizers. Promises are made for benefits to justify the dues that will be extracted. In such a situation, the small school board or private company finds itself matching its own meager resources against huge financial resources paid for by workers in other unions in other places.

> It is a **clear conflict** for public sector employee unions to use funds received as pay from the taxpayer, in order to impose even more taxes in order to fund their own benefits.

Once the unionization of the local entity is successful, the workers find themselves represented by leaders they don't know, with agendas that are not known. Dues paid by smaller local unions are utilized by the large national union to organize the next small school district or private company. The result is that a few immensely powerful unions control public education and governments and several private sector industries across the nation. They use dues to build huge bureaucracies concentrating on national political activism, advancing the cause of making themselves bigger and more powerful.

The national union leadership is permitted to use dues to engage in political activity that may, and often does, conflict with the ideals of some, or much, of its own membership. For example, unions generally support Democratic officials or candidates favorable to the interests of the union, although some of these officials/candidates may be pro-choice, anti-war or have any number of positions that are opposed to the views of some individual union members who pay (voluntarily or involuntarily) dues. In many cases, the issues of pro-life or pro-choice, or support for current military engagements, may be the most significant issue to the individual union member. He may not support the particular candidate or political party being given union campaign funding. This is not fair, and it is not in the best interests of all union members. Private sector unions should be prohibited from making political contributions or engaging in lobbying or advocacy that is not the result of a clear determination by its members. Any political contributions should be allocated to individual and political parties as determined by their own membership.

> All political activity funded by public sector union contributions should be prohibited, because there is a very clear conflict of interest.

There are rules in other areas to prevent such conflicts. For example, Rule G-37 of the Municipal Securities Rulemaking Board prohibits individuals and companies engaged in transactions involved with municipal bonds from making political contributions. It is intended to prevent municipal bonds underwriters and sellers from having undue influence on those who select the underwriters, issuers and sellers of the bonds. **It is based on the recognition of the obvious conflict and potential corruption that would exist if bond underwriters were allowed to contribute to the election of the very people who would then select them as underwriters.**

Why, then, are unions allowed to make political contributions (from dues) to those who will provide benefits that favor these employees? Is that not also a clear conflict of interest? Of course it is. **What's worse is that taxpayer dollars are used to directly support those who want to claim more taxpayer dollars for public employees.**

Large national unions are using membership organization and significant amounts of dues income from their members to provide voter mobilization and campaign finance support to preferred candidates and elected officials. In turn, the elected officials provide legislation to enable more unionization, and also to provide pay and benefits to union members (often their own government employees) in order to keep union members happy and the dues coming in.

The use of taxpayer dollars to coerce unionization so that dues can be funneled to the unions, who then use the money to support the elected officials, who then authorize the expenditure of taxpayer dollars on behalf of public sector employees, is madness.

This whole process is a clear and present danger to private sector taxpayers, and thus to our economy as a whole.

Since employees of the public sector are paid with taxpayer dollars, their union dues should not be used to make political contributions, nor be used in any way to influence public policy, including lobbying. It is a **clear conflict** for public sector employee unions to use funds received as pay from the taxpayer, in order to impose even more taxes in order to fund their own benefits.

Should public sector unions be allowed? My opinion is "No, they should not be." And if they are allowed at all they should be required to be local and unaffiliated with any national organization. They definitely should be forbidden to make political contributions or to engage in any political activity of any kind.

*"For the second time in less than a
decade, we are experiencing another
economic plunge that shows our tax
system is volatile and **unsustainable**..."*

—Ben Westlund, Oregon State Treasurer.
June 18, 2009

_____ Chapter Nine _____

Unrestrained Spending, Debt and Taxes

In fiscal year 2009, the federal government incurred a record-setting deficit of $1.4 trillion. For fiscal year 2010, it plans to spend $3.5 trillion, leaving a deficit shortfall of an additional $1.5 trillion. According to the federal government, our total debt was $13.5 trillion at the end of 2008. Over the next 10 years, the administration is forecasting that budget deficits will total $9.05 trillion more. How, then, are independent analysts coming up with an estimate of the REAL federal debt that exceeds $120 trillion?

The reason for the huge difference is that there are substantial additional liabilities not included in the budget and therefore not reflected in the national debt. **Government accounting practices conceal trillions of dollars of debt the government is essentially hiding from the public as discussed in Chapter Four. This accounting practice is commonly referred to as off-the-balance-sheet financing, the very accounting practice that gave Enron the appearance of being financially stable prior to its sudden collapse.**

The combined debt of the Social Security and Medicare programs alone are "seven times the size of the U.S. economy and 10 times the size of the outstanding national debt," says senior policy analyst Pamela Villarreal of the National Center for Policy

Analysis (NCPA). Our nation's Medicare and Social Security promises exceed its assets by more than $106 trillion, according to the NCPA brief. Using data from 2009 Social Security and Medicare Trustees Reports, the NCPA places the unfunded liability for Social Security at nearly $18 trillion for 2009. In addition, the combined unfunded liability for Medicare is estimated at $89.3 trillion.

The following depicts the status of these programs' unfunded liabilities for 2008 and 2009:

	2008	2009
Social Security	$15.8 trillion	$17.5 trillion
Medicare Part A	$34.7 trillion	$36.7 trillion
Medicare Part B	$34.0 trillion	$37.0 trillion
Medicare Part D	$17.2 trillion	$15.6 trillion
Total	$101.7 trillion	$106.8 trillion

During a meeting of the National Taxpayers Union, David Walker, former head of the Government Accountability Office, claimed, "We suffer from a fiscal cancer" in that "our off balance sheet obligations associated with Social Security and Medicare put us in an America that now owes more than Americans are worth– and the gap is growing!"

To make matters much, much worse, the federal government pension plan is unfunded and the military retirement plan is 97% unfunded. The government has already agreed to bail out Fannie Mae and Freddie Mac with an unlimited financial guarantee, and these two GSE's have TRILLIONS of dollars of horrible loans on their books. The unfunded liabilities of Fannie Mae and Freddie Mac alone are estimated to be $5 trillion but may be greatly underestimated as these two organizations continue the practice of lending to those who are not truly financially qualified to purchase a home. These known liabilities are not reflected in the national debt, either.

In the unlikely event that the federal government wanted to reveal the "real" national debt to us (after all, we're the ones who have to pay it), it appears to lack the capability to do so. Pursuant to the Government Management Reform Act of 1994, the Government Accountability Office (GAO) is required to audit the consolidated financial statements of the federal government. In 2008, the GAO reported that material weaknesses, which are significant deficiencies resulting in the likelihood of misstatements on financial statements, "hamper the federal government's ability to reliably report a significant portion of its assets, liabilities, costs and other related information" as well as "hinder the federal government from having reliable financial information to operate in an efficient and effective manner."

> The GAO further reported that the federal government DID NOT maintain effective internal control over financial reporting and compliance with significant laws and regulations as of September 30, 2008.

Additionally, as a result of the material weaknesses, the GAO was prevented from expressing an opinion from 1997 through 2008. The federal government is clearly unaware of its financial condition and unable to determine its true revenues, true liabilities and other related information. **The federal government is violating and not complying with its own laws, and it has been unable to obtain clean, audited financials for the past 12 years.**

The National Center for Policy Analysis estimate of the unfunded liabilities of Medicare and Social Security of $106.8 trillion must be added to the admitted national debt of $13.5 trillion. That takes us to $120 TRILLION. At 5% interest, the cost to carry this debt is $6 trillion a year. That can't be done. Not even close. And that is why we print trillions of new dollars every year, and incur trillions of new deficits and debt every year.

In 2008, total personal income taxes paid to the federal government were $1 trillion. If the above estimates of $120+ trillion of unfunded liabilities are correct, and if interest rates eventually do increase to 5%, the interest payments, alone, would equal six TIMES the total personal income taxes paid in 2008. And that does not include the ongoing cost of government, or the additional $9 trillion of debt the federal government is planning to incur in the next decade. Nor does it include the debt that will undoubtedly be incurred for health care reform, or for a possible second stimulus package, new government agencies being created, or for a major terrorist attack or natural disaster.

The federal government will say it must take more taxes from us. **It collected $2.5 trillion in tax revenues in 2008, an amount equal to 17.7% of our Gross Domestic Product.** As shown in the following table, using data from the Congressional Budget Office, individual income and payroll taxes, and corporate income and payroll taxes were 93% of the federal government's income in 2008. **That is $2.325 TRILLION dollars. But they spent $3.7 trillion.** And in 2009, tax receipts will be lower (when 10 million people don't work, they don't pay payroll and income taxes). But the government will spend $3.5 trillion, anyway.

Sources of Federal Tax Revenue FY 2008		
Individual Income and Payroll Taxes*	63%	$1,575,000,000,000
Corporate Income and Payroll Taxes*	30%	$ 750,000,000,000
Excise Taxes	3%	$ 75,000,000,000
Other Taxes	4%	$ 100,000,000,000
Total (in dollars)		$2,500,000,000,000

Source: Congressional Budget Office

*Payroll taxes are the state and federal taxes that an employer is required to withhold and to pay on behalf of his employees. Social Security and Medicare taxes, also known as FICA taxes, are withheld from employees' wages. An employer must also pay a matching amount of FICA taxes for its employees. Currently the social security tax rate is 6.2%. The employer withholds 6.2% of an employee's wages for social security taxes and pays a matching amount in social security taxes until the employee reaches the wage base for the year. The wage base for social security tax is $106,500 for the year 2010. Once that amount is earned, neither the employee nor the employer owes any social security tax.

The Medicare tax rate is 2.9% for the employee and the employer. The employer withholds 1.45% of an employee's wages and pays a matching amount for the

Medicare tax. There is no wage base for the Medicare portion of the FICA tax. Both the employer and the employee continue to pay Medicare tax, no matter how much is earned.

State and Local Deficits are Unsustainable, Too

Enormous deficits and debt are not confined to the federal government. State and local governments are accruing unsustainable debt as well. In Connecticut, the state debt reached $417 billion in 2008. Illinois is currently looking at an $11 billion to $12 billion 2011 budget deficit. And on the local level, Atlanta had $1.2 billion in total unfunded pension liabilities for fiscal year 2009. Of its three pension plans, the general employees plan is in the worst financial condition, with liabilities of $634 million. The police pension fund has unfunded liabilities of $313 million, and firefighters have a pension fund with $234 million in unfunded liabilities.

The State of Washington will be giving $83 million in step increases in 2010 for 21,000 state employees, even though their Governor has proposed cutting $1.7 billion from public education, health care and other state programs to meet their budget. In a quiet meeting, the Governor renewed labor contracts, and now the state will be held accountable for those raises until the 2011–2013 budget cycle. It goes on and on, and we keep hearing about the debt crises in California, New York, New Jersey, Illinois, Michigan and more. **While some appear to be identifying and dealing with their shockingly large deficit and debt problems, they are only showing us a portion of the problem because they are utilizing the GASB accounting numbers, not the real unfunded liabilities that truly exist.**

The fact is that no one actually knows what the real combined debt and long-term unfunded obligations of federal and nonfederal public sector entities are. What is remarkable is that the sum total of debt and liability that must be paid by the American taxpayer is unknown. Even if the grossly-understated debt recognized by public sector entities were accurate, **public sector entities continue to** incur more debt each year without reference to the total impact that their collective deficit spending has on the American taxpayer.

> The combination of a huge pool of taxpayer-supported entities, together with the fact that each of them has a virtually limitless ability to incur debt and the ability to hide off-the-balance-sheet liabilities, has resulted in a massive and unrecognized impact on businesses and workers in the private sector.

While federal spending and debt occasionally receive national attention, the combination of federal debt and deficits added to the undisclosed unfunded liabilities, and then added to state, local and public sector debt and spending, and then added to its own hidden and unfunded liabilities, **has created a catastrophic situation for our nation and economy.**

If the current "best guess" is accurate that federal debt is $120 trillion, the average worker in the United States owes $1.2 million, today, just for federal debts and liabilities. If they paid just 5% interest on the debt and never paid the debt off at all, it would cost each worker $60,000 a year just for federal debt. (Since the average private sector worker earns less than $50,000 a year, I don't think this would be feasible.) And workers would, of course, still have to pay for the ongoing costs of government and public education. Add to that our current nonfederal public sector debt and unfunded liabilities of about $6 trillion, and the fact that the federal government plans to INCREASE debt by $9 trillion over the next decade, and you get to $135 trillion!

> What is astonishing, jaw-dropping, eye-popping and mind-boggling is that the federal government wants to fix things with ANOTHER stimulus package (more debt), and wants to create MORE bureaucracies with MORE government employees. It is actually saying the blame lies with fat cats who run American companies and individual taxpayers in the private sector—the ones paying taxes to support them and simply fighting to survive!

In dealing with the issues of national debt and liabilities, the numbers we use are so large that "millions," "billions" or "trillions" all begin to sound pretty much the same and are so overworked that they lose their meaning entirely. Large numbers lose impact when they cannot be related to "real" numbers that the average citizen can understand.

We hear the experts talk about trillions of dollars in deficits and debt and how unsustainable that is for our economy. But to the average American, this talk has little or no impact. "What do those huge numbers mean to me? I hear how bad things are, but I'm doing OK. What's the fuss?"

Florida residents like me get frequent hurricane warnings. Even when told, "There is imminent danger, and tomorrow will likely see 100 mph winds," we take a look outside and say, "That can't be. It's clear and sunny…a beautiful day. What ARE those guys talking about?" But we've learned that before long, the clouds start to develop, the rain starts and the winds pick up. And then it hits. We have learned (his name was Andrew) that if we don't take the necessary steps to protect ourselves when there is still time, we won't get a second chance.

> We are actually in a financial hurricane right now. We have warnings. We've been told by virtually every person or institution that looks at government spending and debt at every level that what has been going on is unsustainable.

Unfortunately cool, calm and collected people, like David Walker, say important things like, "[We are] on a burning platform" but they are saying it dryly and calmly. I get what "burning platform" means. But the press didn't say, "the Comptroller General of the United States of America has said that IF WE DON'T GET OFF THIS THING WE WILL ALL DIE!" Instead, it's as if someone said, "You know, there are some strong winds coming this way tomorrow. You might want to cancel that picnic."

We need people to SCREAM from the rooftops, "A HURRICANE is coming! It has 150 mile per hour winds! It will KILL you! Here's what you need to do RIGHT NOW to protect yourself and your children!" But the intelligentsia doesn't talk that way. They are calm, smart and measured when we need them to talk to us in passionate ways, using information that we all understand. And many typical Americans don't understand deficits, debt, GASB or GDP. And most of all, typical Americans don't understand trillions.

The federal government and the press began adding the word trillion to the American vocabulary in 2008. We began hearing about more than a trillion of deficit and trillions of total debt. Many tried to explain that a trillion is a really big number, not to be treated as just a few more billion. Even billions had lost meaning to most Americans, who are still dealing in thousands when it comes to their own finances.

My two favorite ways to describe a trillion are:

- "A billion seconds is 32 years, and a trillion seconds is 32 THOUSAND years!"
- "If you had a trillion cable channels on your TV set, and wanted to watch each channel for one minute, it would take 80,000 GENERATIONS to see them all!"

These examples can create a comparative understanding, a smile or a "WOW" moment, but like a cute joke, it passes. When we hear the huge numbers related to government spending, debt and liabilities, we tend to react with the same degree of awe as when we were first told, "Light travels at 186,000 miles per SECOND, and a light year is the distance that light travels in a YEAR, and the universe is BILLIONS of light years across. Isn't that AMAZING?" Yes, it sure is. The numbers are beyond comprehension. What's for lunch?

If dealing with huge numbers to explain the truly unsustainable and devastating financial position the public sector has placed us in won't work, how then do we get the message across? **We have to look at the component parts of the problem and bring each of them to ground level so that people can see where the big numbers come from, and how it specifically affects each one of them. Make it personal and understandable.**

What are the component parts that make up the overall financial debacle that is facing our nation? **A partial list includes:**

1. The misinterpretation or clear violation of the U.S. Constitution.

2. Unrecognized or misrepresented government payroll and pension largesse with the accompanying huge costs and liabilities. This includes hidden liabilities and deceptive accounting practices.

3. The enactment of more and larger entitlement programs relying on economic forecasts that cannot possibly be met.

In essence, the public sector and government tactic could be summarized as: "Keep taxpayers from seeing the facts, threaten to take away services and buffalo them with numbers so incomprehensible that their eyes will glaze over."

The Stimulus Wasn't Stimulus—It Was "Pork"

The $787 billion stimulus program has placed a huge burden on taxpayers. It was supposed to create jobs, but instead it went to state governments and into more federal government programs, and hugely increased our debt.

Here are just a few examples:

1. **Education.** $48 billion. (Remember Chapter One? Congress has no authority to tax and spend for education.) It went to things like Pell Grants ($15 billion), data systems and data coordinators ($250 million) and school improvement grants/student aid administrative costs ($60 million).

2. **Energy.** $41 billion. This money went to stimulate things like weatherization assistance ($5 billion) and energy efficiency and conservation block grants ($3 billion).

3. **Health Care.** $18 billion. The money was spent on stimulative National Institutes of Health grants and contracts

to renovate nonfederal research facilities ($1 billion) and for construction, renovation, equipment, and information technology for health centers ($1.5 billion).

4. **Census Bureau** programs. $1 billion.

5. **Distance learning,** telemedicine and broadband programs. $2.5 billion.

6. **Rural Utilities Service** water and waste disposal program. $1.38 billion.

7. **Defense environmental cleanup.** $5 billion.

8. **TSA** checked-baggage machines. $1 billion.

There is so much more, but if I kept on with the list, I would throw up and you might too. Hundreds and hundreds of billions of dollars, and all of it borrowed. All to "stimulate" our economy. I think I am going to be sick.

A "Stimulus" That Could Have Worked

Imagine what would have happened if Congress had allocated the same amount of money and had said, "No federal personal or corporate income taxes will be charged or withheld for the next year." Imagine if every American and every business got to spend their OWN money, the way they wanted to. They may have bought stocks and bonds, or they may have spent it on their businesses, even creating jobs. Or they may have spent it on other things. But they would have put the money where THEY, and not the government, wanted it to go. Now that would be a real stimulus!

> The government stimulus program represents a spending frenzy that created and supported government dependents, and gave Congress enormous amounts of "pork" to dole out to supporters. What it didn't do is create jobs in the private sector.

Until taxpayers started screaming, the government was actually trying to sell us on a new nonsensical and impossible metric: "jobs created or saved." We now know that with the exception of government jobs, no jobs were created at all. **Unemployment in the private sector kept increasing, while public sector jobs grew even more safe and rewarding.** Home-buyer credits and Cash for Clunkers programs have simply provided gifts of your tax dollars, taken from you and provided to someone else.

Government Takes Over and Keeps Spending

Bailout money has led the government to now hold a majority ownership in GMAC, General Motors, Fannie Mae, Freddie Mac and AIG as well as a large share of Citigroup and Chrysler. And the $1+ TRILLION health care reform bill looms as yet another uncontrollable expenditure on the horizon.

Yet despite our current deep recession, the government and public education sectors have not neglected their own salaries, benefits and pensions, with pay disparity between the public sector and the private sector an increasing inequity. While private sector employers have lost 8.5 million jobs since the beginning of the recession, the public sector has added 110,000 jobs, according to research done by the Nelson A. Rockefeller Institute of Government.

The budget woes of cities, counties and states would require a book to summarize. The State of Illinois has a current $13 billion deficit. That amounts to about one-half of what it spends. It is delaying payment of its bills, with a backlog of $5 billion in unpaid bills, and is not funding its pension plans. California has admitted to $500 billion in unfunded liabilities for its three biggest pension plans, and has a budget crisis every year. On the county level, officials in Nevada's Clark County, home to Las Vegas, are worried over their general fund expenditures because public workers' wages and benefits comprise nearly the entire amount: **the county's general fund is $1.5 billion, and county payroll is $1.2 billion.** And on the local level, the city of Columbia, South Carolina, had to dip into its emergency reserves to the tune of $24.7 million but still managed to give a combined $5 million in pay increases to some of the city's highest paid workers.

Taxes, Taxes, Taxes

All public sector entities receive their revenues through taxation. Here's a list of the taxes we pay:

Airfare Tax
Accounts Receivable Tax
Building Permit Tax
Capital Gains Tax
License fees
Cigarette Tax
Corporate Income Tax
Court Fines (indirect taxes)
Dog License fees
Federal Income Tax
Federal Unemployment Tax (FUTA)
Fishing License fees
Food License Tax
Fuel Permit Tax
Gasoline Tax (42 cents per gallon)
Hunting License fee
Inheritance Tax Interest expense (tax on the money)
Inventory Tax IRS Interest Charges (tax on top of tax)
IRS Penalties (tax on top of tax)
Liquor Tax
Local Income Tax
Luxury Taxes
Marriage License Tax

Medicare Tax

Property Tax

Real Estate Tax

Septic Permit Tax

Service Charge Taxes

Social Security Tax

Road Usage Taxes (Truckers)

Sales Taxes

Recreational Vehicle Tax

Road Toll Booth Taxes

School Tax

State Income Tax

State Unemployment Tax (SUTA)

Telephone Federal Excise Tax

Telephone Federal Universal Service fee Tax

Telephone Federal, State and Local Surcharge Taxes

Telephone Minimum Usage Surcharge Tax

Telephone Recurring and non-recurring Charges Tax

Telephone State and Local Tax

Telephone Usage Charge Tax

Toll Bridge Taxes

Toll Tunnel Taxes

Traffic Fines (indirect taxation)

Trailer Registration Tax

Utility Taxes

Vehicle License Registration Tax

Vehicle Sales Tax

Watercraft Registration Tax

Well Permit Tax

Workers Compensation Tax

Americans rarely, if ever, total up all the taxes they pay in a year to determine how much of their earnings go to taxes of one kind or another. The largest numbers come from individual income tax, payroll taxes and corporate tax. According to the Tax Policy Center, **approximately 80% of federal revenue dollars comes from individual income taxes and payroll taxes.** Federal corporate income taxes contribute another 12 percent. The balance of federal taxes is made up of excise taxes, estate and gift taxes, customs duties, and miscellaneous receipts (earnings of the Federal Reserve System and various fees and charges.)

> But we have seen that there are 89,000 taxpayer-supported public sector institutions, all of which can charge taxes, tolls, fees and licenses. There is absolutely no one in charge of limiting their collective taking from taxpayers. Each of them has its own employees to pay, and its own pension plans and benefits plans to maintain. Most of them never get looked at by the taxpayer, because they're assuming that someone else must be overseeing it all. No one is.

When was the last time you looked at where your taxes go to support the pay and benefits of the independent transportation authority, the water management district, the juvenile welfare board or port authority? Virtually all of them have the great pay and benefits that we see provided to federal employees, state employees and public education employees. **And someone has to pay for it. That person is you.** The long list of taxes shown above is misleading. You don't just pay income taxes. If you're in New York or many other states, you pay federal income taxes, state income taxes and city income taxes! If you're in Florida, you pay property taxes to the city, the county, the water management district and the juvenile welfare board.

Where is the "outer limit" on taxes that you can be forced to pay? What is to prevent them from each taking a bit more here and a bit more there, until nothing is left? There is no such limit. The federal government has imposed a minimum tax, saying that after you complete your tax return, if you don't owe what it wants when you comply fully with all tax calculation requirements, you have to pay an Alternative Minimum Tax, anyway! Isn't that a "taking," forbidden by the Constitution? Doesn't your right of equal protection prevent the government from taking even more than all of the tax requirements imposed on you? Where has the Civil Liberties Union been? Whose side are they on, anyway? And, shouldn't there be an Alternative **Maximum** Tax saying that all public sector entities cannot, collectively, have more than X% of what you earn?

Our taxes are going up...way, way up. One of the "neatest" ways government can increase taxes, but not increase taxes, is to allow previous tax cuts to expire. We've all heard that the "Bush tax cuts" will expire on December 31, 2010. Congress loves that! That doesn't even count as a tax increase! President Bush (demonized to the point that even middle-of-the-roaders are saying "Enough, already") did put through tax cuts 10 years ago. And they will expire. And that IS a tax increase. President Obama also put through some tax cuts, and they will also expire at the same time as the Bush tax cuts.

According to Gerald Prante of the Tax Foundation;

"If nothing is done by Congress on tax policy from now until December 31, massive changes in tax policy will take place. The odds of Congress doing absolutely nothing are small, but it is worth considering why Congress is highly likely to address the tax code this year: it is because so many key provisions are scheduled to change when the ball drops on January 1, 2011. Most of the key provisions that expire at the end of 2010 were put in place with the 2001 and 2003 tax cuts, often called the Bush tax cuts. There were other tax changes that took place during Bush's term that are set to expire at the end of 2010, and President Obama has also pushed through some changes in tax law that are set to expire at the end of 2010."

We used Gerald Prante's list of tax cuts that are slated to expire in order to determine what impact these tax expirations will have:

- Decrease the rate bracket for married filers
- Decrease standard deduction for married filers
- Increase the capital gain rates for dividends of individuals taxed at capital gain rates
- Eliminate the 10% individual income tax. Reinstate individual income tax rates of 15%, 28%, 31%, 36% and 39.6%
- Eliminate the increase in the child credit—which was increased from $500 to $1,000
- Decrease eligibility for refundable portion of the credit, AMT relief
- Eliminate the provisions that provide that child credit not be treated as income or resources for purposes of benefit or assistance programs financed in whole or in part with Federal funds
- Earned Income Tax Credit (EITC)—Decrease in the beginning point of the phase-out range for joint filers
- Reinstate personal exemptions phase outs ("PEP") for high income taxpayers
- Reinstate the overall limitation on itemized deductions (the "Pease limitation")
- Decrease amount of Dependent care credit
- Decrease Adoption credit and adoption assistance
- Decrease Student loan interest deduction, and reinstate provision that voluntary payments of interest are not deductible
- Decrease amounts that can be deducted for contribution to Education IRAs
- Reinstate estate and generation-skipping transfer taxes
- Increase the maximum gift tax rate
- Reinstate the qualified family-owned business deduction
- Reinstate tax on awards under the National Health Service Corps Scholarship Program and the F. Edward Hébert

Armed Forces Health Professions Scholarship and Financial Assistance Program

- Eliminate employer-provided educational assistance–expansion to graduate education and making the exclusion permanent
- Eliminate making work pay credit (sec. 36A)
- Eliminate refundable child credit floor amount (sec. 24(d))
- Eliminate American Opportunity Tax credit (sec. 25A(i))
- Eliminate Earned income tax credit
- Reinstate "marriage penalty"
- Decrease in dollar limitations for expensing to $125,000/500,000 (indexed) credit for certain   non business energy property (sec. 25C(g))
- Eliminate enhanced credit for health insurance costs of eligible individuals
- Eliminate election of investment credit in lieu of production tax credit
- Eliminate grants for specified energy property in lieu of tax credits
- Eliminate work opportunity tax credit targeted group status for unemployed veterans and disconnected youth
- Eliminate parity for exclusion from income for employer-provided mass transit and parking benefits
- Eliminate expansion of availability of industrial development bonds to facilities manufacturing intangible property
- Eliminate computer technology and equipment allowed as a qualified higher education expense for section 529 accounts
- Eliminate alternative motor vehicle credit for advanced lean burn technology motor vehicles and qualified hybrid motor vehicles that are passenger automobiles or light trucks

- Eliminate alternative motor vehicle credit for qualified alternative fuel vehicles
- Alternative fuel vehicle refueling property—decrease in credit rate and credit cap
- Eliminate credit for energy efficient appliances
- Premiums for mortgage insurance not deductible as interest that is qualified residence interest

Of course, none of the above counts as a tax increase. The federal government is talking about the need for tax increases as if the expiration of the Bush tax cuts doesn't count at all. As we've discussed earlier, the federal government will do what it usually does. **It will ignore the real reason for the incredible costs (the true cost of its own employees and entitlement and spending programs), and it will keep trying to redistribute what isn't there.** It will redistribute using IOUs from private sector taxpayers in the form of massive additional debt. It will say it is forced to raise taxes, and it will increase payroll taxes, income taxes and will try like heck to put in a brand new tax, a VAT (value added tax).

What Congress is quietly doing today is considering implementing a federal value added tax (VAT). A VAT is a national sales tax (in addition to all the local sales taxes) that charges x% on every transaction in the chain from the raw material to the consumer. If you buy a bicycle, you might be charged a VAT of, say, 6%. (In Europe, 20% and 25% is now commonplace.)

Unseen by you, here's what happens with the VAT:

When the ore came out of the ground to sell to the steel producer, 6% was charged. When the steel went to the bike maker, 6% was charged. When the bike maker sold it to the wholesaler, 6% was charged. When the wholesaler sold it to the retailer, 6% was charged. And when you bought it, 6% was charged.

The beauty is that you only saw 6% as a VAT tax. But the bicycle actually costs a LOT more, because the government kept getting 6% of every transaction along the way, which had to be passed along to you, the ultimate consumer. It is a "preferred" tax for governments to impose because taxpayers never really see anything but the tip of the iceberg.

Governments always start low with VAT to get you to say, "that's not too bad." Then, they've got you! Don't be fooled.

Corporations and Businesses Get Crushed, Too

It isn't only the individual taxpayer who is suffering. Corporations and businesses are also being punished with taxes that take away dollars that could be used to expand the businesses, the economy and create more jobs. In a global marketplace the ability of a business to "plow back" its earnings to expand or to enhance its own ability to compete with other nations is critical. When government takes too much in taxes it takes away capital that could be used to create growth.

The U.S. has traditionally charged corporate income taxes on the profits earned overseas by American companies if they bring their earnings home to America. This is a counter-intuitive concept. **Why would we discourage American companies from bringing home profits earned overseas to invest in our own economy?** As a quick fix to this problem, the government has just opened a one-year window with "only" a 6% corporate tax rate this year for overseas profits to be repatriated. The hope is that this would lead to investment in our own economy, but as usual they included a lot of limiting conditions. The money has to be used in only the specific ways permitted by the government, and not in others, and voluminous reports and permissions are required. And who knows what the tax rate may be after the one-year window. It has not produced the windfall of hoped-for overseas profits coming home because the rules are draconian, complex and unsure.

Many if not most other countries allow profits that their countries earn in the U.S. to be taken home tax-free and invested in their own countries.

So we have a national policy that causes American companies to invest their overseas profits overseas, and foreign companies to invest their U.S. profits back in their own countries.

If you are wondering how we expect any significant corporate investment to be made in the U.S., and where the money will come from, I can only suggest that you look again at the chapter on "Dying Private Sector, Thriving Government" to see the answer to that question. The answer is that the business sector, the free enterprise sector, is dying because of stupid and confiscatory **tax policies that actually punish acts that would be most beneficial to our economy.** But it isn't just repatriated money that is a problem. It also involves the taxation of profits actually earned in the United States.

The Organization for Economic Cooperation and Development (OECD) represents the largest industrialized nations in the world and serves as a benchmark against which U.S. corporate tax rates are compared. **The U.S. has the highest corporate tax rates, at about 40%, of all OECD nations, with an effective rate of 35%, while the OECD average is 19.5%.** The U.S. tax rate is nearly DOUBLE the OECD average. In a report written by Duanjie Chen and Jack Mintz of the University of Calgary's School of Public Policy, they state that, "of the 30 nations in the OECD, **27 cut their general corporate income tax rates since 2000,** with an average cut of more than 7 percentage points." The OECD member nations appear to generally follow what it preaches. In 2008, they produced a paper that said, **"Corporate taxes are found to be most harmful for growth,** followed by personal income taxes, and then consumption taxes." The **U.S. appears to be the only country that isn't listening.**

Think about this. If we are a free enterprise economy, and we know that the only way to add 24 million needed new jobs is for them to be created by the private sector, shouldn't we ALL care as much about business taxes as we do about personal taxes?

Businesses can't vote, and will be targeted for even more tax punishment. We must recognize, as individuals, that business taxes cost us jobs, pay and benefits, and we must oppose business and corporate tax increases as strongly as we oppose personal taxes.

"No Tax Left Behind"

Another tax that is about to increase dramatically is the capital gains tax. It will increase from 15% to 20% on January 1, 2011 with the expiration of the Bush tax cuts. Added to this will be a new Medicare tax on investment income. **At a time that we are desperate for investment in the economy, why would we INCREASE the barrier to investment?**

> It's a simple fact that people will only invest (take risk) if the potential reward justifies the risk. If you take a large risk, then have 25% taken by the government if you are lucky enough to have made a successful investment, your "net" return on the risk dollar is decreased, and thus your willingness to take the risk is also decreased.

For example, if you can make 4% guaranteed, or by accepting a higher risk you could earn 6%, some of us would take that chance. But if government takes 25% of the 6% you earned, your net is only 4.5%. It just isn't worth the risk of your money to MAYBE earn 0.5% more. That is why so much investment capital is sitting on the sidelines in America today.

The need for more tax dollars is not limited to the federal government. States, school districts and every other public entity need more money, too. They also will also be "forced" to raise your personal taxes and business taxes and fees. And they will do really crazy things to raise revenue because there will be huge opposition to personal tax increases. They will do almost anything to get federal money and they will give up long-term assets, and incur long-term debt, to get just enough money to go another year or two.

In the past 24 months, the federal government has loaned more than $39 billion to the states to provide unemployment benefits because the states ran out of money. No problem…the federal government will take income tax dollars and selectively give money to states to pay benefits that they promised, but can't deliver. The states must pay this money back, eventually, and states like Florida have already increased their unemployment tax rate by 1200% this year. The issue doesn't get a lot of national attention because the federal government is still printing money and will give more to the states, as they keep increasing the time for which they will provide unemployment benefits. But federal taxes (FUTA) and state and local taxes must go up to continue these benefits, and the Government Accounting Office and the Department of Labor have already recommended that Congress implement substantial increases.

Don't you love the fact that governments spend OUR tax dollars convincing us to give them even MORE tax dollars? We get to see the "It's only a penny" sales tactic used on us all the time when governments want to increase sales taxes. "It's only a PENNY, and look at all the great things we can do for you!" They rely on the fact that taxpayers are really stupid, and it works every time!

I don't know how much the average person spends per month buying things on which sales taxes are imposed. The amount of sales taxes, and the items on which sales taxes are charged, vary from state to state. Let's use the example of a person who spends $2,000 a month subject to sales taxes. The "It's only a PENNY," sales pitch actually means that you will pay $20 a month more to the government. You're already giving them 6% ($120 a month), and they want it to go to $140 a month. That's an increase from $1,440 a year to $1,680 a year. And if you buy a car, that's another thousand or two. If you're an average private sector worker, you only earn $37,000 a year BEFORE you pay income and property taxes and all of those other taxes. And government is taking $1,400 a year in sales taxes and wants to increase it to $1,680 a year? How are you supposed to save money for your children's college or your own retirement? But, they say, it's only a penny.

When a Tax Is Not a Tax

When is a tax not a tax? It's when your government sells income-producing assets that you have bought and paid for in order to get cash today. You will now pay much higher taxes because government has lost its income-producing asset. It also occurs when your government takes a facility you have bought and paid for, and sells it for quick cash and agrees to tax you to pay RENT on it forever. It is as if I sold YOUR house which you had bought and paid for, to someone else. I get the cash from the sale of your house, and I force you to stay there and pay rent forever.

Here's how some cities and states are picking up quick cash to defer their real problems for another year or two:

- **Arizona** picked up $735 million (for their quick "heroin fix") by selling 14 state buildings to private investors, and then agreeing to lease them back at a tidy profit to the private investors. They sold the legislative office building, the Governor's office, the state archive building, the state hospital, the state coliseum and even their death row facilities.

- **Chicago** needed quick cash and a lot of it. So they gave up an airport and its parking meters for 99 and 75 years, respectively, to bring in a total of a quick $3.6 billion. Chicago's city council approved a deal that privatized the operations of Midway Airport for 99 years and pays Chicago $2.5 billion. The city plans to use $900 million for infrastructure funding and to help offset the $9 billion unfunded pension liability for city employees. (Get it? Sell off revenue-producing assets for the better part of a century, in order to get enough cash to pay a PORTION of unfunded pension costs. Then, of course, police and fire workers will receive $225 million to pay for their services at the airport.) When Chicago privatized the city's 36,000 parking meters last December, the 75 year leasing deal brought over $1.1 billion dollars, but the new parking kiosks and increased rates sparked outrage among residents. In the best flea market tradition, Chicago also obtained quick cash by leasing its major toll-road and parking garages.

- In March 2006 **Indiana** leased its toll roads to a private consortium of Australian and Spanish investors for 75 years (until 2081) for a lump sum payment of $2.8 billion. The one-time infusion of lump sum cash is a way to cover the state's highway funding deficit with no new taxes. However, it covers the shortfall for only 10 years.

- **Detroit** whose bond rating is "junk status" sold $250 million of bonds to investors although it hasn't filed annual financial reports since 2004. It needed the cash to cover a $280 million deficit this year. The city has warned that it may need to file for bankruptcy.

- Meanwhile, **California** sold or is selling $5 billion in bonds, **Washington, D.C.** raised nearly a billion, and other deficit-ridden states like **Massachusetts** and **Connecticut** are selling more bonds to pick up needed cash. Long-term borrowing for a one-year or short-term stopgap is becoming the norm in the public sector.

All of this is done to get quick fixes for immediate financial problems. The fact that Chicago and Indiana lost income for the next 75 to 99 years in order to get cash today is for taxpayers of the future to worry about. "Kicking the can down the road" is the expression used to signify the public sector's need to hide the enormous tsunami of pension costs from unwitting taxpayers. If that doesn't work, they can issue Pension Obligation Bonds to borrow long-term money to pay a year or two of pension payments. Or, they can be like New Jersey and just skip any pension funding payments for years, pushing monstrous numbers into next year or the year after.

In spite of these imaginative one-time fixes, the public sector still needs more money from taxpayers. California is broke, broke, broke in spite of the fact that it raised taxes by $12 billion in 2009, nearly equaling the total of tax increases implemented by all 23 other states that raised taxes in 2009. Illinois is trying to raise state income taxes from 3% to 5%. The state pays pensions for one of the most generous public sector and teacher pay packages (including higher education) in America.

All elected officials have an "out." Those who created or enabled the problem are gone, and those who are new to the job can say, "Don't blame me, I didn't create this mess."

Who's Got $125 Trillion?

The United States has a huge Gross Domestic Product (GDP), which is defined as "the total market value of all final goods and services produced in a country in a given year, equal to total consumer, investment and government spending, plus the value of exports, minus the value of imports."

According to compilations by the Heritage Foundation and publicly available on Wikipedia, Americans are taxed 28% of our entire GDP. That's more than 125 countries, but less than 50 others. Germany is at 40% and Sweden and Denmark are 50%. They have a Value Added Tax that crushes taxpayers. Greece is only at 33%, and it also has provided their population with great social welfare programs. It is literally bankrupt, and it has just agreed, in order to get a $150 billion loan from the European Union (EU),

> Who is big enough to bail out America? Who's got $125 trillion?

to cut back its totally unfunded retirement and other entitlement programs, and people are literally rioting in the streets about the loss of benefits that they were entitled to. Guess that proves if you spend yourself into a very deep hole, someone else might be willing to bail you out. It's working for Greece.

Portugal, Ireland, Italy and Spain may not be far behind. They are referred to as "the PIIGS" by their EU brethren who are now worried that they will be required to bail them ALL out. It worked in the U.S. for General Motors and AIG, too. And California and other states are looking for help from the federal government (that means you and me). Just where does redistribution end? **How long can governments take from those who have acted responsibly and give it to those who have not?** Who is big enough to bail out America? Who's got $125 trillion?

> What government should be doing is to look very seriously at a "flat tax." It solves an enormous amount of problems that just cannot be fairly dealt with by using tens of thousands of pages of IRS provisions that change with the wind, and that very few can understand. Our current system allows too much gamesmanship, permits too many loopholes and results in many people escaping the payment of any income tax.

Government also needs to take a look at what is a "non-profit" and what public need is served by allowing so many business institutions to escape the payment of taxes, and to receive tax-deductible contributions. A public charity needs to be redefined to differentiate a true charity from an institution that may look, act and operate just like the private sector enterprises that it competes with.

Brace yourself for a major assault by governments and school districts getting more tax dollars to support their **unsustainable entitlement programs.** Governments and school districts will use extreme marketing methods on us, including heavy use of the "holy trinity," the "Washington Monument Ploy," and threats to cut off vital services if we don't comply.

You can bet that in spite of our protests, we will see tax increases, and fees, tolls and licenses will go up as never before in the next two years. We are "in extremis" financially at every level of government and public education, and they will act accordingly. To justify taking more tax dollars, government will have to attack those who "caused the problem"...capitalist demons.

*"Over the medium to long term, the nation is on an **unsustainable** fiscal course, and to be responsible, we must begin the process of fiscal reform now."*

—Peter Orszag, Director,
Office of Management and Budget.
March 20, 2009

_____ Chapter Ten _____

Capitalists, Profits and Demons

The free enterprise (capitalist) economy consists of those who hope to earn a profit. There are many definitions for the word profit. Several definition excerpts from the *American Heritage Dictionary* include "a gain or return; benefit" and "increase in the net worth of a business enterprise in a specific period of time" and "derive a benefit from" and "the amount received in excess of the original cost after all charges are paid." There are more definitions, of course, but these seem reasonable to use. In essence, profit means to have a gain, or to take in more than goes out in a given period of time. Capitalism seeks profits. That means we are all capitalists if we expect to invest something (our labor, time, money or investment in our own education or training) and receive a return from it.

The average American (hopefully) seeks a profit each year by taking in more than expended. They know they can't spend more than they make on a long-term basis. And many expect to make a profit by investing their earnings into improving an asset by painting the house, investing in their 401(k), putting new tires on the car or investing in their own education. They will use their profits to advance their own personal aims.

The use of our own profits is determined by the wants and needs of each of us, and it is dependent on how much of our earnings the government will allow us to have. Some of us seek security in owning assets that cannot be taken away, others want to have resources to travel or spend more time in their avocation, and yet others want to send their children to college, get that bigger house or simply to retire securely. Some even want to use their profits to give to the needy, or create institutions that will be of value to all. It doesn't really matter what the individual motivation is or was. Each of us has a motivation, and each of us has the right to pursue it. In the Constitution it's called "life, liberty, and the pursuit of happiness."

There are two types of governments that are the antithesis to profits. One is a socialist state, whereby a central government professes to abhor profit as a motive and seeks to replace it with a collective effort resulting in the equal sharing of resources with all citizens. We know that the theory never worked. In the Soviet Union and in China, the central government decided citizens place in society and the economy. Some were sent to universities and others weren't. People were told where to live and where to work. Goals were always "collective" goals, and seeking individual gain was immoral.

In communist societies, it was quickly learned that the place to "invest" was to become a part of the government itself. If you invested your time properly and moved up in government, you'd be rewarded with the big apartment or house, the "dacha" in the country, the limo and driver and power over others. The leaders of these governments were secretly the capitalists (profit seekers) of their own societies, but they didn't want anyone else to be.

In a redistributive state, profits are allowed, even encouraged. Someone has got to pay the bills! Government can then tax (take away) these profits and give the money to others who support them, or give the money to themselves. In both the socialist and the redistributive states, those who work in government are always the winners. They can take what they want, do what they want with the money, and use their taxing and policing authority to enforce their power.

If each of us who works for a living needs to have a profit by taking in more than goes out, and each needs to build assets for our own future security, why then are corporate or business profits a bad thing? I've run several small businesses, have been Chairman/CEO of a public company and Chairman of another. In every case, here was our aim:

1. **Grow.** A business maxim is, "If you're not growing, you're dying." The reason is simple: every employee, from the entry-level clerk to the president, is free to go work somewhere else. They expect that their contribution to the company through hard work will bring their company success and earn them a reward in the form of more pay. Everyone expects a raise every year. The company must grow in order to have more money to retain the people it needs, and to attract more.

2. **Take in more than goes out, or earn profits.** To do otherwise is to take less in than you spend, or take a loss. Short-term losers can survive by using savings, by borrowing money or by raising more capital to tide them over. Long-term losers go out of business.

The Demonization of Profits

Why have profits and capitalism become such inflammatory and negative words in a nation that was built on those concepts?

> In a recent poll done by Rasmussen Associates, it was found that those under 30 are equally divided in their opinions as to which is the better economy, socialist or capitalist. Our congressional leaders and even our president are blaming "corporate profits" as the demon that must be exorcised. Why do they say such things?

Redistributors want to receive gains because of who they are and what they need, not what they've done. In order to justify redistribution, they must take resources away from those who have earned them. They like to use the word "fair" to justify taking something from one person and giving it another who has less. That's fair, isn't it?

That's the thinking that goes behind our corporate income tax rates that at 39.7% are the 2nd highest in the industrialized world. That is also why small businesses, most of which file business results on personal income tax returns, can be identified as "the rich" and targeted for even higher tax rates. It's easy to get voters to agree to take money from corporations because they can't vote. And it's easy to get voters to support higher taxes on categories defined by the government as the wealthy or rich, because they are only a few million successful small businesses and individuals who don't have many votes, anyway.

What do corporations do with profits? Is there some smoke-filled room where evil old men sit around a huge pile of gold and dole it out to each other? One might think so, if Congress and our president were asked to describe profits to you. **But a corporation does the same thing with profits that you do in your own personal life.** When you take in more than went out, you have to determine if you can raise your standard of living. Get that boat? Nice vacation? Eat out more often? Invest in the markets? Maybe even get that new house? Corporations do the same thing. With the excess of after-tax income over outgo, they must determine if they can give raises to employees, and how to allocate the raises. Usually, they do that first. Raises are scary because they create a new financial floor, requiring that the coming year can be no less profitable. It's like buying a house with a bigger mortgage just because you had a good year. You've got to ask, "Is this good year repeatable and sustainable?"

In "high risk" industries (like Wall Street) corporations tend to pay out bonuses because they are one time, and do not raise the expense floor for the next year. When corporations do budgets, they do almost exactly what you would do in your own personal planning. The first question is, "Was this a windfall, or will it repeat next year?" In your case, you'd think about your own job security, and the likelihood of having the same success again next year. In the same way, the corporation will look at how it made its profit. Will the same circumstances exist next year? What about new competition? The economy? Interest rates?

High Corporate Taxes Hurt Us All

When a corporation brings in more than it pays out, it does the same thing that you do, but with a twist: **they must first pay a huge amount, averaging about 40%, in taxes.** With the 60% that is left, the corporation will consider the following questions: "Are there any large bills coming due? Is there enough in savings, or do we need to put more away for a rainy day? How much can we give in raises to our employees? Can we afford that new equipment we've been looking at? Repay loans? Paint the building? Invest in opening a new location? Hire new employees?" The bigger the corporation, the more complex the job of planning for next year and the years after that. It is all guesswork, because no one knows for sure what the next year will bring.

How do payroll taxes and 40% corporate tax rates affect you? Hang on to your hat and I'll give you an example. Let's say that you work at Behemoth, Inc., making $60,000 a year, which is the average pay at the company. Behemoth employs about 1,000 people and has sales of $100 million a year. When Behemoth paid you your $60,000 last year, they paid approximately 7.5% ($4,500) to the government in payroll taxes. You also paid 7.5% in payroll taxes, or $4,500, taken directly out of your paycheck. So, the corporation spent $64,500 paying you, and you only got $55,500 BEFORE income tax withholding took out another big chunk. The government already got $9,000, and they keep it no matter what.

That bears another look: The company cost to pay you was $64,500. You get $55,500 before you start paying income taxes. The government got the difference. It is a tax you and the corporation must pay, no matter how much the corporation loses, and no matter what your tax deductions are. And you and your corporate employer haven't even started paying income taxes yet!

Now, we get to the end of the year. Behemoth, thanks to the collective efforts of all of its employees, took in $10 million more than it spent. It has ten million in profits. But wait, before they can do anything with it, they have to give the government 40%

or $4 million first. Seems a bit unfair. You and all of your fellow employees are the ones who actually "earned" that $10 million. It doesn't matter, the corporation has to pay $4 million and that means there's only $6 million left. Let's say they want to give it all away in pay raises. (Pretty stupid, and unlikely to occur, but we're just supposing.) So, everyone can get a $6,000 raise, right? Well, not really. The corporation will have to pay 7.5% MORE than they pay you, in payroll taxes. So, they can give you a $5,580 raise. Of this $5,580 raise, the corporation will be forced to deduct $420 for your payroll taxes. So, what you actually get paid in Year 2 is $5,100 more than last year, but actually you will get less, because the government will immediately start deducting "withholding" from this years' pay. But didn't the government already get 40% of everything your company earned from your efforts? Yes, they did. And now you have to pay income taxes, and have it withheld in advance, AGAIN, on what is left? Probably ANOTHER 25%? Yes, you do. If you're thinking, "That doesn't leave very much for me," you're right.

The same thing happens to those who invest in the company. The company has to pay taxes when they earn the money, and the investor is taxed again if/when they are fortunate enough to earn a dividend. **And that, my friend, is what is meant by double taxation, and why you should be VERY concerned about corporate tax rates. It is YOUR money, whether you are an employee or an investor, taken twice.** Remember this–corporations can't vote. But you can.

Many Non-Profits are Big Businesses—But They Don't Pay Taxes to Support Our Economy

There is a type of business in the U.S. that is "neither fish nor fowl," as we discussed in Chapter Two. It is often referred to as a "non-profit" but the IRS calls it an "exempt" organization. Since profit is achieved by taking in more than is paid out, does that mean that non-profits lose money every year? How do they stay in business? Of course they must take in more than they pay out. If they didn't, they too would go out of business. They just don't call excess of income over outgo profits. Like governments, they rename their profits, calling it "surplus." And, unlike profit which is seemingly a very dirty word, surplus is a very good thing.

The really neat thing about that is government and non-profits can take in more than they pay out (sometimes much, much more), but this is surplus and that means they don't have to pay income taxes. The government itself doesn't really know how to categorize these exempt organizations in their census and financial reporting. They are not government, so they are usually counted as being in the private sector. But many look and act much more like government organizations than private sector companies.

Like government, **exempt organizations do not pay income taxes,** because they do not make a so-called profit. **They are exempt from paying most other taxes like property taxes and sales taxes.** They can collect money from tax-deductible donations and they can charge for tuition, admission fees, medical services and a host of other things. They get to keep 100% of what they get, which is a very good thing for their employees! They have a problem if they finish a year with too much in surplus because then the contributors might say, "I think they don't need it, so I'll give my contributions to someone else." That could cause a problem. So the solution is, "We've got to spend it!", and the nicest way to do that is on pay and benefits for officers and employees. That's why, if you look at large non-profits, you'll often see pay and benefits even better than the government gives itself.

There are many kinds of non-profits. There are struggling and small charities like soup kitchens that endeavor to stay afloat to fulfill their basic mission. These are the charitable organizations that most people think of when they think of non-profits. The term conjures up the thought of volunteers or poorly paid people, suffering personal deprivation for the good of others. They do exist, and they help establish the public perception that non-profits are really great because they do not have that ugly profit incentive.

But there are some non-profits that have revenues and assets that will boggle your mind. Would you guess that Goodwill Industries had $2.4 BILLION in revenues last year? Or that the Salvation Army had $3 BILLION in revenues? Some of the biggest non-profits include institutions like Battelle Memorial Institute, Harvard University and the Mayo Clinic. Others include state universities and non-profit hospitals and hospital groups.

All non-profits get a "free ride" in that they don't have to pay taxes for national defense, government bureaucracy, public schools and welfare payments, while private sector businesses do. And we've seen that when private sector business must pay taxes, that is money earned that they cannot give to their own employees or to grow their companies.

> Whether these non-profit organizations are directly paid by taxpayers via grants or service contracts, or whether they just avoid paying taxes because of their exempt status, the taxpayer "supports" them by paying for all the government services that the non-profits don't have to pay for.

Except for the fact that they don't pay taxes, it is difficult to distinguish many huge non-profit institutions from for-profit enterprises. They both provide a service, they charge for it and they usually take in more than they pay out. They use their profits or surplus to expand, give raises, pay off debt or set up reserves. There are colleges, universities and hospitals that fall into both categories. **We're trained by those who want to demonize capitalism to believe that non-profit equals good, while for-profit equals bad.**

What is hardly ever recognized is that 92% of all the publicly-traded businesses in America do not pay dividends. This means that they do NOT distribute profits to their owners. They use their profits to grow, to invest in doing whatever they do, and to become bigger and better. What, then, is the difference between huge non-profit public charities and for-profit publicly-traded corporations?

There is essentially no difference, except that non-profits pay no income taxes, and most don't pay property or sales taxes, either.

> The private sector companies and their 108 million employees must pay, directly or indirectly, the taxes to provide all of the government services and protection that the non-profits don't have to pay for.

Who ever really looks at these non-profit institutions from the perspective of someone whose tax dollars are being used, directly or indirectly, to support them? Perhaps we should take a closer look. Their revenues, surpluses, compensation and benefits might surprise you.

We're helped by a legal requirement that requires non-profits to file Form 990 and make it available to the public. At www.Guidestar.org you can find the Form 990 for virtually any non-profit. We looked at just a few. **The following is just a sampling of what we found:**

- **Battelle Memorial Institute.** It's a non-profit 501(c)3 public charity engaged in research and in operations of nuclear establishments under government contracts, among other things. They employ 9,000 people and revenues in the year ending September 2008 were $4.6 BILLION. Of that, $3.7 billion came from government grants and $851 million came from "program services revenues, including government fees and contracts." The president made $2.2 million and the EVP made $2.7 million. The next 18 officers averaged $497,000 each. Their five highest-paid people who are NOT officers or directors earned $560,000 each. It's nice they all did so well, but the American economy did not get a penny in taxes from these employers.

- **Harvard.** According to an article called "Harvard's role as a Nonprofit" in *The Harvard Crimson* (May 21, 2009), "Harvard built its endowment from $4.7 billion in 1990 to $37 billion in 2008 because it did not pay taxes on those gains. Relative to businesses, the federal government is subsidizing Harvard's investment fund." (Apparently, no one told the Harvard students that the federal government didn't subsidize these gains...the taxpayer did.) The article went on to add, "Harvard received $535 million in federal grants in fiscal 2008 that accounted for 82% of Harvard's research revenue. Under the federal stimulus package, federal grants to Harvard are expected to increase considerably."

According to their form 990, Harvard's total revenue for the period ending June 2008 was $6.7 billion. Of that, $3.8 billion came from tax-free income from investments and $500 million came from government grants. The average full professor salary is $185,000, but *American Scene* said that can easily double because they are allowed to work as consultants to private companies. That's chump change compared to the folks at Harvard that managed those investment portfolios. **They earned up to $35 million EACH in 2007.** You can bet that the pay and benefits for all of their employees is very good. This is a "public charity?" **And did you notice that the article above said Harvard was getting stimulus money? Stimulus money?**

- **Mayo Clinic.** Revenues were $6.5 billion. They got $450 million from contributions and grants. They are the biggest of the big "non-profits" in the health care field. The Cleveland Clinic is at $3.1 billion. Then there's New York-Presbyterian Hospital at $2.3 billion and Mount Sinai at $1.7 billion, with Memorial-Sloan Kettering at $1.6 billion.

- **Other shockingly large non-profits to note:**
    YMCA of the USA at $5.4 billion in revenues
    United Way at $4.1 billion
    The Salvation Army at $5.3 billion
    Goodwill Industries at $2.6 billion
    Boys & Girls Clubs of America at $1.3 billion.

Unions are also considered non-profits. Trade and membership associations are non-profits. Most private K-12 schools, all public colleges and universities, most private universities, most museums and most hospitals are classified non-profits. None of these institutions support the American economy or running of the government through taxes. All gain tax advantages because they are considered non-profit.

To employees working at these places, what's the difference between their job and a private sector job? The difference is that if their employer is non-profit, the employer can take in contributions tax-free, earn investment income tax-free, and avoid paying income, real estate or sales taxes. It means that very little scrutiny is applied to the benefits and compensation provided by these employers to their employees. This means that non-profits can have a LOT of money to spend on themselves and their employees that private sector companies don't have, because the government does make private sector companies pay income taxes, sales taxes, taxes on investment gains and real estate taxes.

> If government doesn't pay taxes, and if non-profits don't pay taxes, and if public sector employees are tax recyclers because they are paid via taxes in the first place, where DO the new, increasing, tax dollars come from that are needed to run our government, our country and public school systems? You know the answer to that one.

The next question should be, "Doesn't that mean that it's only the employers and employees in the free enterprise part of our economy that actually have to bear the **total cost** of government and private education and subsidies to the non-profits?" You know the answer to that one, too.

So, if profits are a bad thing, those who make them must be bad, too, right? Well, it doesn't always work out that way, especially when those who gain strength by demonizing others need the help of people who make an awful lot of money themselves. That results in what I'll call "selective demonization."

Elected Officials Demonizing Capitalism

First, let's take a look at those it is politically correct to demonize, and who is doing the demonizing. Just a few quotes are found below, made recently by our national leaders. They know that, like any major advertiser, they need to repeat and repeat their message:

> *"I did not run for office to be helping out a bunch of fat cat bankers on Wall Street."*
> —President Obama

> *"...why is it that people are mad at the banks?...America's gone through the worst economic year that it's gone through in decades, and you guys caused the problem."*
> —President Obama

> *"...a few companies made out like bandits by exploiting their customers."*
> —President Obama

> *"Senate Republicans have once again chosen to protect the interests of Wall Street over the interests of families on Main Street."*
> —House Majority Leader Steny Hoyer (D-MD

> *"...unless your business model depends on bilking people, there is little to fear from these new rules..."*
> —President Obama

> *"...remind us all of the terrible price our country paid for Wall Street recklessness..."*
> —Senator Chris Dodd (D-CT)

> *"We're going to take things away from you on behalf of the common good."*
> —Secretary of State Hillary Clinton when she was a U.S. Senator (D-NY)

> *"...the fight against the harshest aspects of unrestricted capitalism is therefore a political problem..."*
> —Rep. Barney Frank (D-MA)

Senator Claire McCaskill, Democrat of Missouri, reacting to reports of extravagant perks and bonuses had blasted Wall Street executives as *"a bunch of idiots"* who were *"kicking sand in the face of the American taxpayer."*

"The greed and excess on Wall Street, there is no question that has spiraled out of control." —Senate Majority Leader Harry Reid

"Allowing the market to work is code for letting the greedy insurance companies" deny care to the sick and elderly.

—Majority Leader Reid as quoted by Senator DeMint (R-SC)

"Put me down as clearly as you possibly can as one who wants to have those tax cuts for the wealthiest in America repealed," and the Bush tax cuts have been *"the biggest contributor to the budget deficit."* —House Speaker Nancy Pelosi

"In an age tarnished by corporate greed, how refreshing it is to see a man of obvious gifts choose to lead a life of public service."

—Majority Leader Harry Reid on Tim Geithner's nomination to Treasury Secretary

"A triple punch of corporate greed, consumer debt and lax government oversight has left Nevada and our country facing the worst financial crisis since the Great Depression,"

—Majority Leader Harry Reid

"We are cutting taxes for millions of working families and ending the irresponsible tax giveaways that the Bush Administration doled out to the super wealthy." —Majority Leader Harry Reid

"As you know, the people in Southern Nevada have been hit hard during these tough times caused largely by unbridled corporate greed and complicit government action during the 8 years of the Bush administration…But do the insurance companies care? No they don't…while making record profits and handing out obscene bonuses." —Representative Tina Titus (D-NV)

Those big corporations and their greed. They're stealing your children's future." —Television ad by presidential candidate John Edwards

"Corporate greed has undercut the health of our economy."

—Senator Mark Pryor (D-AR)

"I have said corporate greed…four years ago I spoke against… corporate greed." —Senator John McCain (R-AZ)

"…do what is right for the American people, put government on the side of the American people, stop the greed and corruption on Wall Street." —Sarah Palin (former Alaska governor)

"So when you go up against the Far Right you go up against the big financial special interests like the Halliburtons of the world, the big oil companies, the big energy companies, who work so hard to rip us off." —Senator Barbara Boxer (I-VT)

"We have a duty to protect the American people from the corporate greed of these for-profit, publicly-traded health insurance companies." —Senator Diane Feinstein (D-CA)

SEIU President Andy Stern said business leaders *"believe in this old market-worshipping, privatizing, deregulating, trickle-down (policy) that took the greatest economy on earth and sent it staggering forward because of their greed and their selfishness."*

"One-third of the health care dollar goes to no such thing as health care, it goes to the insurance companies." —Rep. Patrick Kennedy

"We're having trouble growing and strengthening the middle class because corporate power and greed have literally taken over the government." —Senator John Edwards (D-NC)

"Workers and their unions, who were the victims of corporate greed…" —Bernard Sanders (I-VT)

"…the recent financial crisis was not a natural disaster. It was a man-made economic assault. People did it. Extreme greed was the driving force." —Senator Carl Levin (D-MI)

"We met again today to examine yet another massive corporate failure. We have heard this sad song of corporate greed and regulatory breakdowns one too many times… The vents…add another verse to this troubling refrain in American Capitalism."

—Rep. Paul Kanjorski (D-PA)

"Quite simply, corporate greed, collusion and illusion have become legion." —Rep. Bill Pascrell (D-NJ)

"But when we peel back all the layers of this crisis, its foundation is nothing more than a single concept: Greed."

—Senator Harry Reid (D-NV)

"…I refuse to let America go back to the culture of irresponsibility and greed…" —President Barack Obama

"We're not going to have a middle class if we allow a lot of anti-labor, anti-union operators to get in politics and tear to shreds the fundamental things we all agree on."

—Pat Quinn, Governor of Illinois (D)

"What's frustrating to me is when these very wealthy groups that have received the benefits of all these tax cuts then fund lobbyists to come up to Topeka and say we need to cut even more. I mean the greed is getting just beyond me being able to tolerate."

—Mark Parkinson, Governor of Kansas (D)

The Audacity of Hype

Can government demonize those who oppose it, no matter who they are? Consider a ruling by the United States Supreme Court. It recently ruled to allow, under First Amendment rights, broader opportunity for corporations to speak in support of or opposition to candidates or their opinions. Under the "separation of powers" requirements, the Supreme Court must be the watchdog that protects our constitutional rights. The question had come before it, and the court answered with its ruling.

The president of the United States openly criticized the Supreme Court, first in his weekly address to the nation, and then in his State of the Union address. In his weekly address, he said, "The United States Supreme Court handed down a huge victory to special interests and their lobbyists, and a powerful blow to our efforts to rein in corporate influence. This ruling strikes at democracy itself."

Then he berated the Supreme Court again in his nationally-televised State of the Union address, an annual report to Congress. The Supreme Court Justices are invited guests, although there is no official reason for them to be there. Their presence is a courtesy to the president and it provides gravitas to the setting. The president said, "Last week, the Supreme Court reversed a century of law to open the floodgates for special interests—including foreign corporations—to spend without limit in our elections. Well I don't think American elections should be bankrolled by America's most powerful interests, or worse, by foreign entities. They should be decided by the American people, and that's why I'm urging Democrats and Republicans to pass a bill that helps to right this wrong." He is urging Congress to pass a law to override the Supreme Court, to "right this wrong." That is a very chilling statement coming from a president with overwhelming majorities in both houses of Congress.

What was particularly troubling was the blatant hypocrisy of the president's statement to the nation, concerning "opening the floodgates to special interests," clearly meaning private sector corporations. Let's look at one example during Obama's own presidential campaign. National personality Bruce Springsteen performed numerous concerts for then-Senator Obama during the 2008 campaign. Typically, anyone could go online, enter their name and email address (I'll bet it was given to the Democratic party or Obama campaign), and get a free ticket to see "The Boss" perform and hear him express support for Obama. Tens of thousands of people attended these free concerts, for which they collectively would have had to pay many millions to attend if it were a normal concert tour event. Yet, **the millions of dollars that were effectively donated by Springsteen to draw people to see candidate Obama didn't count as campaign contributions.**

Similarly, we've seen how the SEIU **spent more than $65 million** on the Obama campaign, and was rewarded with pro-union Executive Orders and two top government posts. Yet the president told the nation that the Supreme Court decision that allowed disclosed and transparent campaign contributions by those who might not support him "strikes at democracy itself." This is the president of the United States, criticizing the United States Supreme Court in front of the entire nation for taking an action that "strikes at democracy itself?" It is a breathtaking example of the opportunity for an elected official to use his stage to demonize anyone, even if it is a separate branch of government established specifically to keep the power of Congress and the president in check.

When a member of Congress dares to suggest that a piece of proposed legislation has some flaws, the president will attack them, too. Not on the grounds that he disagrees with them, but on the grounds that they have been bought or influenced by persons or parties not to his liking. The *Wall Street Journal* reported that when Senator Richard Shelby (R-Alabama) presented an amendment to modify rules governing a proposed new bureaucracy, The Consumer Finance Protection Bureau, the president said, "I will not allow amendments like this one written by Wall Street's lobbyists to pass for reform." The proposed bureau does not regulate Wall Street at all, and the proposed amendment had nothing to do with Wall Street. But the temptation to demonize was, once again, too great to resist.

Who Gets Demonized? And Who Doesn't?

There are some very rich people, who make huge money and control huge corporate interests who generally do not get demonized, and who do not get accused of greed. In most cases, they are those who support the party in power...for instance, many of our movie stars and folks in the entertainment business. People like Michael Moore, a multimillionaire whose films have grossed hundreds of millions, and who has a number of corporate ventures, or Oprah Winfrey, one of the richest women in America, who heads a corporate empire, or Bruce Springsteen, "The Boss." These are truly exceptional people. They are rare in their abilities. They have risen to the top of their fields through hard work, great skill and sacrifice. They have experienced "the American Dream." We recognize and salute their accomplishments whether we agree with their political views or not. We see them earning millions or tens of millions of dollars a year or more, and we never hear anyone claim that they are greedy.

Why, then, do we not accord similar respect to the extremely rare and gifted individuals who rise to the top of the corporate ladder? These people are every bit as talented and hardworking, and just as rare. They have worked decades and have proven their worth through their performance. They have the proven ability to make the right decisions involving a huge array of complex questions. They can and do make decisions that are life and death to their companies and their shareholders. They can and do earn billions of dollars for their investors. They do contribute to the American economy. Why, then, do we place them in a special category, the category of corporations, and demonize them?

Of course, the federal government doesn't demonize ALL corporations nor ALL fat cats, especially not those who support the government, or that it controls. Top officers in Fannie Mae and Freddie Mac made **millions upon millions in pay and bonuses while they made massive sub-standard loans** that helped tanked the economy. They were lending trillions of dollars to those who did not have adequate down payments to obtain a mortgage, nor adequate income to make the payments. While giving out more and more of the absurdly free money for mortgages, they actually paid themselves and their fellow officers bonuses based on the volume of loans they were making.

> While there certainly is plenty of blame to go around, most of those in the finance field have recognized that it was the **requirement of the federal government** that all banks were forced to loan money to unqualified individuals, thus causing the need to attempt to "bundle" these sub-prime loans with groups of qualified loans in order to have anyone willing to own these mortgages.

While the "greed" of Wall Street has made headlines for months, Congress and the government have deflected attention from their own contributions to the financial collapse by keeping pressure exerted, and the press focused, on the banking industry and away from Fannie Mae and Freddie Mac. Congress recently upped its bailout limit to its two pet GSEs (government sponsored enterprises) to an unlimited maximum. This will in no way deflect its potential to create another massive real estate meltdown, nor does it deal with the issue of incredible executive pay that has been earned by executives of these organizations.

Thanks to Robert Wilmers, CEO of M&T Bank Corporation, the extent of irresponsibility and greed at GSE's Fannie Mae and Freddie Mac received national exposure in a *Wall Street Journal* op-ed piece. Excerpts from his speech addressing the profligacy at Fannie Mae and Freddie Mac are worth recounting here:

> *"At the end of 2009 their total debt—either held directly by them or as guarantees on mortgage securities they'd sold to investors—was $8.1 trillion... To date, the federal government has been forced to pump $126 billion into Fannie and Freddie. That's far more than AIG, which absorbed $70 billion of government largesse, and General Motors and Chrysler, which shared $77 billion... One former CEO, Franklin Raines, received $91 million in compensation from 1998 through 2003. In 2006, the top five Fannie Mae executives shared $34 million in compensation, while their counterparts at Freddie Mac shared $35 million. In 2009, even after the financial crash and as these two GSE's fell deeper into the red, the top five executives at Fannie Mae received $19 million in compensation and the CEO earned $6 million."*

Also pointed out by Wilmers was the fact that between 2001 and 2006, **Fannie Mae and Freddie Mac spent $123 million to lobby Congress, the second highest in the country.** It included sizable contributions to supportive members of Congress. Think about that for a minute. Should a GSE be allowed to "pay back" those who support it **with taxpayer dollars** (millions of them, in this case) by making more than $100 million dollars of campaign contributions? Is that not insane?

Congress created and sustains Fannie Mae and Freddie Mac as government sponsored enterprises. They are the largest political contributors to Messrs. Dodd and Frank, and are among the largest political contributors in the entire nation. **Congress exempted them from paying taxes, yet they are a publicly-traded company.** While appearing to be in the private sector they have given Congress the opportunity to create a proxy that **can incur $8 trillion of debt that does not need to appear on any government financial statements.** And they have never been placed by the federal government as demons that need to be dealt with. They need to attack those who they do not control while rewarding those that they do.

As we said in Chapter One of this book, in order for a political party to gain enough votes to establish a redistributive government, they need a crisis, they need dependents and they need demons. We've shown you how they have moved to establish and continue all three requirements. The result has been to squeeze the private sector, the "engine" of our economy nearly to death. That means the private sector is dying, and that means that jobs in the private sector have disappeared.

The private sector and taxpayers pay for and support the government and education services, yet GSEs (who may make billions of dollars), non-profits (many are large companies that are actually indistinguishable from for-profit companies) and others don't pay taxes. There is an **unsustainable** level of burden and unfunded liabilities, brought on by the government and public sectors, which the private sector pays for. Yet their "profits" are demonized and they are taxed the second-highest corporate tax in the world. What is wrong with this picture?

For America to grow and prosper, creating the 20 million jobs that are needed in our economy today and dealing with our difficult future, voters will have to get government out of the way, and unleash the private sector.

*"...there are few paths forward more destructive, more painful, and more irresponsible than the one advanced by those clinging to the **unsustainable** status quo."*

—Congressman Paul Ryan (Republican).
February 3, 2009

Chapter Eleven

Back to a Sustainable America: Unleash the Private Sector

You've read ten chapters of "gloom and doom", and you are probably depressed about the outlook for free enterprise and for our nation by now. Don't be. There is a lot we can do to bring America back to the vibrant, robust and free economy that it once was. It certainly won't be easy, but it won't be as hard as you may think, either. There are some simple things that we can do, and this chapter will outline many of them.

Before we attack the problem of getting government spending under control, we must face some realities that have not been previously addressed in this book but are vital to our nation's survival and prosperity...to our sustainability. **A free enterprise nation must be kept free from those who want to harm it.** National defense should be the highest priority of the federal government, and it must not be allowed to suffer from the inevitable "belt-tightening" that lies ahead.

Contained in our defense budget are the annual ongoing costs to provide for the retirement benefits of those who have served our nation. It disguises the amount that we are paying for current national defense expenditures, **making it appear that we spend more for national defense than we really do.** That's why it appears that despite the fact that we are spending huge amounts for national defense, we are maintaining our current military readiness at lower than acceptable levels.

We need to put all retirement costs as a separate budget that is funded appropriately, and establish a separate "active force" defense budget so we can see what we are really paying for our nation's defense. We will see that it is not enough. Our Navy has fewer warships than we had in 1911. Our Air Force is using 50 year old bombers and refueling tankers and 40 year old fighter aircraft. Our Army and Marine Corps are too small and they suffer the same deprivation of having the best and most effective equipment our nation can provide. The husbands, wives and children they must leave behind when they fight for us are not given the full support that a grateful nation should provide. We must not allow our federal government to save money at the expense of our national security and national defense. We actually need to spend more to protect our brave men and women who risk their lives every day in service to us, and to nurture their families left behind, sometimes permanently. That means we must do the BEST we can do for them, not the least we can do.

Domestic security is and will continue to be an ongoing challenge that must be met. I can remember when you could visit the Hoover Dam without going through security checks, and when you could arrive at the airport 15 minutes before flight time and get on the plane. We have come to accept that we must live our lives under high security precautions because there are people who want to kill as many of us as they can, regardless of age, sex, religion, color or national origin. With today's powerful weapons, they can accomplish their aim. Many experts believe that a horrific event of mass destruction is inevitable in the U.S.

The U.S. defense policy has been to find and eliminate those who plan our destruction by eliminating these threats at the source. It seems the only viable policy unless you believe that thousands and thousands of Americans should die, and that we should later attempt to find and punish "the guy that did it." Many of us have led long and full lives, but our children and grandchildren haven't.

God bless those who risk their lives to defend them, and if they are willing to go in harm's way to stop the bad guys before they kill our children and our grandchildren, I can only praise their heroism every day, and pray that they come home safely.

Our policy to seek and disable those who are planning to kill us has some negative diplomatic and commercial consequences, and it is expensive. It may also make us unpopular at home with those who don't fully understand the risks of a failure to prevent a strike. It also makes us unpopular with some other nations, usually those nations that are not themselves targets and may be unlikely to face the consequences of a weapon of mass destruction in their own countries. If our efforts mean that we are seen by some as too determined or too aggressive in efforts to prevent deaths of our own citizens at home, then so be it.

Failure of a strong preemptive mission thwarting those who plan to attack us would mean the loss of tens or hundreds of thousands of men, women and children, all of whom are guilty of nothing more than being American. We must never take for granted that our national defense is government's highest priority.

A corollary to our need for a strong defense policy is our space policy. The exploration of space is not "let's go see what's out there." Space is where satellites are, and they are being placed by many nations. Satellites have become critical to our communications and to our national defense. Recent demolition of much of NASA and the manned space program means that we will rely on other nations to carry our astronauts to space when we need to go, and we'll be depending on nations that are not particularly friendly to us. It isn't in our nation's interests to abandon our space program, but we are doing so to "save money," while billions upon billions of dollars are being taken by the federal government and redistributed to those who support it. Very bad idea.

Now that I've addressed my opinion of the need to spend even more on national defense and the space program, it's time to look at the places where we can save our free enterprise economy by implementing changes that will ignite the growth of the private sector, and create millions upon millions of new jobs.

We Must Eliminate "Fear of Government"

I once said, as a joke, the economy would soar if government would take a couple of years off and promise to do nothing. Upon reflection, that's no joke. We live virtually every day in fear of what our own government will do to us next.

Many large businesses are sitting on huge cash assets, as are many individuals. They're afraid to invest or spend because they don't know what the president and Congress will do next. Congress is on television almost every day talking about some new way to implement another tax or a new law. It clobbered America with health care reform, and people are still trying to figure out what the 2,400 pages of mumbo jumbo means, and whether the next Congress will repeal it or the Supreme Court will rule it unconstitutional.

Meanwhile, Congress has moved on to the next series of ways to meddle with our economy and our lives. Will it be Cap and Trade? Value added taxes? Income tax increases? Creation of new bureaucracies? Borrow even more to give more stimulus money to the state governments? Will the rest of the world start telling us, "We want a little more interest on all those Treasuries you want us to buy," creating inflation? Will the Fed keep printing more money? Will our absolutely INSANE Congress borrow even more money? We are in a government bubble, and we're all afraid it will burst. And almost every state, county, city and school board is trying to get even more tax dollars, too.

During the Great Depression, President Roosevelt famously said, "All we have to fear is fear itself." I like to think I would have answered with, "Wrong, Mr. President. All we have to fear is you and your government itself."

Business hates uncertainty. It has enough trouble dealing with the built-in uncertainty that every one of us faces. When you add in government activism, you make uncertainty the major issue for every business. And when there is uncertainty, the best business leaders will "keep their powder dry" to be able to deal with government's next actions.

89,000 Taxing Authorities Is Too Many!

Employers must deal with federal and nonfederal taxation, as do individuals in the private sector. In American football, there is a rule against "piling on." Once the ball carrier has been tackled, numerous referees are in place to protect the ball carrier from being pummeled by opposing players. Unfortunately, there is no rule against "piling on" when it comes to the protection of the private sector taxpayer in the United States.

> America's 89,000 public sector institutions have the ability to tax, or to charge fees or tolls, in order to obtain the funding that they want. There is no ultimate authority with the power to limit the cumulative amount of taxes that can be levied by these institutions. **The result is that each public sector entity independently determines its needs without reference to the total impact on the person or business being taxed.** To make matters worse for the taxpayer, most of these entities are free to incur debt and liabilities that will automatically add even more burdens to the taxpayer with each passing year.

No holistic approach has been taken with respect to the destructive tax impact imposed by the endless list of different taxpayer-supported public sector entities. They are increasing taxes and incurring unlimited debt and hidden liabilities that must be paid by individuals and private sector businesses. **Even with debt and deficits at historic levels, the federal government has plans to continue multitrillions of dollars of deficit spending for the next decade.** Many states are also at historic levels of deficit spending and yet do not reduce the inherent cost of government by eliminating or restraining the cost of unsustainable levels of pay and benefits for public sector employees.

Attempts have been made to control government spending with Taxpayer Bill of Rights (TABOR) legislation. Colorado is the first to implement this well-intended legislation that didn't go far enough.

261

While it limits the ability of government to raise taxes based on inflation and population growth rates, it sets itself up for the Washington Monument ploy. Government can and does say, "OK, if you don't give me more money, I have no choice but to reduce or eliminate _____" (fill in the blank with whatever taxpayers want most).

The fatal flaw is that the legislation does not require full and complete disclosure of pay and benefits costs, and unfunded liabilities calculated to private sector standards. This would allow Colorado taxpayers to actually SEE where the money is going and take steps to confront the problem. Taxpayers in Colorado have already amended TABOR to spend more on education (teacher's pay) and are considering other ways to circumvent the bill's original intentions.

Significant tax reform is definitely needed at every level. U.S. corporate tax rates are among the highest in the industrialized world. Capital gains taxes are slated to increase from 15% to 20%, and a new Medicare tax of an additional 3.5% is being imposed. Individuals face huge income, property and sales taxes.

> Corporations, small businesses and their employees will have to work together if free enterprise is to survive in America. The businesses have the money and the workers have the votes. And, boy, do they have the votes. There are 108 million employed, 12 million unemployed, and about 35 million "stay at home" parents and voting age children in the private sector. Working together they can change anything they want to!

Individuals who work in the private sector have become disconnected from the realization that they ARE the private sector, and they ARE the corporations and companies that are so often demonized by the redistributors in Congress. They must actually fight for, and vote for, corporate taxes to be reduced, because they–and the American economy–will be the direct beneficiaries of those changes. And they must fight for, and vote for those who support legislation that is friendly to the private sector, and fight against those who oppose it. Don't forget, there are billions of dollars fighting on the other side of this issue.

> In essence, all players in the private sector–free enterprise–must get on the same page. They are currently scattered, and unless they unify, they will be conquered.

The problem is that some companies apparently plan on being the "last man standing" as government takes over more and more of our economy. That won't work. Free enterprise needs unity. We rarely see one company or industry fighting in defense of another, or banding together to fight for the basic fundamental preservation of free enterprise. We've got to see that start happening.

There has been remarkable silence as Wall Street, the banking industry, the auto industry and the insurance industry have been targeted as demons to be blamed for the ills of our economy. Where was the unified private sector outrage expressed at the president or Congress blaming an entire industry, as if there were no good players in the entire field? Such talk would be called stereotyping or prejudiced if applied by anyone else.

The private sector employers and employees need to work together and consider the words of Pastor Martin Niemöller, in a poem named "First They Came…" It was part of a speech given in 1946 in Frankfurt, Germany:

> *They came first for the Communists, and I didn't speak up because*
> *I wasn't a Communist.*
> *Then they came for the trade unionists, and I didn't speak up because*
> *I wasn't a trade unionist.*
> *Then they came for the Jews, and I didn't speak up because I wasn't a Jew.*
> *Then they came for me, and by that time no one was left to speak up.*

Rein in Government and Unleash Free Enterprise

We've seen that the federal government collects about $2.5 trillion in taxes and spends $4 trillion. We've seen how the federal government spends billions, even trillions, of tax dollars engaging in activities that are essentially valueless to taxpayers, or in violation of the authority that we provided to them. We've seen that nonfederal public sector entities collect about $2.2 trillion in taxes, and spend countless billions more than that by issuing bonds, leasing assets and by not paying their bills and/or not making required pension deposits. Conservatively, our governments are spending $2 trillion a year more than they are collecting in taxes. A huge portion of their spending is to provide vastly disproportionate pay and benefits to public sector workers. There is too much gamesmanship of the system, and too much waste. In addition they have incurred an estimated $125 trillion in unfunded liabilities for pension, benefits and entitlement programs. And they are not transparent, hiding information about benefits plans and the costs to taxpayers, and fooling the public by establishing their own self-serving "accounting standards."

We've seen that government has set no overall limit on the collective taxes that 89,000 different public sector entities can take from individuals and businesses. And how many entities are not taxed at all. We've seen how unions collect dues from public sector workers that are then funneled back to support elected officials who support the unions and provide more taxpayer dollars to public sector workers. And we've seen that a redistributive government will run rampant over individual constitutionally guaranteed rights.

As this book was being prepared for final editing before printing, I received the Free Enterprise Nation **Top Ten Research Cites of the Week** (FEN Top Ten). Weekly updates are available from FEN for free. Subscribe at TheFreeEnterpriseNation.org. Highlights this particular week included:

- Congress is furiously debating the passage of financial reform that will create a new bureaucracy and implement even more government control over our banking system.

- Eighteen states have said they will be unable to form the high-risk insurance pools required in the health care reform act.

- Harrisburg, PA is considering bankruptcy because they owe $68 million in bond payments and don't have the money to pay.

- Oakland, CA teachers will strike for another day because they want raises the city can't afford (creating havoc for parents who must find a way to care for their children while they are at work).

- The National Education Association and the American Federation of Teachers voiced support for the Keep Our Teachers Working Act pending in Congress that would provide another $23 billion in federal funding to states to pay teachers.

- Another bill, the Local Jobs for America Act, also contains provisions for paying public school teachers.

We are beyond the point of mere tweaking of tax and public policy. Massive changes must be made, and started immediately. To save our American free enterprise economy, we must rein in the public sector and unleash the private sector. This will require immediate and determined steps to be taken by elected officials at every level of government and public education.

The changes that must be made are fair and moral. They are necessary to level the playing field between public and private sector employees, and they are necessary to provide American citizens with the knowledge they need to elect government that will serve their individual and collective interests. It is our government and we have the right to do that and to require our elected officials at every level to do so. And we must do that, now.

The following are not things that you can do unless you are an elected official. But they are things you can tell your elected official, whether a President, Governor, Senator, Congressman or a member of a local town council or school board. You can say, "If you want my vote, you must accomplish these things, and if you don't, I will vote against you when you come up for reelection."

Here's what we should tell our elected officials that we want:

A. Insist on Financial Transparency

First and foremost, we must demand that every single public sector entity, all 89,000 of them, provide reporting and accounting to us in accordance to the standards that we require and in a clear and uniform way. That means the actuarial, accounting and financial reporting must be done in accordance with our standards, not GASB standards—not the kind of standard that Enron used before it toppled, which is what government uses now.

Taxpayers must see what the actual debt and unfunded liability is in order to fully recognize the emerging costs, and to prudently deal with the issues related to them. If we really do have $125 trillion in debt and unfunded liabilities, we can deal with it. We are a great nation with amazing resources. **But we cannot deal with what we cannot see.**

We must have a Taxpayer Disclosure requirement at every public sector entity, from the federal government down to the smallest town and school district. The disclosure should be done in a uniform, clear format—not mumbo jumbo that no one will be able to read—and it must be provided annually on a website and upon request, in writing. It should contain the following:

For nonfederal governments and public school districts:

1. There must be an independent actuarial valuation of the current liabilities of existing health insurance and pension plans. The valuation must use actual data from retirements during the past 5 years for the purposes of establishing assumptions about pension payments. Do not allow spiking and gamesmanship any further with pensions. This is taxpayer money used unethically. But if past spiking or disability designations have created a higher than planned retirement benefit, it must be built in to the assumptions. The discount

rate (interest rate assumption) must be the average of U.S. bond rates for the preceding 5 years. Actuarial calculations must be completed by independent actuaries, in accordance with private sector (FASB) standards, at least every 5 years.

2. The actuarially determined "present value of future liabilities" must be incorporated as debt on all financial statements.

3. The public sector must provide Balance Sheet, Profit and Loss and Cash Flow statements annually.

4. Compensation for every public sector employee (without name) must be listed online, and with the direct compensation, overtime and employer portion of payments for each employee for each and every benefits plan. This is taxpayer money and we have a right to know how it is spent.

5. Outlines of the benefits provided in each and every employee benefits plan should be readily available online and in writing.

6. Pensions paid (without name) for every retiree and beneficiary of the plan must be listed online at least annually, and must include the employer paid portion of each and every benefits plan.

For the federal government:

1. Require that the federal government obtain audited financial statements that are not qualified by the auditors, in accordance with existing law.

2. Provide a unified balance sheet, showing all debt and unfunded liabilities. Audited financial statements must be produced annually as a condition of any elected federal official or civilian federal employee receiving a paycheck.

3. The actuarially determined "present value of future liabilities" must be incorporated as debt on all financial statements.

B. Take Immediate Corrective Action on Pay and Benefits

1. Establish systems and standards to assure that public sector pay and benefits are appropriate to the job, and consistent with private sector norms in the same locale.

2. Do what the private sector did in the late 1980s and early 1990s. **Except** for military and high-risk occupations, immediately terminate all public sector defined benefits pension plans, vest everyone in their accrued benefits to date and replace those plans with defined contribution plans such as 403(b) or thrift plans. No one would lose anything they have accrued as benefits for past service. But from that day on, future benefits would come from newly established defined contribution plans as opposed to defined benefits.

3. DO NOT ACCEPT the offer that these changes will be effected only for future new hires. That won't solve our immense problem. It will be the solution offered by those who think you are dumb enough to accept it. It would take 30 to 40 years for the new programs to begin to have any real impact, and we do not have 30 to 40 years to continue piling on even more deficits for programs we absolutely cannot afford.

4. Pre-age 65 retirement would be continued for all military in accordance with current DOD policies. Defined civilian high-risk occupations would be entitled to retirement at age 50, or 25 years of service. Pre-age 65 retirement would be restricted to those actually engaged in high risk functions, i.e. clerical, administrative or teaching employees of high-risk departments would NOT qualify for early retirement. Eliminate all abusive practices like spiking, too-easy disability definitions and overtime/holidays included in final pay.

5. Freeze all federal employee and nonfederal public sector employee salaries until defined benefits plans have been terminated and replaced with defined contribution plans. Pay parity should be the aim, and studies undertaken to determine

appropriate levels, and adjust accordingly, both upwards and downwards. It is possible that many public sector jobs may be below comparable private sector pay levels in the same locale. If so, salaries and hourly rates should be increased to parity with average LOCAL private sector pay scales.

6. Increase contributions required from employees for public sector benefits plans to accurately and fairly reflect a fair portion of the costs of these benefits.

7. All abuses of public sector benefits plans must be eliminated. No cash for untaken sick or vacation days. They must be used when earned, or given up. Only spouses could be named as beneficiaries for pensions. Disability benefits should be based on Social Security disability definitions.

8. Where other changes are not permitted by law or bargaining agreements, establish a federal tax on excessive employee benefits, including early pensions, large pensions and paid health insurance premiums.

9. Immediately eliminate all DROP plans.

C. Change Public Policy Re: Unions

1. Either disallow public sector unions entirely, or only allow local unions not affiliated with national or statewide unions.

2. No public sector union should be permitted to make political contributions of any kind.

3. No government contract would be allowed to prefer, coerce or otherwise promote the unionization of any private sector government contractor.

D. Reduce the Size of Government

1. All public sector jobs, and every function currently performed by any public sector entity that could be performed by the private sector should be ceded to, or outsourced, to the private sector.

2. There should be no such thing as a Government Sponsored Enterprise (GSE). Functions appropriate to the government should be undertaken by the government and subject to all disclosure and reporting requirements. Other functions should be eliminated or moved to the private sector. We cannot allow our government to establish private sector corporations which are then exempted from taxes and reporting requirements.

3. The unconstitutional Department of Education should be eliminated. Responsibility for public education should be returned to the states, and to the people.

4. Downsize bloated bureaucracy that is not "serving the people" using our tax dollars, and are simply a drag to the deficit and economy (and unfunded liabilities). Government bureaucracies are created to serve the people and funded by the people as monopolies. Terminate or downsize agencies that no longer serve a purpose or are simply eating up tax dollars with little or no return of service to the people.

E. Guarantee Social Security for All Over Age 50 and Create a New Program for Others

1. Guarantee Social Security benefits for those over the age of 50. Move unfunded liability to federal debt, and commit and recognize it as federal debt.

2. Create a new Social Security Defined Contribution program for all citizens entering or currently in the work force who are below the age of 50.

F. Reform Tax Policy Immediately

1. Extend current tax code indefinitely, until new tax code is implemented. Extend "Bush Tax Cuts."

2. Create new, more simplified tax code. Consider a "Flat Tax" to be applied to all Americans. All citizens who earn

compensation should be required to pay at least some taxes. They must know that nothing is free.

3. Create "Alternative Maximum Tax" for corporations and individuals, including all taxes paid to all taxing authorities. There must be an overall limit to the cumulative taxes that can be taken from a business or an individual.

4. Eliminate (or drastically reduce) capital gains taxes, encouraging investment in our economy.

5. Cut the corporate tax rate to 15% immediately. That will provide several hundred billion dollars to be invested into the economy as they wish, to create jobs and to grow their companies.

6. Allow profits earned overseas to be returned to the United States without taxation. This will allow up to an estimated $600 billion of reserves held by U.S. companies to be returned to the United States and invested in our own economy.

G. Eliminate Intrusive and Irresponible Government

1. Repeal the Patient Protection and Affordable Care Act

2. Eliminate proposal for Cap and Trade legislation

H. Create a Sane Energy Policy and a Long-Term Energy Plan

1. Draw up a plan and implement it. The U.S. does not have a long-term energy plan, unlike many countries. Create jobs, reduce imports and use what we have rather than demonize the oil and gas industry.

2. Promote the building or expansion of new refineries.

3. Drill ANWR and any other place we can find oil in the U.S., especially if it is not offshore.

4. Use and drill for natural gas. We have huge amounts of it. Encourage use of it and create jobs.

5. Continue development of clean coal technology. We are among the world's greatest resources of coal. Find a safe and clean way to use it.

6. Create tax incentives (but not gifts) for the creation of new sustainable energy resources. This is a fast-growing industry at home that can create new jobs, and is needed for a long-term energy plan.

7. Recognize that for the foreseeable future, we must depend on oil. While alternative energy sources will undoubtedly be developed, it will take decades before we can even begin to get by without huge quantities of oil. We must be willing to take risks and bear expense (even in the form of more expensive gasoline) in order to STOP paying billions upon billions of dollars to those who use their profits to support our nation's destruction.

I. Do Not Tolerate Demonization

1. Speak up whenever anyone in elected office, including our president, demonizes any segment of our population. There is no politically correct object of demonization in America. Tell them to stop!

2. Recognize that you ARE the corporations and businesses being demonized. Your employer is a name on a piece of paper. You are the "business," whether you are CEO or mail clerk. Speak up and defend yourself of any claims against you or the company you work. You are guilty of nothing but working hard to grow. You and your efforts are the jobs creator of America. Never apologize for what you've accomplished, no matter how successful you are. It takes a heck of a team to survive and prosper in today's world. Wear your success with pride.

J. Get Out of That Union

1. Most states are not "right to work" states. If you work in a place that has been unionized, you have to pay union dues

whether you want to or not. And it means your union can use your dues in opposition to your own wishes.

2. If your employer is unionized, you are controlled by the policies established by the union, whether you like it or not.

3. You may be able to get out of the union if you want to. See the National Right to Work Committee website. It provides what you need to know about your rights.

4. Consider decertifying your union and going without one, or forming your own.

K. VOTE and WORK to Preserve Free Enterpise

1. Whether you are in the private sector or the public sector, all of this matters, and all of it affects you. It affects the health of the U.S., our economy and our future.

2. Scrutinize who is advertising during campaigns and what they are saying. Don't take anything at face value. Verify before you vote.

3. Whether you are in the private sector or work in the public sector (but want to escape from unionization and preserve personal freedom), and if you want to be rewarded for achievement and not time served, then don't sit on the sidelines. Get in the game. Stay informed. Support political candidates who will rein in big and redistributive government at every level. Make sure you know exactly what they are committing to do, and hold them accountable. Support them with your vote, but also with your time and your money. Share your knowledge with your friends. Speak up whenever you have the opportunity. Help to "get the word out" that we can fix America, but that it can't happen unless we all get involved to fix it.

All it Takes is You

Think about the changes that are outlined above. First consider the problems that we have—many of which are hidden from taxpayers.

Make yourself aware of the various problems. Then consider the changes and possible solutions. Lower taxes—less government—less intrusion into our personal lives—less debt—less unfunded liabilities—less unknowns. Elimination of inappropriate or anti-business tax policies. Elimination of unfair practices that hurt the U.S. and its hardworking taxpayers. Help fix the economy to rebuild a robust and strong America. Let's move from an unsustainable America to one that is sustainable and vibrant.

Is there anything suggested above that is not fair or right to do? Don't the suggestions consistently maintain a morally correct way to operate? Do you think that if we do these things we can create 22 million jobs, and put everyone back to work? If we did create all those jobs, do you think the economy would improve? Then let's do them!

The American economy and the American way of life are the most successful on earth in spite of our currently unsustainable levels of spending and debt. They can be brought under control and the U.S. can resume its long path toward freedom, security and the greatest avenue to personal achievement that has ever been created anywhere. All it takes is for you to make it so.

A friend of mine, Keni Thomas, served as a Sergeant with the US Army Rangers in the Battle of Mogadishu, known widely due to the book and movie by Mark Bowden, *Black Hawk Down*. Sergeant Thomas lost many friends in Somalia and now is a singer/song-writer living in Nashville. One of my favorite songs he wrote is "Not Me." The refrain says:

The world becomes a better place,
When someone stands and leads the way,
Steps forward,
When they'd rather say,
"Not Me"

It's your turn now. Step forward. For America.

About the Author

James E. MacDougald is an entrepreneur with personal experience as a member of almost every part of the economy addressed in this book, including both public and private sectors.

MacDougald was born in Providence, Rhode Island. His father spent his career in the U.S. Army, and his mother was a Civil Service employee. MacDougald's early work experience included jobs with the Federal Reserve Bank and as a group health insurance salesman.

In 1982, MacDougald began a new endeavor as a start-up entrepreneur with no money, a 20 year old automobile costing $400, mountainous debt and working from his home. He and his wife, Suzanne, founded the company that eventually became ABR Information Services, Inc. The company went public in 1994 and was named one of "The Best 200 Small Companies in America" by *Forbes Magazine* in 1995, 1996 and 1997, and was named one of the "100 Fastest Growing Public Companies in America" by *Fortune* magazine in 1998. MacDougald served as its President and Chairman with its stock becoming the darling of Wall Street before its merger with Ceridian Corporation in 1999. He later became Chairman of the Board of Directors of Odyssey Marine Exploration, Inc.

MacDougald has been a registered Independent voter for the past 12 years. He has run for public office in New Jersey as a Democrat (he lost) and has also been a significant financial contributor to the Republican Party. A true "independent," he votes for and supports those candidates who support limited government, fiscal openness and responsibility.

MacDougald is Chairman and CEO of The Free Enterprise Nation, Inc. He is currently also the Chairman of the Board of Trustees of the International Council of the Tampa Bay Region, a trustee of the University of Tampa and a member of the Board of Directors of the Special Operations Warrior Foundation. He has an honorary doctorate from Eckerd College, and has served on the board of trustees of numerous other organizations.

Appendices

Text of The Declaration of Independence

Source: http://www.archives.gov/exhibits/charters/declaration.html

The Declaration of Independence: A Transcription

IN CONGRESS, July 4, 1776.

𝕿𝖍𝖊 𝖚𝖓𝖆𝖓𝖎𝖒𝖔𝖚𝖘 𝕯𝖊𝖈𝖑𝖆𝖗𝖆𝖙𝖎𝖔𝖓 of the thirteen united 𝕾𝖙𝖆𝖙𝖊𝖘 𝖔𝖋 𝕬𝖒𝖊𝖗𝖎𝖈𝖆,

𝖂𝖍𝖊𝖓 in the Course of human events, it becomes necessary for one people to dissolve the political bands which have connected them with another, and to assume among the powers of the earth, the separate and equal station to which the Laws of Nature and of Nature's God entitle them, a decent respect to the opinions of mankind requires that they should declare the causes which impel them to the separation.

We hold these truths to be self-evident, that all men are created equal, that they are endowed by their Creator with certain unalienable Rights, that among these are Life, Liberty and the pursuit of Happiness.—That to secure these rights, Governments are instituted among Men, deriving their just powers from the consent of the governed,—That whenever any Form of Government becomes destructive of these ends, it is the Right of the People to alter or to abolish it, and to institute new Government, laying its foundation on such principles and organizing its powers in such form, as to them shall seem most likely to effect their Safety and Happiness. Prudence, indeed, will dictate that Governments long established should not be changed for light and transient causes; and accordingly all experience hath shewn, that mankind are more disposed to suffer, while evils are sufferable, than to right themselves by abolishing the forms to which they are accustomed. But when a long train of abuses and usurpations, pursuing invariably the same Object evinces a design to reduce them under absolute Despotism, it is their right, it is their duty, to throw off such Government, and to provide new Guards for their future security.—Such has been the patient sufferance of these Colonies; and such is now the necessity which constrains them to alter their former Systems of Government. The history of the present King of Great Britain is a history of repeated injuries and usurpations, all having in direct object the establishment of an absolute Tyranny over these States. To prove this, let Facts be submitted to a candid world.

He has refused his Assent to Laws, the most wholesome and necessary for the public good. __ He has forbidden his Governors to pass Laws of immediate and pressing importance, unless suspended in their operation till his Assent should be obtained; and when so suspended, he has utterly neglected to attend to them. __ He has refused to pass other Laws for the accommodation of large districts of people, unless those people would relinquish the right of Representation in the Legislature, a right inestimable to them and formidable to tyrants only. __ He has called together legislative bodies at places unusual, uncomfortable, and distant from the depository of their public Records, for the sole purpose of fatiguing them into compliance with his measures. __ He has dissolved Representative Houses repeatedly, for opposing with manly firmness his invasions on the rights of the people. __ He has refused for a long time, after such dissolutions, to cause others to be elected; whereby the Legislative powers, incapable of Annihilation, have returned to the People at large for their exercise; the State remaining in the mean time exposed to all the dangers of invasion from without, and convulsions within. __ He has endeavoured to prevent the population of these States; for that purpose obstructing the Laws for Naturalization of Foreigners; refusing to pass others to encourage their migrations hither, and raising the conditions of new Appropriations of Lands. __ He has obstructed the Administration of Justice, by refusing his Assent to Laws for establishing Judiciary powers. __ He has made Judges dependent on his Will alone, for the tenure of their offices, and the amount and payment of their salaries. __ He has erected a multitude of New Offices, and sent hither swarms of Officers to harrass our people, and eat out their substance. __ He has kept among us, in times of peace, Standing Armies without the Consent of our legislatures. __ He has affected to render the Military independent of and superior to the Civil power. __ He has combined with others to subject us to a juris-diction foreign to our constitution, and unacknowledged by our laws; giving his Assent to their Acts of pretended Legislation: __ For Quartering large bodies of armed troops among us: __ For protecting them, by a mock Trial, from punishment for any Murders which they should commit on the Inhabitants of these States: __ For cutting off our Trade with all parts of the world: __ For imposing Taxes on us without our Consent: __ For depriving us in many cases, of the benefits of Trial by Jury: __ For transporting us beyond Seas to be tried for pretended offences __ For abolishing the free System of English Laws in a neighbouring Province, establishing therein an Arbitrary government, and enlarging its Boundaries so as to render it at once an example and fit instrument for introducing the same absolute rule into these Colonies: __ For taking away our Charters, abolishing our most valuable Laws, and altering fundamentally the Forms of our Governments: __ For suspending our own Legislatures, and declaring themselves invested with power to legislate for us in all cases whatsoever. __ He has abdicated Gov-ernment here, by declaring us out of his Protection and waging War against us. __ He has plundered our seas, ravaged our Coasts, burnt our towns, and destroyed the lives of our people. __ He is at this time transporting large Armies of foreign Mercenaries to compleat the works of death, desolation and tyranny, already begun with circumstances of Cruelty & perfidy scarcely paralleled in the most barbarous ages, and totally unworthy the Head of a civilized nation. __ He has constrained our fellow Citizens taken Captive on the high Seas to bear Arms against their Country, to become the executioners of their friends and Brethren, or to fall themselves by their Hands. __ He has excited domestic insurrections amongst us, and has endeavoured to bring on the inhabitants of our fron-tiers, the merciless Indian Savages, whose known rule of warfare, is an undistinguished destruction of all ages, sexes and conditions.

In every stage of these Oppressions We have Petitioned for Redress in the most humble terms: Our repeated Petitions have been answered only by repeated injury. A Prince whose character is thus marked by every act which may define a Tyrant, is unfit to be the ruler of a free people.

Nor have We been wanting in attentions to our Brittish brethren. We have warned them from time to time of attempts by their legislature to extend an unwarrantable jurisdiction over us. We have reminded them of the circumstances of our emigration and settlement here. We have appealed to their native justice and magnanimity, and we have conjured them by the ties of our common kindred to disavow these usurpations, which, would inevitably interrupt our connections and correspondence. They too have been deaf to the voice of justice and of consanguinity. We must, therefore, acquiesce in the necessity, which denounces our Separation, and hold them, as we hold the rest of mankind, Enemies in War, in Peace Friends.

We, therefore, the Representatives of the **united States of America,** in General Congress, Assembled, appealing to the Supreme Judge of the world for the rectitude of our intentions, do, in the Name, and by Authority of the good People of these Colonies, solemnly publish and declare, That these United Colonies are, and of Right ought to be Free and Independent States; that they are Absolved from all Allegiance to the British Crown, and that all political connection between them and the State of Great Britain, is and ought to be totally dissolved; and that as **Free and Independent States,** they have full Power to levy War, conclude Peace, contract Alliances, establish Commerce, and to do all other Acts and Things which Independent States may of right do. __ And for the support of this Declaration, with a firm reliance on the protection of divine Providence, we mutually pledge to each other our Lives, our Fortunes and our sacred Honor.

Georgia:
Button Gwinnett
Lyman Hall
George Walton

North Carolina:
William Hooper
Joseph Hewes
John Penn

South Carolina:
Edward Rutledge
Thomas Heyward, Jr.
Thomas Lynch, Jr.
Arthur Middleton

Massachusetts:
John Hancock

Maryland:
Samuel Chase
William Paca
Thomas Stone
Charles Carroll of Carrollton

Virginia:
George Wythe
Richard Henry Lee
Thomas Jefferson
Benjamin Harrison
Thomas Nelson, Jr.
Francis Lightfoot Lee
Carter Braxton

Pennsylvania:
Robert Morris
Benjamin Rush
Benjamin Franklin
John Morton
George Clymer
James Smith
George Taylor
James Wilson
George Ross

Delaware:
Caesar Rodney
George Read
Thomas McKean

New York:
William Floyd
Philip Livingston
Francis Lewis
Lewis Morris

New Jersey:
Richard Stockton
John Witherspoon
Francis Hopkinson
John Hart
Abraham Clark

New Hampshire:
Josiah Bartlett
William Whipple

Massachusetts:
Samuel Adams
John Adams
Robert Treat Paine
Elbridge Gerry

Rhode Island:
Stephen Hopkins
William Ellery

Connecticut:
Roger Sherman
Samuel Huntington
William Williams
Oliver Wolcott

New Hampshire:
Matthew Thornton

Text of The Constitution of the United States

Source: http://www.archives.gov/exhibits/charters/constitution_transcript.html

The Constitution of the United States: A Transcription

Note: *The following text is a transcription of the Constitution in its **original** form. Items that are hyperlinked have since been amended or superseded.*

We the People of the United States, in Order to form a more perfect Union, establish Justice, insure domestic Tranquility, provide for the common defence, promote the general Welfare, and secure the Blessings of Liberty to ourselves and our Posterity, do ordain and establish this Constitution for the United States of America.

Article. I.

Section. 1: All legislative Powers herein granted shall be vested in a Congress of the United States, which shall consist of a Senate and House of Representatives.

Section. 2: The House of Representatives shall be composed of Members chosen every second Year by the People of the several States, and the Electors in each State shall have the Qualifications requisite for Electors of the most numerous Branch of the State Legislature.

No Person shall be a Representative who shall not have attained to the Age of twenty five Years, and been seven Years a Citizen of the United States, and who shall not, when elected, be an Inhabitant of that State in which he shall be chosen.

Representatives and direct Taxes shall be apportioned among the several States which may be included within this Union, according to their respective Numbers, which shall be determined by adding to the whole Number of free Persons, including those bound to Service for a Term of Years, and excluding Indians not taxed, three fifths of all other Persons. The actual Enumeration shall be made within three Years after the first Meeting of the Congress of the United States, and within every subsequent Term of ten Years, in such Manner as they shall by Law direct. The Number of Representatives shall not exceed one for every thirty Thousand, but each State shall have at Least one Representative; and until such enumeration shall be made, the State of New Hampshire shall be entitled to chuse three, Massachusetts eight, Rhode-Island and Providence Plantations one, Connecticut five, New-York six, New Jersey four, Pennsylvania eight,

Delaware one, Maryland six, Virginia ten, North Carolina five, South Carolina five, and Georgia three.

When vacancies happen in the Representation from any State, the Executive Authority thereof shall issue Writs of Election to fill such Vacancies.

The House of Representatives shall chuse their Speaker and other Officers; and shall have the sole Power of Impeachment.

Section. 3: The Senate of the United States shall be composed of two Senators from each State, chosen by the Legislature thereof for six Years; and each Senator shall have one Vote.

Immediately after they shall be assembled in Consequence of the first Election, they shall be divided as equally as may be into three Classes. The Seats of the Senators of the first Class shall be vacated at the Expiration of the second Year, of the second Class at the Expiration of the fourth Year, and of the third Class at the Expiration of the sixth Year, so that one third may be chosen every second Year; and if Vacancies happen by Resignation, or otherwise, during the Recess of the Legislature of any State, the Executive thereof may make temporary Appointments until the next Meeting of the Legislature, which shall then fill such Vacancies.

No Person shall be a Senator who shall not have attained to the Age of thirty Years, and been nine Years a Citizen of the United States, and who shall not, when elected, be an Inhabitant of that State for which he shall be chosen.

The Vice President of the United States shall be President of the Senate, but shall have no Vote, unless they be equally divided.

The Senate shall chuse their other Officers, and also a President pro tempore, in the Absence of the Vice President, or when he shall exercise the Office of President of the United States.

The Senate shall have the sole Power to try all Impeachments. When sitting for that Purpose, they shall be on Oath or Affirmation. When the President of the United States is tried, the Chief Justice shall preside: And no Person shall be convicted without the Concurrence of two thirds of the Members present.

Judgment in Cases of Impeachment shall not extend further than to removal from Office, and disqualification to hold and enjoy any Office of honor, Trust or Profit under the United States: but the Party convicted shall nevertheless be liable and subject to Indictment, Trial, Judgment and Punishment, according to Law.

Section. 4: The Times, Places and Manner of holding Elections for Senators and Representatives, shall be prescribed in each State by the Legislature thereof; but the Congress may at any time by Law make or alter such Regulations, except as to the Places of chusing Senators.

The Congress shall assemble at least once in every Year, and such Meeting shall be on the first Monday in December, unless they shall by Law appoint a different Day.

Section. 5: Each House shall be the Judge of the Elections, Returns and Qualifications of its own Members, and a Majority of each shall constitute a Quorum to do Business; but a smaller Number may adjourn from day to day, and may be authorized to compel the Attendance of absent Members, in such Manner, and under such Penalties as each House may provide.

Each House may determine the Rules of its Proceedings, punish its Members for disorderly Behaviour, and, with the Concurrence of two thirds, expel a Member.

Each House shall keep a Journal of its Proceedings, and from time to time publish the same, excepting such Parts as may in their Judgment require Secrecy; and the Yeas and Nays of the Members of either House on any question shall, at the Desire of one fifth of those Present, be entered on the Journal.

Neither House, during the Session of Congress, shall, without the Consent of the other, adjourn for more than three days, nor to any other Place than that in which the two Houses shall be sitting.

Section. 6: The Senators and Representatives shall receive a Compensation for their Services, to be ascertained by Law, and paid out of the Treasury of the United States. They shall in all Cases, except Treason, Felony and Breach of the Peace, be privileged from Arrest during their Attendance at the Session of their respective Houses, and in going to and returning from the same; and for any Speech or Debate in either House, they shall not be questioned in any other Place.

No Senator or Representative shall, during the Time for which he was elected, be appointed to any civil Office under the Authority of the United States, which shall have been created, or the Emoluments whereof shall have been encreased during such time; and no Person holding any Office under the United States, shall be a Member of either House during his Continuance in Office.

Section. 7: All Bills for raising Revenue shall originate in the House of Representatives; but the Senate may propose or concur with Amendments as on other Bills.

Every Bill which shall have passed the House of Representatives and the Senate, shall, before it become a Law, be presented to the President of the United States: If he approve he shall sign it, but if not he shall return it, with his Objections to that House in which it shall have originated, who shall enter the Objections at large on their Journal, and proceed to reconsider it. If after such Reconsideration two thirds of that House shall agree to pass the Bill, it shall be sent, together with the Objections, to the other House, by which it shall likewise be reconsidered, and if approved by two thirds of that House, it shall become a Law. But in all such Cases the Votes of both Houses shall be determined by yeas and Nays, and the Names of the Persons voting for and against the Bill shall be entered on the Journal of each House respectively. If any Bill shall not be returned by the President within ten Days (Sundays excepted) after it shall have been presented to him, the Same shall be a Law, in like Manner as if he had signed it, unless the Congress by their Adjournment prevent its Return, in which Case it shall not be a Law.

Every Order, Resolution, or Vote to which the Concurrence of the Senate and House of Representatives may be necessary (except on a question of Adjournment) shall be presented to the President of the United States; and before the Same shall take Effect, shall be approved by him, or being disapproved by him, shall be repassed by two thirds of the Senate and House of Representatives, according to the Rules and Limitations prescribed in the Case of a Bill.

Section. 8: The Congress shall have Power To lay and collect Taxes, Duties, Imposts and Excises, to pay the Debts and provide for the common Defence and general Welfare of the United States; but all Duties, Imposts and Excises shall be uniform throughout the United States;

To borrow Money on the credit of the United States;

To regulate Commerce with foreign Nations, and among the several States, and with the Indian Tribes;

To establish an uniform Rule of Naturalization, and uniform Laws on the subject of Bankruptcies throughout the United States;

To coin Money, regulate the Value thereof, and of foreign Coin, and fix the Standard of Weights and Measures;

To provide for the Punishment of counterfeiting the Securities and current Coin of the United States;

To establish Post Offices and post Roads;

To promote the Progress of Science and useful Arts, by securing for limited Times to Authors and Inventors the exclusive Right to their respective Writings and Discoveries;

To constitute Tribunals inferior to the supreme Court;

To define and punish Piracies and Felonies committed on the high Seas, and Offences against the Law of Nations;

To declare War, grant Letters of Marque and Reprisal, and make Rules concerning Captures on Land and Water;

To raise and support Armies, but no Appropriation of Money to that Use shall be for a longer Term than two Years;

To provide and maintain a Navy;

To make Rules for the Government and Regulation of the land and naval Forces;

To provide for calling forth the Militia to execute the Laws of the Union, suppress Insurrections and repel Invasions;

To provide for organizing, arming, and disciplining, the Militia, and for governing such Part of them as may be employed in the Service of the United States, reserving to the States respectively, the Appointment of the Officers, and the Authority of training the Militia according to the discipline prescribed by Congress;

To exercise exclusive Legislation in all Cases whatsoever, over such District (not exceeding ten Miles square) as may, by Cession of particular States, and the Acceptance of Congress, become the Seat of the Government of the United States, and to exercise like Authority over all Places purchased by the Consent of the Legislature of the State in which the Same shall be, for the Erection of Forts, Magazines, Arsenals, dock-Yards, and other needful Buildings;—And

To make all Laws which shall be necessary and proper for carrying into Execution the foregoing Powers, and all other Powers vested by this Constitution in the Government of the United States, or in any Department or Officer thereof.

Section. 9: The Migration or Importation of such Persons as any of the States now existing shall think proper to admit, shall not be prohibited by the Congress prior to the Year one thousand eight hundred and eight, but a Tax or duty may be imposed on such Importation, not exceeding ten dollars for each Person.

The Privilege of the Writ of Habeas Corpus shall not be suspended, unless when in Cases of Rebellion or Invasion the public Safety may require it.

No Bill of Attainder or ex post facto Law shall be passed.

No Capitation, or other direct, Tax shall be laid, unless in Proportion to the Census or enumeration herein before directed to be taken.

No Tax or Duty shall be laid on Articles exported from any State.

No Preference shall be given by any Regulation of Commerce or Revenue to the Ports of one State over those of another; nor shall Vessels bound to, or from, one State, be obliged to enter, clear, or pay Duties in another.

No Money shall be drawn from the Treasury, but in Consequence of Appropriations made by Law; and a regular Statement and Account of the Receipts and Expenditures of all public Money shall be published from time to time.

No Title of Nobility shall be granted by the United States: And no Person holding any Office of Profit or Trust under them, shall, without the Consent of the Congress, accept of any present, Emolument, Office, or Title, of any kind whatever, from any King, Prince, or foreign State.

Section. 10: No State shall enter into any Treaty, Alliance, or Confederation; grant Letters of Marque and Reprisal; coin Money; emit Bills of Credit; make any Thing but gold and silver Coin a Tender in Payment of Debts; pass any Bill of Attainder, ex post facto Law, or Law impairing the Obligation of Contracts, or grant any Title of Nobility.

No State shall, without the Consent of the Congress, lay any Imposts or Duties on Imports or Exports, except what may be absolutely necessary for executing it's inspection Laws: and the net Produce of all Duties and Imposts, laid by any State on Imports or Exports, shall be for the Use of the Treasury of the United States; and all such Laws shall be subject to the Revision and Controul of the Congress.

No State shall, without the Consent of Congress, lay any Duty of Tonnage, keep Troops, or Ships of War in time of Peace, enter into any Agreement or Compact with another State, or with a foreign Power, or engage in War, unless actually invaded, or in such imminent Danger as will not admit of delay.

Article. II.

Section. 1: The executive Power shall be vested in a President of the United States of America. He shall hold his Office during the Term of four Years, and, together with the Vice President, chosen for the same Term, be elected, as follows:

Each State shall appoint, in such Manner as the Legislature thereof may direct, a Number of Electors, equal to the whole Number of Senators and Representatives to which the State may be entitled in the Congress: but no Senator or Representative, or Person holding an Office of Trust or Profit under the United States, shall be appointed an Elector.

The Electors shall meet in their respective States, and vote by Ballot for two Persons, of whom one at least shall not be an Inhabitant of the same State with themselves. And they shall make a List of all the Persons voted for, and of the Number of Votes for each; which List they shall sign and certify, and transmit sealed to the Seat of the Government of the United States, directed to the President of the Senate. The President of the Senate shall, in the Presence of the Senate and House of Representatives, open all the Certificates, and the Votes shall then be counted. The Person having the greatest Number of Votes shall be the President, if such Number be a Majority of the whole Number of Electors appointed; and if there be more than one who have such Majority, and have an equal Number of Votes, then the House of Representatives shall immediately chuse by Ballot one of them for President; and if no Person have a Majority, then from the five highest on the List the said House shall in like Manner chuse the President. But in chusing the President, the Votes shall be taken by States, the Representation from each State having one Vote; A quorum for this purpose shall consist of a Member or Members from two thirds of the States, and a Majority of all the States shall be necessary to a Choice. In every Case, after the Choice of the President, the Person having the greatest Number of Votes of the Electors shall be the Vice President. But if there should remain two or more who have equal Votes, the Senate shall chuse from them by Ballot the Vice President.

The Congress may determine the Time of chusing the Electors, and the Day on which they shall give their Votes; which Day shall be the same throughout the United States.

No Person except a natural born Citizen, or a Citizen of the United States, at the time of the Adoption of this Constitution, shall be eligible to the Office of President; neither shall any Person be eligible to that Office who shall not have attained to the Age of thirty five Years, and been fourteen Years a Resident within the United States.

In Case of the Removal of the President from Office, or of his Death, Resignation, or Inability to discharge the Powers and Duties of the said Office, the Same shall devolve on the Vice President, and the Congress may by Law provide for the Case of Removal, Death, Resignation or Inability, both of the President and Vice President, declaring what Officer shall then act as President, and such Officer shall act accordingly, until the Disability be removed, or a President shall be elected.

The President shall, at stated Times, receive for his Services, a Compensation, which shall neither be increased nor diminished during the Period for which he shall have been elected, and he shall not receive within that Period any other Emolument from the United States, or any of them.

Before he enter on the Execution of his Office, he shall take the following Oath or Affirmation:—"I do solemnly swear (or affirm) that I will faithfully execute the Office of President of the United States, and will to the best of my Ability, preserve, protect and defend the Constitution of the United States."

Section. 2: The President shall be Commander in Chief of the Army and Navy of the United States, and of the Militia of the several States, when called into the actual Service of the United States; he may require the Opinion, in writing, of the principal Officer in each of the executive Departments, upon any Subject relating to the Duties of their respective Offices, and he shall have Power to grant Reprieves and Pardons for Offences against the United States, except in Cases of Impeachment.

He shall have Power, by and with the Advice and Consent of the Senate, to make Treaties, provided two thirds of the Senators present concur; and he shall nominate, and by and with the Advice and Consent of the Senate, shall appoint Ambassadors, other public Ministers and Consuls, Judges of the supreme Court, and all other Officers of the United States, whose Appointments are not herein otherwise provided for, and which shall be established by Law: but the Congress may by Law vest the Appointment of such inferior Officers, as they think proper, in the President alone, in the Courts of Law, or in the Heads of Departments.

The President shall have Power to fill up all Vacancies that may happen during the Recess of the Senate, by granting Commissions which shall expire at the End of their next Session.

Section. 3: He shall from time to time give to the Congress Information of the State of the Union, and recommend to their Consideration such Measures as he shall judge necessary and expedient; he may, on extraordinary Occasions, convene both Houses, or either of them, and in Case of Disagreement between them, with Respect to the Time of Adjournment, he may adjourn them to such Time as he shall think proper; he shall receive Ambassadors and other public Ministers; he shall take Care that the Laws be faithfully executed, and shall Commission all the Officers of the United States.

Section. 4: The President, Vice President and all civil Officers of the United States, shall be removed from Office on Impeachment for, and Conviction of, Treason, Bribery, or other high Crimes and Misdemeanors.

Article III.

Section. 1: The judicial Power of the United States shall be vested in one supreme Court, and in such inferior Courts as the Congress may from time to time ordain and establish. The Judges, both of the supreme and inferior Courts, shall hold their Offices during good Behaviour, and shall, at stated Times, receive for their Services a Compensation, which shall not be diminished during their Continuance in Office.

Section. 2: The judicial Power shall extend to all Cases, in Law and Equity, arising under this Constitution, the Laws of the United States, and Treaties made, or which shall be made, under their Authority;—to all Cases affecting Ambassadors, other public Ministers and Consuls;—to all Cases of admiralty and maritime Jurisdiction;—to Controversies to which the United States shall be a Party;—to Controversies between two or more States;—between a State and Citizens of another State,—between Citizens of different States,—between Citizens of the same State claiming Lands under Grants of different States, and between a State, or the Citizens thereof, and foreign States, Citizens or Subjects.

In all Cases affecting Ambassadors, other public Ministers and Consuls, and those in which a State shall be Party, the supreme Court shall have original Jurisdiction. In all the other Cases before mentioned, the supreme Court shall have appellate Jurisdiction, both as to Law and Fact, with such Exceptions, and under such Regulations as the Congress shall make.

The Trial of all Crimes, except in Cases of Impeachment, shall be by Jury; and such Trial shall be held in the State where the said Crimes shall have been committed; but when not committed within any State, the Trial shall be at such Place or Places as the Congress may by Law have directed.

Section. 3: Treason against the United States, shall consist only in levying War against them, or in adhering to their Enemies, giving them Aid and Comfort. No Person shall be convicted of Treason unless on the Testimony of two Witnesses to the same overt Act, or on Confession in open Court.

The Congress shall have Power to declare the Punishment of Treason, but no Attainder of Treason shall work Corruption of Blood, or Forfeiture except during the Life of the Person attainted.

Article. IV.

Section. 1: Full Faith and Credit shall be given in each State to the public Acts, Records, and judicial Proceedings of every other State. And the Congress may by general Laws prescribe the Manner in which such Acts, Records and Proceedings shall be proved, and the Effect thereof.

Section. 2: The Citizens of each State shall be entitled to all Privileges and Immunities of Citizens in the several States.

A Person charged in any State with Treason, Felony, or other Crime, who shall flee from Justice, and be found in another State, shall on Demand of the executive Authority of the State from which he fled, be delivered up, to be removed to the State having Jurisdiction of the Crime.

No Person held to Service or Labour in one State, under the Laws thereof, escaping into another, shall, in Consequence of any Law or Regulation therein, be discharged from such Service or Labour, but shall be delivered up on Claim of the Party to whom such Service or Labour may be due.

Section. 3: New States may be admitted by the Congress into this Union; but no new State shall be formed or erected within the Jurisdiction of any other State; nor any State be formed by the Junction of two or more States, or Parts of States, without the Consent of the Legislatures of the States concerned as well as of the Congress.

The Congress shall have Power to dispose of and make all needful Rules and Regulations respecting the Territory or other Property belonging to the United States; and nothing in this Constitution shall be so construed as to Prejudice any Claims of the United States, or of any particular State.

Section. 4: The United States shall guarantee to every State in this Union a Republican Form of Government, and shall protect each of them against Invasion; and on Application of the Legislature, or of the Executive (when the Legislature cannot be convened), against domestic Violence.

Article. V.

The Congress, whenever two thirds of both Houses shall deem it necessary, shall propose Amendments to this Constitution, or, on the Application of the Legislatures of two thirds of the several States, shall call a Convention for proposing Amendments, which, in either Case, shall be valid to all Intents and Purposes, as Part of this Constitution, when ratified by the Legislatures of three fourths of the several States, or by Conventions in three fourths thereof, as the one or the other Mode of Ratification may be proposed by the Congress; Provided that no Amendment which may be made prior to the Year One thousand eight hundred and eight shall in any Manner affect the first and fourth Clauses in the Ninth Section of the first Article; and that no State, without its Consent, shall be deprived of its equal Suffrage in the Senate.

Article. VI.

All Debts contracted and Engagements entered into, before the Adoption of this Constitution, shall be as valid against the United States under this Constitution, as under the Confederation.

This Constitution, and the Laws of the United States which shall be made in Pursuance thereof; and all Treaties made, or which shall be made, under the Authority of the United States, shall be the supreme Law of the Land; and the Judges in every State shall be bound thereby, any Thing in the Constitution or Laws of any State to the Contrary notwithstanding.

The Senators and Representatives before mentioned, and the Members of the several State Legislatures, and all executive and judicial Officers, both of the United States and of the several States, shall be bound by Oath or Affirmation, to support this Constitution; but no religious Test shall ever be required as a Qualification to any Office or public Trust under the United States.

Article. VII.

The Ratification of the Conventions of nine States, shall be sufficient for the Establishment of this Constitution between the States so ratifying the Same.

The Word, "the," being interlined between the seventh and eighth Lines of the first Page, the Word "Thirty" being partly written on an Erazure in the fifteenth Line of the first Page, The Words "is tried" being interlined between the thirty second and thirty third Lines of the first Page and the Word "the" being interlined between the forty third and forty fourth Lines of the second Page.

Attest William Jackson Secretary

Done in Convention by the Unanimous Consent of the States present the Seventeenth Day of September in the Year of our Lord one thousand seven hundred and Eighty seven and of the Independence of the United States of America the Twelfth In witness whereof We have hereunto subscribed our Names,

G°. Washington
Presidt and deputy from Virginia

Delaware
Geo: Read
Gunning Bedford jun
John Dickinson
Richard Bassett
Jaco: Broom

Maryland
James McHenry
Dan of St Thos. Jenifer
Danl. Carroll

Virginia
John Blair
James Madison Jr.

North Carolina
Wm. Blount
Richd. Dobbs Spaight
Hu Williamson

South Carolina
J. Rutledge
Charles Cotesworth Pinckney
Charles Pinckney
Pierce Butler

Georgia
William Few
Abr Baldwin

New Hampshire
John Langdon
Nicholas Gilman

Massachusetts
Nathaniel Gorham
Rufus King

Connecticut
Wm. Saml. Johnson
Roger Sherman

New York
Alexander Hamilton

New Jersey
Wil: Livingston
David Brearley
Wm. Paterson
Jona: Dayton

Pennsylvania
B Franklin
Thomas Mifflin
Robt. Morris
Geo. Clymer
Thos. FitzSimons
Jared Ingersoll
James Wilson
Gouv Morris

Text of The Bill of Rights

Sources: http://www.archives.gov/exhibits/charters/bill_of_rights.html and http://www.archives.gov/exhibits/charters/constitution_amendments_11-27.htm

The Bill of Rights: A Transcription

The Preamble to The Bill of Rights

Congress of the United States

begun and held at the City of New-York, on Wednesday the fourth of March, one thousand seven hundred and eighty nine.

THE Conventions of a number of the States, having at the time of their adopting the Constitution, expressed a desire, in order to prevent misconstruction or abuse of its powers, that further declaratory and restrictive clauses should be added: And as extending the ground of public confidence in the Government, will best ensure the beneficent ends of its institution.

RESOLVED by the Senate and House of Representatives of the United States of America, in Congress assembled, two thirds of both Houses concurring, that the following Articles be proposed to the Legislatures of the several States, as amendments to the Constitution of the United States, all, or any of which Articles, when ratified by three fourths of the said Legislatures, to be valid to all intents and purposes, as part of the said Constitution; viz.

ARTICLES in addition to, and Amendment of the Constitution of the United States of America, proposed by Congress, and ratified by the Legislatures of the several States, pursuant to the fifth Article of the original Constitution.

> *Note:* The following text is a transcription of the first ten amendments to the Constitution in their original form. These amendments were ratified December 15, 1791, and form what is known as the "Bill of Rights."

Amendment I: Congress shall make no law respecting an establishment of religion, or prohibiting the free exercise thereof; or abridging the freedom of speech, or of the press; or the right of the people peaceably to assemble, and to petition the Government for a redress of grievances.

Amendment II: A well regulated Militia, being necessary to the security of a free State, the right of the people to keep and bear Arms, shall not be infringed.

Amendment III: No Soldier shall, in time of peace be quartered in any house, without the consent of the Owner, nor in time of war, but in a manner to be prescribed by law.

Amendment IV: The right of the people to be secure in their persons, houses, papers, and effects, against unreasonable searches and seizures, shall not be violated, and no Warrants shall issue, but upon probable cause, supported by Oath or affirmation, and particularly describing the place to be searched, and the persons or things to be seized.

Amendment V: No person shall be held to answer for a capital, or otherwise infamous crime, unless on a presentment or indictment of a Grand Jury, except in cases arising in the land or naval forces, or in the Militia, when in actual service in time of War or public danger; nor shall any person be subject for the same offence to be twice put in jeopardy of life or limb; nor shall be compelled in any criminal case to be a witness against himself, nor be deprived of life, liberty, or property, without due process of law; nor shall private property be taken for public use, without just compensation.

Amendment VI: In all criminal prosecutions, the accused shall enjoy the right to a speedy and public trial, by an impartial jury of the State and district wherein the crime shall have been committed, which district shall have been previously ascertained by law, and to be informed of the nature and cause of the accusation; to be confronted with the witnesses against him; to have compulsory process for obtaining witnesses in his favor, and to have the Assistance of Counsel for his defence.

Amendment VII: In Suits at common law, where the value in controversy shall exceed twenty dollars, the right of trial by jury shall be preserved, and no fact tried by a jury, shall be otherwise re-examined in any Court of the United States, than according to the rules of the common law.

Amendment VIII: Excessive bail shall not be required, nor excessive fines imposed, nor cruel and unusual punishments inflicted.

Amendment IX: The enumeration in the Constitution, of certain rights, shall not be construed to deny or disparage others retained by the people.

Amendment X: The powers not delegated to the United States by the Constitution, nor prohibited by it to the States, are reserved to the States respectively, or to the people.

Constitutional Amendments 1–10 make up what is known as The Bill of Rights.

The Constitution: Amendments 11–27 are listed below.

AMENDMENT XI
Passed by Congress March 4, 1794. Ratified February 7, 1795.
> *Note:* Article III, section 2, of the Constitution was modified by amendment 11.
> The Judicial power of the United States shall not be construed to extend to any suit in law or equity, commenced or prosecuted against one of the United States by Citizens of another State, or by Citizens or Subjects of any Foreign State.

AMENDMENT XII
Passed by Congress December 9, 1803. Ratified June 15, 1804.
> *Note:* A portion of Article II, section 1 of the Constitution was superseded by the 12th amendment.

The Electors shall meet in their respective states and vote by ballot for President and Vice-President, one of whom, at least, shall not be an inhabitant of the same state with themselves; they shall name in their ballots the person voted for as President, and in distinct ballots the person voted for as Vice-President, and they shall make distinct lists of all persons voted for as President, and of all persons voted for as Vice-President, and of the number of votes for each, which lists they shall sign and certify, and transmit sealed to the seat of the government of the United States, directed to the President of the Senate;—the President of the Senate shall, in the presence of the Senate and House of Representatives, open all the certificates and the votes shall then be counted;—The person having the greatest number of votes for President, shall be the President, if such number be a majority of the whole number of Electors appointed; and if no person have such majority, then from the persons having the highest numbers not exceeding three on the list of those voted for as President, the House of Representatives shall choose immediately, by ballot, the President. But in choosing the President, the votes shall be taken by states, the representation from each state having one vote; a quorum for this purpose shall consist of a member or members from two-thirds of the states, and a majority of all the states shall be necessary to a choice. [And if the House of Representatives shall not choose a President whenever the right of choice shall devolve upon them, before the fourth day of March next following, then the Vice-President shall act as President, as in case of the death or other constitutional disability of the President.—]* The person having the greatest number of votes as Vice-President, shall be the Vice-President, if such number be a majority of the whole number of Electors appointed, and if no person have a majority, then from the two highest numbers on the list, the Senate shall choose the Vice-President; a quorum for the purpose shall consist of two-thirds of the whole number of Senators, and a majority of the whole number shall be necessary to a choice. But no person constitutionally ineligible to the office of President shall be eligible to that of Vice-President of the United States.

*Superseded by section 3 of the 20th amendment.

AMENDMENT XIII

Passed by Congress January 31, 1865. Ratified December 6, 1865.

> *Note:* A portion of Article IV, section 2, of the Constitution was superseded by the 13th amendment.

Section 1: Neither slavery nor involuntary servitude, except as a punishment for crime whereof the party shall have been duly convicted, shall exist within the United States, or any place subject to their jurisdiction.

Section 2: Congress shall have power to enforce this article by appropriate legislation.

AMENDMENT XIV

Passed by Congress June 13, 1866. Ratified July 9, 1868.

> *Note:* Article I, section 2, of the Constitution was modified by section 2 of the 14th amendment.

Section 1: All persons born or naturalized in the United States, and subject to the jurisdiction thereof, are citizens of the United States and of the State wherein they reside. No State shall make or enforce any law which shall abridge the privileges or immunities of citizens of the United States; nor shall any State deprive any person of life, liberty, or property, without due process of law; nor deny to any person within its jurisdiction the equal protection of the laws.

Section 2: Representatives shall be apportioned among the several States according to their respective numbers, counting the whole number of persons in each State, excluding Indians not taxed. But when the right to vote at any election for the choice of electors for President and Vice-President of the United States, Representatives in Congress, the Executive and Judicial officers of a State, or the members of the Legislature thereof, is denied to any of the male inhabitants of such State, being twenty-one years of age,* and citizens of the United States, or in any way abridged, except for participation in rebellion, or other crime, the basis of representation therein shall be reduced in the proportion which the number of such male citizens shall bear to the whole number of male citizens twenty-one years of age in such State.

Section 3: No person shall be a Senator or Representative in Congress, or elector of President and Vice-President, or hold any office, civil or military, under the United States, or under any State, who, having previously taken an oath, as a member of Congress, or as an officer of the United States, or as a member of any State legislature, or as an executive or judicial officer of any State, to support the Constitution of the United States, shall have engaged in insurrection or rebellion against the same, or given aid or comfort to the enemies thereof. But Congress may by a vote of two-thirds of each House, remove such disability.

Section 4: The validity of the public debt of the United States, authorized by law, including debts incurred for payment of pensions and bounties for services in suppressing insurrection or rebellion, shall not be questioned. But neither the United States nor any State shall assume or pay any debt or obligation incurred in aid of insurrection or rebellion against the United States, or any claim for the loss or emancipation of any slave; but all such debts, obligations and claims shall be held illegal and void.

Section 5: The Congress shall have the power to enforce, by appropriate legislation, the provisions of this article.

*Changed by section 1 of the 26th amendment.

AMENDMENT XV
Passed by Congress February 26, 1869. Ratified February 3, 1870.

Section 1: The right of citizens of the United States to vote shall not be denied or abridged by the United States or by any State on account of race, color, or previous condition of servitude—

Section 2: The Congress shall have the power to enforce this article by appropriate legislation.

AMENDMENT XVI
Passed by Congress July 2, 1909. Ratified February 3, 1913.

Note: Article I, section 9, of the Constitution was modified by amendment 16.

The Congress shall have power to lay and collect taxes on incomes, from whatever source derived, without apportionment among the several States, and without regard to any census or enumeration.

AMENDMENT XVII

Passed by Congress May 13, 1912. Ratified April 8, 1913.

Note: Article I, section 3, of the Constitution was modified by the 17th amendment.

The Senate of the United States shall be composed of two Senators from each State, elected by the people thereof, for six years; and each Senator shall have one vote. The electors in each State shall have the qualifications requisite for electors of the most numerous branch of the State legislatures.

When vacancies happen in the representation of any State in the Senate, the executive authority of such State shall issue writs of election to fill such vacancies: Provided, That the legislature of any State may empower the executive thereof to make temporary appointments until the people fill the vacancies by election as the legislature may direct.

This amendment shall not be so construed as to affect the election or term of any Senator chosen before it becomes valid as part of the Constitution.

AMENDMENT XVIII

Passed by Congress December 18, 1917. Ratified January 16, 1919. Repealed by amendment 21.

Section 1: After one year from the ratification of this article the manufacture, sale, or transportation of intoxicating liquors within, the importation thereof into, or the exportation thereof from the United States and all territory subject to the jurisdiction thereof for beverage purposes is hereby prohibited.

Section 2: The Congress and the several States shall have concurrent power to enforce this article by appropriate legislation.

Section 3: This article shall be inoperative unless it shall have been ratified as an amendment to the Constitution by the legislatures of the several States, as provided in the Constitution, within seven years from the date of the submission hereof to the States by the Congress.

AMENDMENT XIX

Passed by Congress June 4, 1919. Ratified August 18, 1920.

The right of citizens of the United States to vote shall not be denied or abridged by the United States or by any State on account of sex.

Congress shall have power to enforce this article by appropriate legislation.

AMENDMENT XX

Passed by Congress March 2, 1932. Ratified January 23, 1933.

Note: Article I, section 4, of the Constitution was modified by section 2 of this amendment. In addition, a portion of the 12th amendment was superseded by section 3.

Section 1: The terms of the President and the Vice President shall end at noon on the 20th day of January, and the terms of Senators and Representatives at noon on the 3d day of January, of the years in which such terms would have ended if this article had not been ratified; and the terms of their successors shall then begin.

Section 2: The Congress shall assemble at least once in every year, and such meeting shall begin at noon on the 3d day of January, unless they shall by law appoint a different day.

Section 3: If, at the time fixed for the beginning of the term of the President, the President elect shall have died, the Vice President elect shall become President. If a President shall not have been chosen before the time fixed for the beginning of his term, or if the President elect shall have failed to qualify, then the Vice President elect shall act as President until a President shall have qualified; and the Congress may by law provide for the case wherein neither a President elect nor a Vice President shall have qualified, declaring who shall then act as President, or the manner in which one who is to act shall be selected, and such person shall act accordingly until a President or Vice President shall have qualified.

Section 4: The Congress may by law provide for the case of the death of any of the persons from whom the House of Representatives may choose a President whenever the right of choice shall have devolved upon them, and for the case of the death of any of the persons from whom the Senate may choose a Vice President whenever the right of choice shall have devolved upon them.

Section 5: Sections 1 and 2 shall take effect on the 15th day of October following the ratification of this article.

Section 6: This article shall be inoperative unless it shall have been ratified as an amendment to the Constitution by the legislatures of three-fourths of the several States within seven years from the date of its submission.

AMENDMENT XXI
Passed by Congress February 20, 1933. Ratified December 5, 1933.

Section 1: The eighteenth article of amendment to the Constitution of the United States is hereby repealed.

Section 2: The transportation or importation into any State, Territory, or Possession of the United States for delivery or use therein of intoxicating liquors, in violation of the laws thereof, is hereby prohibited.

Section 3: This article shall be inoperative unless it shall have been ratified as an amendment to the Constitution by conventions in the several States, as provided in the Constitution, within seven years from the date of the submission hereof to the States by the Congress.

AMENDMENT XXII
Passed by Congress March 21, 1947. Ratified February 27, 1951.

Section 1: o person shall be elected to the office of the President more than twice, and no person who has held the office of President, or acted as President, for more than two years of a term to which some other person was elected President shall be elected to the office of President more than once. But this Article shall not apply to any person holding the office of President when this Article was proposed by Congress, and shall not prevent any person who may be holding the office of President, or acting as President, during the term within which this Article becomes operative from holding the office of President or acting as President during the remainder of such term.

Section 2: This article shall be inoperative unless it shall have been ratified as an amendment to the Constitution by the legislatures of three-fourths of the several States within seven years from the date of its submission to the States by the Congress.

298

AMENDMENT XXIII
Passed by Congress June 16, 1960. Ratified March 29, 1961.

Section 1: The District constituting the seat of Government of the United States shall appoint in such manner as Congress may direct:

A number of electors of President and Vice President equal to the whole number of Senators and Representatives in Congress to which the District would be entitled if it were a State, but in no event more than the least populous State; they shall be in addition to those appointed by the States, but they shall be considered, for the purposes of the election of President and Vice President, to be electors appointed by a State; and they shall meet in the District and perform such duties as provided by the twelfth article of amendment.

Section 2: The Congress shall have power to enforce this article by appropriate legislation.

AMENDMENT XXIV
Passed by Congress August 27, 1962. Ratified January 23, 1964.

Section 1: The right of citizens of the United States to vote in any primary or other election for President or Vice President, for electors for President or Vice President, or for Senator or Representative in Congress, shall not be denied or abridged by the United States or any State by reason of failure to pay poll tax or other tax.

Section 2: The Congress shall have power to enforce this article by appropriate legislation.

AMENDMENT XXV
Passed by Congress July 6, 1965. Ratified February 10, 1967.
   Note: Article II, section 1, of the Constitution was affected by the 25th amendment.

Section 1: In case of the removal of the President from office or of his death or resignation, the Vice President shall become President.

Section 2: Whenever there is a vacancy in the office of the Vice President, the President shall nominate a Vice President who shall take office upon confirmation by a majority vote of both Houses of Congress.

Section 3: Whenever the President transmits to the President pro tempore of the Senate and the Speaker of the House of Representatives his written declaration that he is unable to discharge the powers and duties of his office, and until he transmits to them a written declaration to the contrary, such powers and duties shall be discharged by the Vice President as Acting President.

Section 4: Whenever the Vice President and a majority of either the principal officers of the executive departments or of such other body as Congress may by law provide, transmit to the President pro tempore of the Senate and the Speaker of the House of Representatives their written declaration that the President is unable to discharge the powers and duties of his office, the Vice President shall immediately assume the powers and duties of the office as Acting President.

   Thereafter, when the President transmits to the President pro tempore of the Senate and the Speaker of the House of Representatives his written declaration that no inability exists, he shall resume the powers and duties of his office unless the Vice President and a majority of either the principal officers of the executive department or of such other body as Congress may by law provide, transmit within four days to the President pro tempore of the Senate and the Speaker of the House of Representatives their written declaration that the President is unable to discharge the powers and duties of his office. Thereupon Congress shall decide the issue, assembling within forty-eight hours for that purpose if not in session. If the Congress, within twenty-one days after receipt of the latter written declaration, or, if Congress is not in session, within twenty-one days after Congress is required to assemble, determines by two-thirds vote of both Houses that the President is unable to discharge the powers and duties of his office, the Vice President shall continue to discharge the same as Acting President; otherwise, the President shall resume the powers and duties of his office.

AMENDMENT XXVI
Passed by Congress March 23, 1971. Ratified July 1, 1971.

> *Note:* Amendment 14, section 2, of the Constitution was modified by section 1 of the 26th amendment.

Section 1: The right of citizens of the United States, who are eighteen years of age or older, to vote shall not be denied or abridged by the United States or by any State on account of age.

Section 2: The Congress shall have power to enforce this article by appropriate legislation.

AMENDMENT XXVII
Originally proposed Sept. 25, 1789. Ratified May 7, 1992.

No law, varying the compensation for the services of the Senators and Representatives, shall take effect, until an election of representatives shall have intervened.

References

The following resources were among those used to research, learn and gather information for this book. Many more were accessed in the creation of The Free Enterprise Nation's huge database, available at www.TheFreeEnterpriseNation.org. We salute the intrepid journalists and think tanks whose work has helped us to shed light on unsustainable practices.

AARP. "Retirement security or insecurity? The experience of workers aged 45 and older." 2008.

Alanez, T. "Double Dippers: Florida public officials cash in on retirement payouts, then go back to work." *South Florida Sun-Sentinel*. April 25, 2009.

Alexander, Ralph B. *Global Warming False Alarm: The Bad Science Behind the United Nations' Assertion that Man-Made CO2 Causes Global Warming*. Canterbury Publishing: Royal Oak, MI, 2009.

Altimari, D. and Kauffman, M. "Some retired state workers get big paychecks on top of pensions; our tax dollars." *Hartford Courant*. February 8, 2009..

Anderson, Z. "State employees enjoy a pension and a salary." *Herald-Tribune. com*. February 22, 2009.

Annis, Edward R. *Code Blue: Health Care in Crisis*. Regnery Gateway: Washington, D.C., 1993.

Associated Builders and Contractors, Inc. "Before the United States Department of Labor, Office of Labor-Management Standards, Notice of Proposed Rulemaking 29 CFR Part 471 Notification of Employee Rights Under Federal Labor Laws RIN 1215-AB70 to Implement Executive Order 13496 (74 Fed. Reg. at 38488)." September 2, 2009.

Associated Builders and Contractors. "ABC Member Files Protest Against U.S. Department of Labor Project Labor Agreement." October 6, 2009. *PRNewswire*. http://www.reuters.com/article/pressRelease/idUS164244+06-Oct -2009+PRN20091006.

Bandler, J. "Public workers enjoy golden nest eggs." *The LoHud Journal*. October 25, 2009.

Bang-Jensen, L. "Public workers feel no pain in recession." *The New York Post*. February 14, 2010.

Barr, Andy. "Nancy Pelosi: Health care was 'hijacked.'" *Politico*. March 11, 2010. http://www.politico.com/news/stories/0310/34265.html#ixzz0ijbkhYOg

Bego, David A. *The Devil at My Doorstep*. Ebook. 2009.

Bellante, Don and David Denholm, Ivan G. Osorio. "Vallejo Con Dios: Why public sector unionism is a bad deal for taxpayers and representative government." *Cato Institute.* (No. 645). Retrieved May 25, 2010. http://www. cato.org/pub_display.php?pub_id=10569.

Benton, E. "$10G bonuses total in millions: City school administrators double dip after early retirement." *New Haven Register.* August 24, 2009.

Biggs, Andrew. "Public pensions cook the books." *Wall Street Journal.* July 6, 2009. http://online.wsj.com/article/SB124683573382697889.html.

Biggs, Andrew G. "Truth in Accounting: Calculating the Market Value of Unfunded Obligations in State and Local Government Pensions." *Free Enterprise Nation.* 2009.

Biggs, Andrew. "Why Kevin Drum Is Right on Social Security." November 30, 2009. *The Enterprise Blog.* http://blog.american.com.

Bogdanich, W. "A disability epidemic among a railroad's retirees." *The New York Times.* September 2, 2008.

Boren, J. "Pittsburgh: Pension liability slips in at under $1 billion." *Pittsburgh Tribune Review.* April 1, 2010.

Bridges, A. "Pension Scenarios tough to compare." *Springfield Missouri News-Leader.* September 6, 2009.

British North American Committee. "The need for transparency in public sector pensions." June 2009.

Burger, J. "Retirement agency goes forward with $5.5 million digs." *Bakersfield. com.* February 10, 2010.

California Pension Reform Database. "Facts at a Glance." CalPERS and CalSTRS. February 8, 2010.

"Card Check: Learn the Basics." *U.S. Chamber of Commerce.* http://www.uschamber.com/wfi/cardcheckbasics.htm.

Carlson, K. "Practice of boosting Stanislaus employees' last year's salary draws public eye, ire." *The Modesto Bee.* December 20, 2009.

Cauchon, D. "For feds, more get 6-figure salaries." *USA Today.* December 11, 2009.

Causey, M. "Federal workers had excellent '09." *The Washington Times.* December 28, 2009.

CBSnews.com. "Federal Budget Deficit Hits $120.3 Billion." December 10, 2009. http://www.cbsnews.com/stories/2009/12/10/national/main5963445.shtml.

Censky, A. "Record monthly deficit for U.S.: $221 billion." *CNNMoney.com.* March 10, 2010.

Center for Responsive Politics. http://www.opensecrets.org/orgs/list.php?order=A.

Chao, Elaine. "Two Steps Back on Labor Rights." *Heritage Foundation.* April 20, 2009. http://www.heritage.org/Press/Commentary/ed050409c.cfm.

Chen, D., & Mintz, J. "U.S. Effective corporate tax rate on new investments: Highest in the OECD." *Cato Institute.* May 2010.

Choate, A. "Ex-firefighters sue over cut in retirement." *Las Vegas Review-Journal.* September 30. 2009.

Chon, G. "States skip pension payments, delay day of reckoning." *Wall Street Journal.* April 9, 2010.

"Cities shouldn't get a pass – exemptions unwise in smart pension board reform." *Dallas Morning News*. April 29, 2009.

Citizens Against Government Waste. *The pig book: How government wastes your money*. Thomas Dunne Books/St. Martin's Griffin: New York, 2005.

Colavecchio, S. "Gov. Charlie Crist signs law limiting state employees' ability to double-dip." *St. Petersburg Times*. June 18, 2009.

Cook, J. "DROP pays big dividends to some educators." *The Dothan Eagle, State and Regional News*. March 30, 2008.

"Council passes measure modifying DROP program." *Philadelphia Inquirer*. March 19, 2010.

Davis, A. "State lets employees get pension and salary." *Arkansas Democrat-Gazette*. July 28, 2009.

Dobbs, L. "The federal bonus." *CNN*, transcript. May 12, 2009.

Donovan, L. "Blame state lawmakers for pension debacle, critic says." *Chicago Sun Times*. March 8, 2010.

Edelman, S. "Taxpayer pension pain." *The New York Post*. October 18, 2009.

Edelman, S., Boniello, K. and Fagen, C. R. "Exiled Queens teacher on payroll despite knocking up student." *New York Post*. February 11, 2010.

Edwards, Chris. "Public-sector unions." *Tax & Budget Bulletin*, No. 61. March 2010.

Edwards, C. "Federal pay continues rapid ascent." *Cato Institute*. August 24, 2009.

Ehrenberg, Ronald G., Ed. *What's happening to public higher education? The shifting financial burden*. The Johns Hopkins University Press: Baltimore, MD, 2006.

Epstein, Richard, A. "*Regulation*. The Ominous Employee Free Choice Act." *Cato Institute*. Spring 2009. http://www.cato.org/pubs/regulation/regv32n1/v32n1-7.pdf

Erdley, D. "School taxes in Pennsylvania may soar to pay for pension promises." *The Pittsburgh Tribune Review*. November 1, 2009.

Fahey, T. "Retiree hike hits with thud." *The Union Leader*. November 11, 2009.

Fanelli, J. "This guy gets paid $283G to repair trains. MTA workers pull in outrageous OT fortunes." *New York Post*. June 7. 2009.

Firey, Thomas. "What's Another Taxpayer Liability?" *Cato Institute*. August 8, 2006. http://www.cato-at-liberty.org/2006/08/08/whats-another-taxpayer-liability/.

Fitch, S. "Gilt-Edged Pensions." *Forbes.com. February 16, 2009*.

Fox, Jeffrey, "What are Executive Orders?" *ThisNation.com*. http://www.thisnation.com/question/040.html.

Fox, P. "Gwinnett to limit how long retirees draw paycheck and pension." *Atlanta Journal-Constitution*. July 19, 2009.

Fullhart, Steve. "New BPD chief done in Omaha; pension checks to be bigger." *Pension Tsunami*. June 18, 2009.

Futty, J. "Police, fire retirements to come at high price." *Columbus Dispatch*. March 21, 2010.

Gao, H. "Millions needed for city pensions." *Union-Tribune*. January 19, 2010.

Gibson, G. "Audit rips retiree 'double-dipping.' " *The News Journal*. August 10, 2009.

Goodwin Procter LLP. "Labor & Employment Alert, New Executive Orders Favoring Organized Labor Will Affect Many Employers That Provide Goods or Services to the Federal Government." March 18, 2009. http://www.goodwinprocter.com/Publications/Newsletters/Labor-and-Employment-Alert/2009/New-Executive-Orders-Will-Affect-Many-Employers-That-Provide-Goods-or-Services-to-the-FG.aspx.

Gordon, Rachel. "1 in 3 San Francisco employees earned $100,000." *San Francisco Chronicle.* April 26, 2010.

"Governor plans emergency address on budget." *The Washington Times.* February 8, 2010.

Greenhouse, Stephen. "Democrats Drop Key Part of Bill to Assist Unions." *New York Times.* July 16, 2009. http://www.nytimes.com/2009/07/17/business/17union.html?_r=3&hp.

Greenhut, S. "6 Reps sign on to union giveaway." *Cal Watchdog.* March 1, 2010.

Greenhut, Steven. *Plunder! How public employee unions are raiding treasuries, controlling our lives and bankrupting the nation.* The Forum Press: Santa Ana, CA, 2009.

Gross, Martin L. *The government racket 2000: All new Washington waste from A to Z.* Avon Books: New York, 2000.

"Hey, even chiefs can use some extra cash." *Lowell Sun.* September 14, 2008.

Hinkel, D. "PERFectly secret: Taxpayers can't see pension payouts." *Northwest Indiana and Illinois Times.* October 5, 2009.

Hollingsworth, H. "Plan would close half of public schools." *Lawrence Journal-World.* March 8, 2010.

Hollis, M. "In prison and on the payroll." *The Huntsville Times.* June 16, 2009.

Horstman, B. "Pension packages top $1 million for Cincinnati's police, fire chiefs." *Cincinnati Enquirer.* December 12, 2009.

"How does the pension funding and fairness act work? *The Illinois Policy Institute.* January 22, 2010.

John, David C. "Social Security's Unexpected Deficits Show Urgent Need for Reform", WebMemo #2632. *Heritage Foundation.* September 29, 2009. http://www.heritage.org/Research/SocialSecurity/wm2632.cfm.

"Kansas City looks at plan to close half of its school." *News-Leader.* February 15, 2010.

Keating, C. "More than 1,000 state employees are paid more than Gov. Rell; 175 retired state employees have 100K pensions." *Hartford Courant.* February 9, 2010.

Kelleher, S. "Hospital CEO collects special $1.7M payoff." *The Seattle Times.* September 29, 2009.

Kerkstra, P. "Her payday was no DROP in the bucket." *Philadelphia Inquirer.* January 18, 2010.

"Kicking out your union." *Unionfacts.com.* Retrieved 2010.

Kolodner, Meredith. "Home-based day care workers get raises, but city to cut 1,100 kids from program to pay for it." *New York Daily News.* May 14, 2009.

"Labor Day: The price of success." *St. Louis Today.* September 6, 2009.

Langley, K. "Towns to sue over retirement cuts." *The Concord Monitor.* October 26, 2009.

"Lawmakers must tackle pension costs." *The Burlington Free Press, Editorial.* November 8, 2009.

Lawrence, G. "Wait…you say there's a recession?" *Nevada Policy Research Institute.* February 10, 2010.

Lieb, D. A. "Analysis: Nixon seeks power to seize overdue taxes from bank accounts." *News-Leader.* February 1, 2010.

Lieberman, Myron. *Understanding the teacher union contract: A citizen's handbook.* Transaction Publishers: New Brunswick, 2000.

Linskey, A. "Unions agree to scale back pension plan." *Baltimore Sun.* March 17, 2009.

Lipsky, Seth. *The Citizen's Constitution: An Annotated Guide.* Basic Books, a member of the Perseus Books Group: New York, 2009.

Lucas, Fred. "Union Elections Should Keep Secret Ballot, Chamber of Commerce Says." *Cybercast News Service, CNSnews.com.* August 19, 2008. http://cnsnews.com/news/print/34314.

Maher, Kris. "Service Union chief met with Blagojevich." *Wall Street Journal.* January 7, 2009.

Maher, Kris. "SEIU Campaign spending pays political dividends." *Wall Street Journal.* May 16, 2008. http://online.wsj.com/article/SB124243785248026055.html

Matthews, A. W. "Drug Prices Rose 9.1% Last Year, Ahead of Federal Health Overhaul." *Wall Street Journal.* April 20, 2010.

McKenna, Long and Aldrich, LLP. "President Obama Signs Executive Order Allowing Agencies to Require Project Labor Agreements (PLA's) on Large Construction Projects." February 10, 2009. http://www.mckennalong.com/news-advisories-2072.html.

McKitrick, C. "Double dippers adding to the pension fund problem?" *The Salt Lake Tribune.* August 18, 2009.

McNichol, D. "Pennsylvania cities stake pensions on pennies and parking lots." *Bloomberg.* September 18, 2009.

Melloan, George. *The great money binge: Spending our way to socialism.* Threshold Editions, a division of Simon & Schuster Inc., New York, 2009.

Merrion, P. & Hinz, G. & Strahler, S. R. "Illinois enters a state of insolvency." *Crain's Chicago Business.* January 18, 2010.

Merritt, G. E. "UConn to limit double-dipping by retirees." *Hartford Courant.* April 22, 2009.

Montgomery, L. "Senate Democrats face hurdles getting votes to increase nation's debt limit." *Washington Post.* January 21, 2010.

Morgan, L. "Double dipping rises despite outrage." *St. Petersburg Times.* December 30, 2008.

Morgan, L. "Six wardens among double dippers at Florida Department of Corrections." *St. Petersburg Times.* May 5, 2008.

Morris, Charles R. *The trillion dollar meltdown: Easy money, high rollers and the great credit crash.* PublicAffairs: New York, 2008.

Mullen, S. "As state pension debt rises, so do payouts over $100,000." *Asbury Park Press.* October 16, 2009.

National Right to Work Committee, National Right to Work Newsletter. "Card-Check Survivor Tells His Story: A 'Nasty, Ugly, Three-Year, Million-Dollar War I Did Not Ask For.'" Nov/Dec 2009. http://www.nrtwc.org/nl/nl200912p8.pdf.

National Right to Work Legal Defense Foundation. "Public Sector Decertification/Deauthorization Laws" (as of 2/6/2004). Retrieved 2010 from http://www.nrtw.org/.

Novy-Marx, Robert, & Rauh, Joshua D. "The liabilities and risks of state-sponsored pension plans." *Journal of Economic Perspectives.* Fall 2009. Volume 23, Number 4, pp. 191–210.

O'Brien, M. "Pension panel ready to work." *Omaha World-Herald.* February 27, 2009.

Official complaint filed at the United States Northern District Court, in Pensacola, Fl. March 23, 2010. Case 3:10-cv-00091-RV-EMT. http://www.healthcarelawsuit.us/webfiles.nsf/WF/MRAY-83TKWB/$file/HealthCareReformLawsuit.pdf.

Olson, B. "Mayor blasts raise plan for pension fund staff." *The Houston Chronicle.* August 27, 2009.

Oregon Public Employee Retirement System. July 2009.

Paige, Rod. *The war against hope: How teachers' unions hurt children, hinder teachers and endanger public education.* Thomas Nelson, Inc.: Nashville, TN, 2006.

Peebles, J. "Banked vacation, sick time equal big bucks in Corpus Christi." *Texas Watchdog.* March 26, 2009.

"Pension Plan for Missouri state employees show mixed results." *The Kansas City Star.* August 18, 2009.

"Pension bomb ticks louder." *Wall Street Journal.* April 27, 2010.

Peoples, Steve. "R.I. public employee unions align to sue over pension changes." *Providence Journal.* July 30, 2009.

Peoples, Steve. "State pension costs are soaring." *Providence Journal.* March 7, 2010.

Peter G. Peterson Foundation. "National Debt." Based on 2008 Financial Report of the United States Government. Social Security and Medicare benefits are present values as of January 1, 2008. Burden per person calculated using estimated December 2008 US Census Bureau data, other data as of September 30, 2008, http://www.pgpf.org/about/nationaldebt/.

Pew Center on the States. "The trillion dollar gap: Underfunded state retirement systems and the roads to reform." February 2010.

Pew Center on the States. "Pew study finds states face $1 trillion shortfall in retiree benefits." *Pew Press Release.* February 18, 2010.

"Phoenix alters retiree-hire plan." *Associated Press.* January 15, 2009.

Powers, S. "State 'retirees' can double 6-figure paychecks." *Orlando Sentinel*. April 26, 2009.

Prante, Gerald. "List of tax provisions scheduled to expire on December 31, 2010." *The Tax Foundation*. May 26, 2010. www.taxfoundation.org.

Prince, J. "Copping a comfy retirement." *Fort Worth Weekly*. July 22, 2009.

"Report: GA's university presidents well rewarded." *Atlanta Business Chronicle*. January 18, 2010.

Ring, D. "Massachusetts pension system overhaul proposed by special state commission." *Republican Newsroom*. September 1, 2009.

Rio Grande Foundation. "Government Pensions: New Mexico's Next Crisis." January 7, 2010.

Salzer, J. "Bonus pay stokes anger." *Atlanta Journal-Constitution*. January 31, 2010.

Scanlon, Terrence. "Will 2010 be labor's turn?" *Washington Times*. January 4, 2010. http://www.washingtontimes.com/news/2010/jan/04/will-2010-be-labors-turn.

Scharper, J. "Pension fix draws speedy criticism." *The Baltimore Sun*. April 19, 2010.

Schoenmann, J. "Clark County cost-cutting ideas center on salaries." *The Las Vegas Sun*. December 30, 2009.

Schulman, S. "Police chiefs share in big retirement benefits." *Buffalo News*. January 12, 2009.

Schulman, S. "For retiring firefighters, a lifetime of overtime." *Buffalo News*. March 15, 2009.

Scott, B. "$8 billion benefits bombshell." *The New York Post*. February 1, 2010.

Scott, B. "Pension reform's gift to teachers." *The New York Post*. March 31, 2010.

Secter, B. "Illinois stuck in a 'historic, epic' budget crisis." *Chicago Tribune*. February 23, 2010.

Sherk, James. "How Union Card Checks Block Workers' Free Choice." Web-Memo #1366. *Heritage Foundation*. February 21, 2007. http://www.heritage.org/Research/Labor/wm1366.cfm.

Shields, J. "Now, high-level city employees at center of DROP controversy." *Philadelphia Inquirer*. March 1, 2010.

Sisk, C. "Tennessee workers rack up overtime." *The Tennessean*. October 5, 2009.

Smith, G., & Wenger, Y. "Early release of prisoners discussed." *The Post & Courier*. February 24, 2010.

Smith, H. "KPERS facing bankruptcy if changes are not made, report says." *Kansas Liberty*. September 16, 2009.

"Survey: CO seniors will delay retirement without economic improvement." *Public News Service*. October 2008.

Sweeney, S. M. "Sen. Stephen Sweeney: N.J. unions had hand in pension crisis." *NJ.com*. March 3, 2010.

Tanner, Michael, D. "Social Security's Sham Guarantee." *Cato Institute*. May 29, 2005. http://www.cato.org/pub_display.php?pub_id=3785.

"The government pay boom." *Wall Street Journal*, editorial. March 26, 2010.

"The need for transparency in public sector pensions." British North-American Committee. June 1, 2009.

"The Numbers: What are the Federal Government's Sources of Revenues." *Tax Policy Center, Urban Institute and Brookings Institution; The Tax Policy Briefing Book*. April 22, 2009. http://www.taxpolicycenter.org/briefing-book/background/numbers/revenue.cfm.

"The separation of health and state." *Wall Street Journal*, op-ed. April 6, 2010.

"The state cannot afford the benefits it promised." *Daily Mail*. November 11, 2009.

"There he goes again." *Wall Street Journal*. May 7, 2010. p.46.

THOMAS. Library of Congress. http://thomas.loc.gov/cgi-bin/query/z?c111:H.R.1409.

Troy, Leo. *The new unionism in the new society: Public sector unions in the redistributive state*. George Mason University Press: Fairfax, VA, 1994.

Tuerck, David G., PhD, Glassman, Sarah, MSEP, Bachman, Paul, MSIE. "Project Labor Agreements on Federal Construction Projects: A Costly Solution in Search of a Problem." *The Beacon Hill Institute at Suffolk University*. August 2009. http://www.beaconhill.org/BHIStudies/PLA2009/PLAFinal090923.pdf.

U.S. Department of Commerce, Bureau of Economic Analysis. "Regional economic accounts. Tables SA06N, SA07N and SA27N." October 2009.

U.S. Department of Commerce, Bureau of Economic Analysis. "National Economic Accounts." http://www.bea.gov/national/index.htm#gdp.

U.S. Department of Labor, Bureau of Labor Statistics. "Union Members in 2008." January 28, 2009. http://www.bls.gov/news.release/union2.nr0.htm.

"U.S. Federal Budget; Overview." *New York Times*. July 22, 2009. http://topics.nytimes.com/top/reference/timestopics/subjects/f/federal_budget_us/index.html.

U.S. Government Accountability Office. "Federally Created Entities." October 2009. GAO-10-97

Velie, K. "Top two sheriff officials double and triple dipping." *Calcoastnews.com*. January 24, 2010.

Villarreal, P. "Social Security and Medicare Projections: 2009." *National Center for Policy Analysis*. June 11, 2009.

Wickline, M. "$19.5 million teacher benefits raise passed by board." *Arkansas Democrat-Gazette*. May 23, 2009.

Wickline, M. "State police retirement fund's investments lose, regain some." *Arkansas Democrat-Gazette*. May 15, 2009.

Wilmers, R. "What about Fan and Fred reform?" *Wall Street Journal*. May 4, 2010. p.47.

Wright, P. J. & Jahr, M. D. "Michigan forces business owners into public sector unions." *The Wall Street Journal*. December 25, 2009.

Zettler, B. "Gov. Quinn: Raise taxes on $10/hr workers by 41% to pay for $10 million pensions." *Champion News*. June 22, 2009.

Index

LaVergne, TN USA
06 September 2010
196013LV00008B/25/P